BEYOND EXPECTATION:
LESBIAN/BI/QUEER WOMEN AND ASSISTED CONCEPTION

An in-depth study of lesbian, bisexual, and queer women's experiences of thinking about and trying to become a parent, *Beyond Expectation* draws on extensive interviews conducted with eighty-two women during the late 1990s in British Columbia. Jacquelyne Luce chronicles these women's reproductive experiences, which took place from 1980 to 2000, a period that saw significant changes in attitudes toward and regulation of assisted reproduction and in the status of lesbian, gay, bisexual, and transgender parents and same-sex partners.

Beyond Expectation looks closely at the changing contexts in which these women's experiences took place and draws attention to complex issues such as 'contracting' relationships, mediating understandings of biology and genetics, and decision-making amid various social, legal, and medical developments. Luce juxtaposes the stories of her interviewees with the wider public discourses about lesbian/bi/queer parenting and reproductive technology, while highlighting gaps in existing legislative reforms. Most important, *Beyond Expectation* gives voice to the lived experiences of lesbian, bisexual, and queer women in their endeavour to negotiate kinship at the intersection of reproduction, technology, and politics.

JACQUELYNE LUCE is a research fellow at Zeppelin University.

JACQUELYNE LUCE

Beyond Expectation

Lesbian/Bi/Queer Women and Assisted Conception

UNIVERSITY OF TORONTO PRESS
Toronto   Buffalo   London

ISBN 978-1-4426-4063-4 (cloth)
ISBN 978-1-4426-1008-8 (paper)

Printed on acid-free, 100% post-consumer recycled paper with vegetable-based inks.

Library and Archives Canada Cataloguing in Publication

Luce, Jacquelyne Marie, 1971–
   Beyond expectation : assisted conception and the politics of recognition /
Jacquelyne Luce.

Includes bibliographical references.
ISBN 978-1-4426-4063-4 (bound). – ISBN 1-4426-1008-8 (pbk.)

1. Lesbian mothers – Canada.   2. Lesbians – Family relationships – Canada.
3. Lesbians – Canada – Social conditions.   4. Lesbians – Health and hygiene
– Canada.   5. Reproductive technology – Canada.   6. Motherhood –
Political aspects – Canada.   I. Title.

HQ75.53.L83 2010   306.874'3086643   C2009-905687-9

This book has been published with the help of a grant from the Canadian
Federation for the Humanities and Social Sciences, through the Aid to
Scholarly Publications Programme, using funds provided by the Social
Sciences and Humanities Research Council of Canada.

University of Toronto Press acknowledges the financial assistance to its
publishing program of the Canada Council for the Arts and the Ontario
Arts Council.

University of Toronto Press acknowledges the financial support for its
publishing activities of the Government of Canada through the
Book Publishing Industry Development Program (BPIDP).

Contents

Preface

Beyond Expectation explores the experiences of women whose narratives of conception are part of what has been called 'the lesbian baby boom.' The majority of the fieldwork for this project was conducted between September 1998 and October 2000 in British Columbia, Canada, with the temporal parameters of the research extending both backwards and forwards from 1996 to 2008. The book has emerged from what could perhaps be considered meeting points between discourses of lesbian health and queer politics and simultaneously, but not distinctly, assisted reproduction and kinship, inviting mediation of the normative language employed within these spheres. Throughout the book I draw attention to many of the implications of assumptions about shared use and meaning of language, turning to focus on stories about experiences and the practices and politics of meaning-making within specific contexts.

The meanings of the terms *assisted reproduction* and *assisted conception* are often represented as self-evident on fertility clinic websites or in regulatory guidelines governing the use of assisted reproductive technologies (ARTs), or what used to be more commonly referred to as new reproductive technologies (NRTs).[1] Both terms, however, can refer to a broad variety of clinical practices, including, for example, ovulation stimulation, in vitro fertilization (IVF), intrauterine insemination (IUI), donor insemination (DI), and gamete intrafallopian transfer (GIFT). Within the discipline of anthropology, the multiple meanings of *assistance, conception,* and *reproduction* facilitate a conceptual play with the novel materialities of social, biological, and technological reproduction and have contributed significantly to a new set of anthropological studies of kinship and relatedness (Franklin and Ragoné 1998; Edwards, Franklin, et al. 1999; Davis-Floyd and Dumit 1998).

Ethnographic studies at and about the intersections between assisted reproduction and kinship studies provided starting points from which to trace the movement of language, terminology, and ideas that contextualize assisted conception experiences through the various spaces of everyday, legal, clinical, and political life. The so-called age of assisted conception (Edwards, Franklin, et al. 1999) marks an era in which the possibility to conceive by in vitro fertilization may be more visible than by insemination at home with donor semen. A close analysis of narratives of experiences which took place inside and outside of clinical settings sheds light on the transference of knowledge, concepts, and understanding of reproductive 'science' between both. Paying attention to the 'paper tools' (Landecker 2003) that facilitate parental recognition and/or displacement further emphasizes the changing role of information and knowledge transfer during the past few decades. My use, thus, of the terms *assisted conception* and *assisted reproduction* throughout this book is a means of invoking their multiple meanings and further displacing *assisted reproduction* from its normative location within social, legal, and medical discourses and practices.

Assumptions about the language used to refer to sexual identity, sexual orientation, and sexuality are also common. I use the terms *lesbian* and *queer woman* throughout the book, and in their narratives women use the language with which they are familiar and that they find relevant. I would suggest that there are no fixed meanings of the labels associated with sexual identity and sexual orientation. The usage of particular words changes over time and is sometimes (or often) restricted to particular contexts. The images that certain labels sometimes carry can have very significant effects, and as the chapters of this book illustrate, the need to 'label' identities, projects, and techniques is greater in certain contexts than in others. Some labels which may be incredibly important are unattainable at times, require constant negotiation, or cannot be expressed.

Over the course of my fieldwork I conducted fifty-nine in-depth 'formal' interviews with eighty-two women.[2] The interviews were with women who ranged in age from 24 to 58 and whose experiences spanned two decades, from 1980 to 2000. Although I had initially developed an interview guide, after the first few interviews I found myself simply inviting women to tell their story about having thought about becoming a parent or having brought a child into their life. I sometimes did not know prior to an interview what the context of the woman's narrative would be, and I realised as my research progressed that sometimes parts of a story were so present in a woman's mind that other aspects almost disappeared (Luce 2005b). This awareness disrupted the attempt to think about women's stories as being told by single women or women in a relationship, by women who had used semen from known donors or women who had tried to become pregnant at a fertility clinic or with semen from a sperm bank. For the most part, I came to *deny* the categories by which much of the literature on lesbian parenting and assisted reproduction has been organized: specifically, biological and non-biological mother; single or partnered parent; mother by self or clinic-based insemination; and user of anonymous or known donor semen. Some women clearly spoke about how being single shaped their decisions, and others who had been in a relationship when trying to become pregnant were single at the time of our interview, having separated from or lost their former partner. Other women, in a relationship, spoke about how getting pregnant was 'their own project' or how they had become a parent together with someone other than their partner. Women planning their first pregnancy were already, or had already been, parents. Women combined intrauterine inseminations and home inseminations in the same cycle. Women miscarried and never became a mother. Women never became pregnant and experienced loss. The stories cannot be captured by a set of common parameters (of religion, socio-economic status, level of education) because their richness lies in the contours of everyday life experiences that make us believe something is possible and that we use to make sense of happenings that just do not make sense. The stories were varied and shaped by the past, the present, and an imagined future.

In re-presenting the narratives in this book, I have done my best to find ways to retain women's individuality, as well as the nuances and complexities of their experiences, by recounting in their stories what they defined as significant. Within the course of interviews, different histories and varied cultural (broadly imagined) experiences appeared in women's narratives. Religious affiliation (primarily Anglican, Quaker, and Catholic), first-generation Canadian status, experience living in remote areas, growing up on the tundra, living in a multiracial family, experiencing the death of a parent or a partner, being adopted, losing a child, exploring a transgender identity, 'passing' for white, and claiming a lesbian, bisexual, or queer 'sexual identity,' 'sexual preference,' 'sexual orientation,' or 'sexuality' were some of the aspects of experience that women pointed to as shaping and influencing their thoughts, reflections, and decisions.

At the end of the book I have provided a set of short biographies to support readers in keeping track of the various narratives of particular individuals. These biographies purposefully do not include information about a woman's occupation, geographical location, nor the exact year in which she may have tried to become pregnant, as presenting each of these key aspects of identification alongside each other and alongside the detailed backgrounds of other women renders individuals much more identifiable. The women's biographies are ordered according to temporal categories which relate to key developments within the governance of assisted conception and lesbian, gay, bisexual, and transgender (LGBT) rights and relationships in Canada and, specifically, British Columbia. Thus, readers can situate women's stories clearly within the social, legal, and medical contexts that might have influenced them and which are discussed in the different chapters herein.

There have been times over the years when I have been listening to a story and thought that it sounded similar to one or more of the narratives of the women I had interviewed. I suspect that some readers may believe their own experiences to be reflected here, perhaps also in the narratives of others. In order to maintain the privacy of not only the women I interviewed but also the donors, partners, ex-lovers, co-parents, parents, friends, and children who may not have participated in the interviews, but who make appearances in the stories included here, all names have been changed.

The chapters in *Beyond Expectation* are organized according to the three main lenses through which I look at women's narratives of assisted conception and through which discourses and practices of assisted reproduction and parental recognition are mediated. An introductory chapter explores the academic, political, medical, legislative, and popular contexts within which *Beyond Expectation* is embedded.

Part I, 'Re-Imagining Relations,' focuses on the myriad social contexts in which women's experiences were situated, reconstructing accounts of how the women in my study acquired information about becoming a parent and the strategies they employed to create a supportive environment in which to attempt to conceive and raise a child. Drawing on the narratives of women whose experiences ranged from attempts to get pregnant in an era when 'people didn't have children' (meaning, lesbians didn't, visibly, have children) to exuberantly staking their membership in a 'lesbian baby boom' ('It's massive, don't you think?'), I examine the disconnections and reconnections that women made between queer sexuality, reproduction, and parenting. Women's stories demonstrate how queer women mobilized social networks and social knowledge in order to acquire information about how to get pregnant in a context in which lesbian parenting is increasingly visible, but the process of becoming a queer parent remains (surprisingly) shrouded in mystique. Coming out[3] as a (queer) prospective parent was nerve-racking and, often, required an appropriate setting, an appropriate audience, and an appropriate tale with an appropriate ending. Queer women planning to parent not only explicitly called attention to their sexual identity but often challenged individuals to acknowledge their sexuality (the everyday lived and embodied expressions of desire, attraction, and relatedness) via practices of, and claims for, recognition. What I call *strategic outings* rendered assisted reproduction and queer (attempted) conceptions visible and broadened the spheres in which women were out. For many women I interviewed, their ability to be out, as well as their ability to provide their children with images of, and access to, other children living with LGBT parents, was important.

Part II, 'Negotiating Relatedness,' contextualizes queer women's narratives about choosing donors within the framework of women's concerns about the legal status of LGBT parents and the possible configurations of legal and non-legal relationships between certain parents, certain donors, and children. Queer women's use of clinic-based donor insemination is often explained as a result of, and as a solution to, the potential 'risk' of HIV transmission (Kahn 2000; Weston 1991). However, most of the women I interviewed expressed more concern about their ability to negotiate a *relationship* with a donor (and the donor's friends and family) than their sense of being able to negotiate a safe(r) insemination. Women pursued a number of avenues in order to secure a recognized relationship to their child or children. In this section, the narratives of women who chose anonymous, known, unknown, or willing-to-be-known donors, and who attempted to get pregnant at various points in time over the past two decades, highlight the interrelated discourses of legal kinship, queer sexuality, and assisted reproduction.

Part III, 'Reproductive "Assistance,"' addresses the 'locations' of queer women within dominant medical narratives of assisted reproduction and assisted reproduction legislation. The first chapters address the situated meaning of screening donors for women choosing to inseminate with semen from known or sperm bank donors. Donor-screening practices are talked about in relation to sexually (insemination) transmitted infections and HIV, as well as perceived hereditary traits and genetic conditions. The manners in which women included references to HIV/AIDS in their narratives about trying to become a parent facilitates an extension of an analysis of the implications of HIV and AIDS on women's experiences of assisted reproduction to the social and political meanings of HIV testing and living with HIV/AIDS. Women's narratives argued for the inextricability and contingency of women's practices of screening for sexually transmitted infections (STIs), and more broadly defined health attributes, which leads to a discussion of what women perceived to be hereditary and what has been popularly discussed as genetically determined. The final chapter in the book looks beyond the experiences of women I interviewed to address some of the perhaps coming, and certainly already there but not widely visible, decisions that queer women may be faced with as the definitions and practices of medically assisted reproduction and the reasons for engaging them continue to expand.

Beyond Expectation situates queer women's experiences within broader discussions and analyses of the politics of reproduction, reproductive and genetic technologies, recognition and kinship, and ultimately health. Throughout the book I aim to retain the sense of the bodily, emotive, and enduring relationships, and the cultural challenges to which these experiences contribute, that women presented in their narratives of trying to become a parent within shifting social, legal, and medical contexts. The stories that the women shared are replete with representations of and references to experiences that are taken up in various chapters of this book and in other writing but which are also at times left uncommented, perhaps to be addressed by other scholars in the future. My aim has been to write an ethnographic account of particular experiences of assisted conception which retain the contestability of any one narrative. What is left unanalysed I have tried not to leave invisible. Rather, I invite readers to also conduct their own additional analyses and to seek out the comparability of the stories.

Acknowledgments

As with all research and writing projects, one always benefits from the experiences of others, the opportunities of engaging in critical dialogue, and the various forms of institutional support. *Beyond Expectation* has literally travelled with me from the early days of my doctoral studies, taking shape in relation to the numerous legislative, political, medical, and social transformations which have occurred. A number of organizations supported various phases of research over this project's lifetime, for which I am thankful: York University, where I completed my doctoral studies (1996–2002) in the Department of Anthropology, awarded professional development grants to facilitate my participation in conferences and academic exchange, as well as a Dean's Academic Excellence Award (1997–8) and a President's Dissertation Fellowship (2000–1). The Social Sciences and Humanities Research Council of Canada supported the research with doctoral (1998–2000) and postdoctoral (2002–4) fellowships. A seed grant from the British Columbia Centre of Excellence for Women's Health (BCCEWH) provided support for fieldwork and interviews with women living in northern British Columbia (1998–9), as well as the opportunity to present and publish an early account of the research (Luce 2002). A grant from the Lesbian Health Fund of the Gay and Lesbian Medical Association and a Health Services Research Dissertation grant (no. R03HS1126-01), awarded by the U.S. Agency for Healthcare Research and Quality, enabled further intensive fieldwork phases (1999–2000) to be conducted across British Columbia, including in rural and remote areas.

Naomi Adelson, Lorna Weir, Ken Little, Margaret Rodman, and Shubhra Gururani at York University and, earlier, Gavin Smith and

Belinda Leach at the University of Toronto played very significant roles in the development of my engagement with ethnographic research and my sustained belief in the power of stories. My understanding of the shaping influences of health care systems and regulatory acts benefited immensely from my work with Ivy Bourgeault and Margaret MacDonald on two projects which addressed the integration of midwives into the British Columbia (BC) and Ontario health care systems. Participation as a graduate student researcher in activities of the BC Centre of Excellence for Women's Health in 1998–9 offered a solid foundation upon which to begin the fieldwork for this project. In 2002, during the final stages of completing my dissertation, I was asked challenging questions by students in the Politics of the Family course, which I taught at Simon Fraser University, and they helped me to think through ways in which to render the politics of recognition and reproductive health more broadly accessible.

During a postdoctoral fellowship at Lancaster University in the United Kingdom (2002–4), a strong culture of workshops and lectures focusing on feminist technoscience studies, the meanings of genes, and the intersections of political and academic work led my research further into the spaces at which technologies, science, and 'the everyday' meet. Sarah Franklin, Maureen McNeil, Michal Nahman, Celia Roberts, and Jackie Stacey especially were engaging interlocutors in a 'postmodern genealogies' reading group and numerous other conversations. Between 2004 and 2006 I was based at the Policy, Ethics, and Life Sciences Research Centre in the United Kingdom, where I had the opportunity to further develop my understanding of the contemporary implications of the Human Fertilisation and Embryology Act and Authority; the timing was especially important given the implementation of the Assisted Human Reproduction Act in Canada in 2004. I am thankful to colleagues, especially Erica Haimes, Tom Shakespeare, and Simon Woods, for exchanges about the ethics and politics of research governance in the life sciences.

Since 2006, I have been a research fellow within the Karl Mannheim Chair in Cultural Studies at Zeppelin University in Germany, where I have expanded my perspectives on knowledge governance and the politics of access to knowledge of various forms. I returned to the ideas and stories which make up *Beyond Expectation* with the support of Zeppelin University, and especially Nico Stehr, in 2007–8. The final revisions to the manuscript were completed with the support of a European Commission Marie Curie International Incoming Fellowship in cooperation with the Research Centre for Biotechnology, Society, and Environment at Hamburg University.

Thank you to Amelia Needoba, Monica Sheridan, and Michelle Walks for research assistance at various states of the project. For their insightful comments my thanks are extended to the anonymous reviewers and editorial staff at the University of Toronto Press, as well as to Virgil Duff for his support of the project. To my family, friends, and neighbours who have supported this project over the years, listening as I tried to make sense of stories, sending me news clippings about recent developments, and providing me with chocolate cake, thank you. I am especially grateful to my parents, Donna Martin and Jack Luce, for always encouraging me to pursue the projects that I imagine to be possible. S. Star, to you I am indebted and deeply obliged for the sustenance and colours which you offer during your visit from universe.

I have remained ever grateful to the women who have shared their experiences with me over the years: your stories were often told so that someone else could benefit, so that the experiences would become visible. Your worlds and your words are the core of this book.

BEYOND EXPECTATION:
LESBIAN/BI/QUEER WOMEN AND ASSISTED CONCEPTION

1 Introduction

When a woman decides that she wants a child, that's what she's going to do. If you are so in love with this woman, how do you choose to leave? I never wanted children. I never wanted to be a parent. When I came out as a dyke, I thought, thank God, that's not something I ever have to do. (Rae)

I'm going to be thirty and I have always thought that I didn't want to wait until after the age of thirty – thirty-two at the latest – to have my first child. And so over the past ten years I've been preparing myself for motherhood. (Bryn)

Beginnings

While doing research in a low-risk maternity care unit in Ontario in 1996, I met Kate Oslo and Gwen Michaels, who were expecting their second child. Gwen had conceived their first child, a girl, using donor semen three years earlier. When I interviewed Kate, who was pregnant with their second child, she commented on the importance that she and Gwen had placed on their decision to use sperm from the same donor to conceive both children. Kate described the establishment of a genetic relationship between the two children as a gift of continuity and stability, a gift that could potentially outlive her relationship with Gwen. She also represented the genetic tie as a form of insurance in the event that either child should ever need a genetic match for health reasons.

Shortly following this interview I attended a lecture by anthropologist Sarah Franklin at which she argued that genes as symbols of genetic relatedness were replacing earlier cultural investments in the symbol of blood, which has been understood anthropologically to define European and North American (and socially, legally, and medically normative) kinship (Franklin 1997; Strathern 1992; cf. Schneider 1980, 1984, 1997). Why did Kate and Gwen describe their wish to create what is commonly understood as a biological relationship between their children (as half-siblings) in terms of the value genetic relatedness could have with respect to potential future health needs? Why did the use of the *same* donor to create a relationship normatively recognized as significant (that is, biological half-siblings) represent the creation of a potentially more enduring tie than the children's lived experiences of sharing a history with the same parents, regardless of whether the parents continued their relationship with each other? *Beyond Expectation* responds to such questions by exploring the imbrications of concepts and experiences of health, relatedness, and sexuality through the stories of women interviewed in the late 1990s who had thought about becoming or had tried to become a parent between 1980 and 2000, during what is at times referred to as 'the age of assisted conception' (Edwards, Franklin, et al. 1999). While the experiences of some of the women whose narratives form the core of this book may have occurred well before anyone would have thought of so characterizing this time period, the stories as a whole are informed by a general shift in the possibility to envisage conception, contractual reproductive relations, genetic significance, and lesbian parenting differently.

Since the 1990s, ethnographic studies have documented the ways in which new technologies of assisted reproduction (be they medical, legal, or social) have transformed understandings of conception, pregnancy, and parenthood. Helena Ragoné described the boundary work involved in gestational surrogacy arrangements in which the significance of biological conception is displaced by 'conception in the heart,' the emotional imagining of a child-to-be marking the beginning of a familial relationship (Ragoné 1994). Sarah Franklin's account of women's experiences with in vitro fertilization (IVF) in England located the *possibility* of IVF and the advent of a new technology within political discourses of scientific progress and family values (Franklin 1997). Deborah Lynn Steinberg focused on the relationship between clinical practice and the legislation governing new assisted reproduction practices, illustrating the privileging of embryo research in legislation and identifying discursive constructions of technology and infertility care as scarce resources – rhetoric which was then used to justify restricted access to services (1997b).[1] Jeanette Edwards conducted a community-based study of understandings of new reproductive relations, exploring the ways in which practices of egg or sperm donation or IVF are understood by people who are perhaps not intimately involved in so-called treatment or donation processes (2000). More broadly, social scientists from various interdisciplinary backgrounds have located themselves over the years within clinical spaces, parliamentary discussions, laboratories, and people's homes, providing rich analyses of how relationships are created and maintained within the context of assisted reproduction developments.

Family and kinship questions were also a key interrelated area of development, explored not necessarily in relation to technology but in relation to gender. In 1991, Kath Weston published the influential *Families We Choose: Lesbians, Gays, Kinship,* in which she explores the kinship narratives of lesbians and gay men living in the San Francisco Bay area. Ellen Lewin's publication of *Lesbian Mothers: Accounts of Gender in American Culture* (1993) documents the narration of lesbian motherhood at a time when the concept of lesbian mother was still considered to be an oxymoron, single motherhood was devalued, and numerous custody cases hinged on whether or not homosexuality was viewed as pathological. Both Weston's and Lewin's publications are significant beyond their contribution to anthropological studies of kinship; they are pivotal studies within what would become a critical area of queer studies within the discipline of anthropology. Ethnographic studies of sexuality and same-sex or same-gender sexuality gained visibility and recognition throughout the 1990s (see also Kennedy and Davis 1993; Blackwood and Wieringa 1999) and were published alongside key methodologically oriented texts describing the hazards and rewards of conducting academic research in the area of 'lesbian and gay studies' or being 'out in the field' (Kulick and Wilson 1995; Lewin and Leap 1996; Newton 2001; Weston 1997).

The ethnographic project on which *Beyond Expectation* is based developed within the midst of these emerging publications and intradisciplinary and interdisciplinary conversations. It was also significantly informed by my interest in the politics of women's health, transformations in health care provision, and the legal status of caregivers, 'patients,' and 'clients.'[2] I have endeavoured, in both my research and writing, to take an ethnographic approach that facilitates a continual emphasis on the interrelatedness of influential contexts such as access to health services, normative societal images of lesbian parenting, and notions of fixed and fluid identity. In doing so, I aim to open up the seemingly constraining concepts of biological and non-biological mother, medically assisted or self insemination, or use of anonymous or known donor sperm, according to which the women in (and findings of) lesbian mother studies are often framed. The stories in this book are framed by my perspective that categories and classifications of relatedness and assisted reproductive technologies, which carry with them significant weight in terms of the lived experiences of being a woman, mothering, and parenting, are culturally normative and prescriptive identifications (of people and services) which need to be brought into question. In the following pages I introduce developments in the study of reproductive technologies, assisted conception and kinship; the representation of lesbians within interrelated narratives; and the potential to address queer women's experiences of assisted reproduction and kinship with an emphasis on the politics of health.

Social Science, Ethnography, and Assisted Reproduction

Early feminist writing on what was referred to as the *new* reproductive technologies[3] made disturbing predictions about the implications of these technological developments for women, highlighting the ever-increasing medicalization of women's bodies and reproduction (Arditti, Duelli Klein, and Minden 1984; Corea 1985). New reproductive technologies were viewed as reinforcing the relationships between women and nature, women and biology, and women and motherhood (see for example Spallone 1989; Spallone and Steinberg 1987; Stanworth 1987b). Publications during the 1980s, following reports of in vitro fertilization (IVF), gamete intrafallopian transfer (GIFT), and shifts from practices of so-called genetic surrogacy to gestational surrogacy, strongly critiqued reproductive technologies, offering politically astute analyses that contextualized the new developments and expectations in a history of scholarship regarding the role of women in society as mothers and carers. At the time, however, while women's bodies were in focus as sites of technological change and experimentation, women's *experiences* with the new technologies were not. As Michelle Stanworth points out in her 1987 publication, the representation of science and medicine as 'realms of boundless possibility, in the face of which mere human beings have no choices other than total rejection or capitulation' obscures the ways in which women do resist 'abuses of medical power and techniques they have found unacceptable' (1987a,17). She argues: 'The ideology of motherhood attempts to press women in the direction of child-bearing, and ... in this sense women's motivations are socially shaped. But "shaped" is not the same as "determined"; and a rejection of child-bearing (for infertile women or fertile) is not necessarily a more authentic choice (Stanworth 1987a, 17).'

What was missing from feminist analyses was attention to the ways in which women were mediating technology and playing an active role in its constitution. Women were not simply pawns in a patriarchal game in which science had the upper hand, but they were becoming knowledgeable about new reproductive possibilities and actively seeking out and using medical technologies in their attempts to become pregnant. The narratives of women presented in *Beyond Expectation* illustrate the decisions that women made against the particular uses of technology with which they did not agree; the stories also demonstrate the reframing of what might once have seemed unacceptable within, for example, the language of consumption and the exchange of money for treatment value or safety. In one interview two women, Pam and Caroline, felt that, in contrast to the at-home process they had planned using semen from a U.S. sperm bank, they received 'more bang for [their] buck' upon attending a local fertility clinic. The extra value of the clinical donor insemination service included a hormone level investigation, a hysterosalpingogram, the importation of 'washed' semen from the United States, ovulation monitoring, and intrauterine insemination. As discussed later, there are expected and potentially accepted uses of technology which represent a broad spectrum in between the points of total rejection and capitulation to available technologies. It was the negotiation of these points in-between, including the definition of what actually counts as technology, that shaped the experiences of women in this study. Thus, it is important to ask in what ways women have not only resisted, or actively promoted and made use of, assisted reproductive technologies, but also inscribed them with particular meanings and meaningful representations.

Social science contributions to the analysis of reproductive technologies which began to emerge in the 1980s and early 1990s (Stanworth 1987b; Franklin and McNeil 1988; McNeil 1990) focused on women's *experiences* of infertility, the decisions women make with respect to using various methods of assisted conception, and the co-production of scientific knowledge in the field of reproductive medicine. Science and discursive representations of reproductive knowledge became the subjects of study *as culture* (Franklin 1995b; Kaplan and Squier 1999; Hartouni 1997; Haraway 1991). The reconceptualization of conception was explored in relation to older social science and, specifically, anthropological topics of family and kinship (Strathern 1992; Carsten 2004) and emerging 'sites' of the anthropology of science, such as genetic testing (Katz Rothman 1986; Rapp 1999, 2000; Rapp, Health, and Taussig 2001) and preimplantation genetic diagnosis (Franklin and Roberts 2006). Within the discipline of anthropology, ethnographic research in the field of assisted reproduction contributed to the emergence of a renewed emphasis on the study of kinship and what came to be called the new kinship studies.[4]

'New' Kinship Studies

Kinship has a long and significant history as a subject of study and analytical concept within anthropology. It has undergone and withstood numerous critiques throughout the history of the discipline, perhaps the most influential of which addressed the concentration of kinship studies in so-called non-Western geographical locations (see Yanagisako and Collier 1987) and the importation of Western notions of kinship as a lens through which to study (and create a typology of) non-familiar forms of relatedness. The critique of kinship emerged from various directions, namely, feminist work on gender, anthropological studies of nature, and post-colonial anthropological emphases on reflexivity and the politics of the field. In 1968 David Schneider published *American Kinship: A Cultural Account* and then in 1984 *A Critique of the Study of Kinship*. While Schneider's work addressed kinship as a social construction – a cultural expression of biological 'facts' or knowledge – it left intact the concept of factual biology. New critical engagements with the concept of kinship in the 1990s, influenced by Schneider's work, pushed the critique further in order to address so-called biological facts as cultural constructions as well (Yanagisako and Delaney 1995). Since the late 1980s there has been an interest in exploring kinship within the context of social transformations holding the potential to challenge normative understandings of relatedness (Carsten 2000; Franklin and Ragoné 1998; Peletz 1995). In their introduction to *Relative Values: Reconfiguring Kinship Studies*, Franklin and McKinnon write: 'The naturalization of kinship within a reproductive model – where kinship is a "hybrid" institution, connecting nature and culture – depended on the way in which nature could provide not only a grounding function or context for society but indeed a model for context itself' (2001,5). Destabilizing the potential for nature to be thought of as the grounding function simultaneously destabilized the context.

The relationship between kinship and reproduction has proven to be enduring, having generated thought-provoking analyses in many realms including 'off-spring' areas of research such as embryonic stem cell research and preimplantation genetic diagnosis (see Franklin and Roberts 2006; Williams et al. 2008). In the introduction to the second edition of *Technologies of Procreation: Kinship in the Age of Assisted Conception*, the authors write: 'Why kinship? To a greater or lesser extent, part of everyone's identity as a person is derived from knowledge about their birth and about how they were brought up. It follows that such knowledge is also social knowledge, in that it presumes connection and relationship with others. Those others are persons with their own identities, so that kinship entails intimate participation in the way other people construe their identity too' (Edwards, Franklin, et al. 1999).

One could also ask, why technologies of procreation? One of the reasons that anthropological work on assisted reproduction and, increasingly, genetics and genomics has so strongly contributed to new kinship studies is perhaps the broader dissemination of new 'facts' of reproductive and genetic science. Narratives of procreation, conception, genealogy, and family are questioned, destabilized, and re-narrated through individual and collective experiences of kinship in the age of assisted conception (Edwards, Franklin, et al. 1999). Additionally, and increasingly, both what is understood to be reproductive and genetic knowledge and what is understood as the narratives that make sense of this knowledge must articulate a new foundation upon which they are based. It still seems that only recently egg and sperm cells were the point beyond which narratives of the constructed nature of conception could not go. However, the birth of a cloned sheep in 1996, the isolation of embryonic stem cells in 1998, and the growing number of scientific projects devoted to differentiating stem cells into germ cells and establishing human embryos without fertilization or hybrid embryos without human eggs offer new opportunities to study the cultural and literal making of nature.[5]

Ethnographies such as *Families We Choose* (Weston 1991), *Render Me, Gender Me* (Weston 1996), *Lesbian Mothers* (Lewin 1993), and *Recogniz-*

ing Ourselves (Lewin 1998a) expanded the parameters of gender and kinship studies in anthropology, repatriating lesbians and gay men to discourses of kinship and kinship studies from which they had been historically exiled (Weston 1991). While studies of lesbian and gay kinship were noted as burgeoning contributions to the new kinship studies (Franklin and McKinnon 2001), social science, and specifically ethnographic, research on lesbians' and gay men's experiences of assisted reproduction and genetics continues to be minimal (with the exception of the oft-cited contributions of Kath Weston's chapter 'Parenting in the Age of AIDS' in *Families We Choose*, Cori Hayden's article 'Gender, Genetics, and Generation: Reformulating Biology in Lesbian Kinship' published in *Cultural Anthropology* [1995], and Laura Mamo's recent book, *Queering Reproduction: Achieving Pregnancy in the Age of Technoscience* [2007]). This contrasts dramatically with the relationships established between lesbians, gay men, and emerging reproductive and genetic technologies in both academic texts and popular media, as will be discussed further below.

New Reproductive Autonomies?
Debating Assisted Reproduction in the United Kingdom and Canada

Analyses of reproductive technologies during the early 1980s created distinctions between different forms of practice and their relationship to women's reproductive autonomy. In contrast to newly visible practices of egg collection and either GIFT or IVF, donor insemination was represented as enhancing the abilities of women who wished to become pregnant without having sex with a man to exercise their reproductive autonomy outside of a clinical setting (Hornstein 1984; Duelli Klein 1984; Wolf 1982). The donor insemination practised by the women featured in these analyses was often of the so-called no-tech variety, involving fresh semen, known or anonymous donors, and, most likely, a diaphragm or needleless syringe to deposit the semen close to the cervix. In other cases, small 'sperm banks' enabled some women to use frozen sperm from anonymous donors. Many of these early sperm banks did not have sperm motility testing technologies, nor technical facilities to screen for sexually transmitted infections and genetic conditions, but rather were simply repositories for donor semen. The use of sperm banks, though, was viewed as facilitating even greater reproductive autonomy, distancing the recipient from the donor and thus obviating potential paternity concerns. As increasing knowledge of HIV transmission became available, small sperm banks ceased to exist. The dates of some of the publications mentioned above indicate that, although it may have generally been perceived as such, this time period was not part of a pre-AIDS era.

The period of the 1980s and early 1990s was marked not only by the increasing availability of reproductive technologies but also by debates regarding their appropriate regulation. Unlike the distinction between high, low, or no-tech technologies in feminist critiques, donor insemination (both within and outside of clinical contexts) became the topic of regulatory discussion. Throughout my research I have been influenced by developments in the United Kingdom and Canada, with my Canadian-based fieldwork influencing my reading and analyses of literature emerging from UK-based research, and my research experiences in the United Kingdom having influenced (also retrospectively) my analyses of developments in Canada. In the following pages I point to developments in the United Kingdom and Canada in order to draw attention to the contrasting modes of governing the practices of and access to assisted reproduction technologies and parental status and recognition.

United Kingdom

It was in England that Louise Brown, the first child conceived following IVF, was born. The United Kingdom was and still is viewed as a leader in the enactment of governance frameworks pertaining to assisted reproductive technologies. The Warnock Report, published in 1985, proposed the implementation of an act and a regulatory body – which eventually were, respectively, the Human Fertilisation and Embryology Act (1990) (HFE Act) and the Human Fertilisation and Embryology Authority (HFEA) which came into being in 1991(cf. Edwards, Franklin, et al. 1999; Franklin 1997). The legislation contained the possible permeations of the 'natural' family by constellations facilitated by medical technologies (see Haimes 1990; Dalton 2001). Most relevant to women trying to become pregnant outside of a relationship with a man was a clause included within the HFE Act (Section 13[5]) which stipulated that, prior to the provision of services, health professionals were required to take into account a would-be child's need for a mother and father. Clinics providing services that involved the storage of gametes (for example, cryopreserved semen) were within the remit of the Act. Single women's and lesbians' access to donor insemination services were subject to clinicians' reading of the 'welfare of the child' clause. Although it left room for interpretation and thus transgression as a hard and fast rule, restricting access to reproductive technologies was perceived by many to be inscribed in law. When Deborah Lynn Steinberg conducted the survey work that was reported in *Bodies in Glass*, published in 1997, a significant majority of UK fertility clinics maintained policies that excluded access by lesbian women. Interestingly, although section 13(5) could be invoked as a justification for this policy, Steinberg reports that the discursive rationale was related to the conservation of gametes, which were deemed to be in short supply, for those in need (that is, heterosexual couples having difficulty conceiving).[6] Section 13(5) became subject to an open consultation entitled *Tomorrow's Children*, only in 2005 (United Kingdom Human Fertilisation and Embryology Authority 2005). The revised guidelines published by the HFEA in 2006 maintained the so-called welfare of the child clause, but provided clear statements on its interpretation, including that it is discriminatory to refuse fertility treatment on the basis of sexual orientation.

The clarification regarding the right of lesbian women to fertility treatment (or, rather, their right not to be discriminated against) evoked a particular form of response that in relation to other challenges to the regulatory framework points to the continuing significance that male involvement in reproduction holds within the rhetoric. A newspaper report on the changes to the HFE Act, published in December 2006 under the headline 'Fatherless Babies in the Fertility Revolution,' claimed that the amendment would 'give single women and lesbians the right to treatment.' Discussing the revisions to the Act, Health Minister Caroline Flint pre-empted a particular thread of commentary, making it clear that restrictions will still be in place. The article states, 'Some medical advances will be outlawed, including the possible creation of a child by combining genetic material of two women, which would render males redundant altogether.' The sexuality of women trying to conceive outside of a relationship with a man does not seem to have maintained much hold within UK culture, with the emphasis remaining focused instead on how men will remain involved: what will or could *fatherless* actually mean? The HFE Act had previously been amended in a widely publicized case brought forward by Diane Blood to facilitate the inclusion on a child's birth certificate of a man who died prior to the child's conception, thereby illustrating the cultural significance of naming fathers. Minister Flint's clarification then can be placed in this context of and in relation to developments in reproductive science and representations of new fertility or reprogenetic practices.

In May 2001, the front page of the *Calgary Herald* featured a report on a new development in the field of assisted reproduction in Australia. The headline read 'Eggs of Two Moms Make One Baby' (Rogers 2001). Rogers writes, 'Scientists have created children who have two mothers' (2001, A1). The reason for articulating the new procedure in such a way is tied to the *partiality* of the genetic material that is to constitute genetic relatedness. Donor egg in vitro fertilization and gestational surrogacy (in which the surrogate is genetically unrelated to the fetus) both rely on discourses of reproductive intent and what Charis Cussins (1998b) articulates as distinctions between opaque and transparent kinship relations (see chapter 8) in order to define only one mother. In this case, however, the procedure is described as 'combining the genetic material of two donor mothers into one egg ... Scientists take a small amount of genetic material from the egg of a younger woman and place it into the older woman's egg to make fertilization more likely' (Rogers 2001, A1). The discourse of intent is still applicable, yet the distinction between the contributions of individual women will now perhaps rest on emphasizing the amount or origin of the genetic material contributed rather than a 'simple' designation of genetic, gestational, or social mother.

Shortly before the announcement of the revisions to the code of practice governing the implementation of the HFE Act, another set of 'dual mother' headlines was featured in UK newspapers.[7] The reports concerned research which had just been licensed by the HFEA and involved the combination of reproductive material from two women. The project was designed to look at the potential to transfer an egg nucleus of one woman into the enucleated egg of another woman in order to avoid the transmission of mitochondrial DNA disorders to potential children. In this case, if used as a 'therapeutic' practice, the combined genetic material would then be fertilized with sperm. This distinguishes it from the medical application which was mentioned by Minister Flint as quoted earlier, in which the combination of genetic material *only* from two women to create a baby would be banned. Reports that emerged when the license was issued, though, focused on the image of male redundancy and female-only reproduction – an aim that is not recorded in the license description. As an interesting contrast, techniques of parthenogenesis which are being used in embryonic stem cell research and reports about the possibility to control the differentiation of stem cells into germ cells (for example, sperm or eggs) did not evoke such commentary on redundancy but, rather, remarks on the potential discovery of new research and treatment resources.[8]

In January 2004, the UK government announced the review of the HFE Act (1990), a process which culminated in the Royal Assent of the Human Fertilisation and Embryology Act (2008) in November 2008. The new HFE Act transforms into law some of the policies and recommendations which had been guiding the interpretation and implementation of the Act in the preceding years as new technological possibilities emerged. Two of the provisions of the new Act noted on the Department of Health website, which may play key roles in the experiences of a woman trying to become a parent on her own or in the context of a relationship with a woman, are to 'recognise same-sex couples as legal parents of children conceived through the use of donated sperm, eggs or embryos' and 'retain a duty to take account of the welfare of the child in providing fertility treatment, but replace the reference to "the need for a father" with "the need for supportive parenting" – hence valuing the role of all parents.'[9] There is mention of some of the coverage of the parliamentary debates concerning the Human Fertilisation and Embryology Bill [HL] 2007–08 which led to the Act, within *Beyond Expectation*, but a full analysis of its implications will be left to future research.

Canada

In early reviews of current and pending legislation governing new reproductive and genetic technologies, Canada was expected to implement broad-reaching federal legislation (Spallone and Steinberg 1987). The Canadian government established the Royal Commission on New Reproductive Technologies (RCNRT) in 1989, just four years following the publication of the Warnock Report, which had provided the foundation for the Human Fertilisation and Embryology Act (1990) and the accompanying regulatory body, the Human Fertilisation and Embryology Authority, in the UK. The final report of the RCNRT, published in 1993, made over three hundred recommendations reflecting research on Canadian attitudes toward the use of assisted reproductive technologies and possibilities for governance. In 1995 a voluntary moratorium on particular practices was implemented, but although recommendations for regulation were revised and bills were tabled, they were consistently shelved.[10] It was not until March 2004 that the Assisted Human Reproduction Act was proclaimed, which includes the implementation of a regulatory oversight body, the Assisted Human Reproduction Agency of Canada (or Assisted Human Reproduction Canada).[11] A number of technological developments and new directions in research (especially as related to preimplantation genetic diagnosis, mammalian cloning by cell nuclear replacement, and investments in regenerative medicine and stem cell research) occurred during the late 1990s and early 2000s, providing perhaps the final impetus for the implementation of the Act. Thus, although voluntary and self-regulatory measures were in effect between 1995 and 2004, as well as legislation pertaining to particular aspects of assisted reproduction – specifically, donor insemination and semen storage – there was often ambiguity and uncertainty about the governance of reproductive technologies. In contrast to the framework implemented in the UK, the status of relationships arising from the use of assisted reproduction technologies and donor gametes was and is not governed by assisted reproduction legislation.

The narratives of women I interviewed are contextualized by a history of exclusion from clinic-based donor insemination or other assisted reproduction practices and access to programs that facilitated other options with respect to donor anonymity and place of insemination. Although a formal legislative framework did not exist, the experiences of the women and the options perceived to be available were affected by the implementation of moratoriums, directives, and guidelines and by the anticipation of forthcoming assisted reproduction legislation, and, importantly, decisions in human rights cases and changes to family law.

Assisted Reproduction Governance

Women whom I interviewed had accessed clinic-based donor insemination in British Columbia during the early 1980s, but most women told me that the one local (that is, British Columbia) physician who had provided access to donor semen would not inseminate a woman who disclosed her sexual identity.[12] During this period there were a few women's health clinics and community organizations in Washington, a northern state of the United States, and individual physicians in

British Columbia providing health services to women who were trying to conceive both within and outside of medical settings. These services were not always accessible to lesbians and bisexual women (but rather to women without husbands) and were not perceived to be viable options. Sperm banks located in other Canadian provinces would only distribute semen to a physician, a further restriction on women's access to donor semen and to the possible choices with respect to how and where to inseminate. A private fertility clinic opened in Vancouver in 1995 and openly facilitated access to assisted reproduction services by women identifying themselves as lesbian. A second fertility practice providing donor insemination services in Vancouver at the time of my fieldwork was mentioned by only three women – one who was trying to conceive and two who were deciding on donors and methods.

Between the early 1980s and 1995, and continuing to 1999, a number of the women I interviewed ordered semen from one of a few feminist and 'lesbian friendly' sperm banks which had opened in California. This enabled women to decide on the level of medical involvement in the conception process.[13] These organizations ran both anonymous and willing-to-be-known donor programs and would deliver semen to a physician or an individual, including those based in Canada. In 1999 a quarantine was issued by Health Canada on all semen currently stored at Canadian facilities, and Canada Customs employees were directed to detain the importation of human semen from international sources (Luce 2000, 2009). A case of Chlamydia trachomatis was reported to have been contracted from donor semen stored in Canada. Upon inspection, Health Canada discovered that many storage facilities for semen in Canada were not compliant with the 1996 Semen Regulations.[14] Some of the women in my study were unable to access semen that they had purchased from U.S. sperm banks – but which had not yet been delivered or which was being stored at Canadian facilities – due to variations between some of the screening tests used by the sperm banks and those necessitated by the Semen Regulations.

Although the interviewees who had accessed sperm banks in California during the 1980s and early 1990s were unclear about the legal status of importing semen, their concerns were most often framed within familiar North American narratives of cross-border shopping in the 1980s. The Health Canada quarantine reconfigured women's perceptions of the 'risk' of 'smuggling' semen into Canada. Thus, during my fieldwork, some women chose to use the donor insemination (intrauterine insemination) services of a local fertility clinic rather than do self-inseminations with semen purchased from California sperm banks because bringing sperm across the border was then considered 'illegal.' The storage, importation, and release of donor semen in Canada are governed by the Semen Regulations (2000), enforced by the Health Canada Therapeutic Products Programme. The quarantine ended with the implementation of new guidelines in July 2000, and the importation of semen from sperm banks conforming to the regulations was permitted. However, the California-based sperm banks that were mentioned by the women interviewed did not have the facilities to so conform.[15]

In 1991, in a survey conducted as part of the Royal Commission on New Reproductive Technologies, nineteen out of the thirty-three assisted insemination programs surveyed in Canada indicated that insemination services would not be provided to single heterosexual women, single lesbians, or lesbian couples (Canada 1993, 454). When the *Final Report of the Royal Commission on New Reproductive Technologies* was published, it was recommended that all women, including lesbians, be given equitable access to fertility services in compliance with the Canada Health Act and the Canadian Charter of Rights and Freedoms (RCNRT 1993, 456). In 1995 the British Columbia Council of Human Rights awarded $2,400 in compensation and $834 in expenses to a lesbian couple who had been denied access to donor insemination services by a BC physician. The council found that the physician had discriminated against the women on the 'basis of sexual orientation and/or family status' (Capen 1997). Although this case related specifically to one couple, the article by Capen (1997) with the title 'Can Doctors Place Limits on their Medical Practice?' in the *Canadian Medical Association Journal* offers an indication of its broader implications. The decision reinforced the principle of equitable access to health services, including fertility services and regardless of sex or family status.

Parental Rights and Family Law

In British Columbia, occurrences in the framework of family law, rather than claims to reproductive rights, contributed more often to the growing visibility and status of lesbians and gay men as parents or potential parents. Key changes took place in the late 1990s and early in the new millennium. In 1996 the provincial government of British Columbia amended the Adoption Act[16] to read 'any person or any two persons may adopt,' thus enabling single and partnered lesbians and gay men to file adoption applications in the province. In 1997, Bills 31 and 32 amended the Family Relations Act, which was proclaimed into force in 1998 and conferred legal recognition on same-sex partners in the definition of *spouse*, and thereby allocated to same-sex parents the rights and obligations of child support, custody, and access in the event of the dissolution of a relationship. In July 2000, Bill C-23 was proclaimed by the federal government, giving same-sex common-law partners in Canada the same rights and obligations as those of hetero-sexual common-law couples in the areas of legislation that confer rights or obligations through the category of spouse.[17] In August 2001 the BC Human Rights Tribunal determined that the BC Vital Statistics Agency had discriminated against same-gender partners by refusing the inclusion of two women's names on a child's birth registration form and, ultimately, the child's birth certificate. The decision facili-tated the recognition of a 'non-biological birth mother' and now allows a female partner of a biological birth mother to be recognized as her child's parent (co-parent) from the time of birth. In 2003 the Province of British Columbia legalized same-sex marriage, and in 2005 same-sex marriage became inscribed in federal legislation.

These legislative changes are recognized as having positioned British Columbia and Canada as leaders in formalizing lesbian and gay rights in North America. Importantly, though, the early changes did not confer rights to non-biological parents throughout the course of a relationship. During my fieldwork same-gender couples were still required to pay fees for a second-parent adoption in order to establish legal parental ties *within* the context of the relationship. Single lesbians and lesbian couples choosing to self-inseminate were (and are) still at risk of custody disputes by men legally recognized as biological fathers, regardless of whether or not a donor insemination contract has been signed (Arnup 1995). My interviews with queer women about their experiences of trying to become a parent prior to and shortly fol-lowing some of the recent changes in the BC provincial legislation defining same-sex parenting rights offer insight into gaps in the legis-lation. These stories also highlight the impact that the potential for legal recognition could have on queer women's thoughts about and experiences of health, health care, and parenting.

Intersecting Spheres of Governance

In a number of jurisdictions the regulation of kinship (including the legal status of parents, gamete donors, women who act as surrogate mothers, and so forth) is embedded within the governance of medical practice. For example, many of the shifts related to the definition of *mother* or *father* in the UK in circumstances where assisted reproductive technologies are used are the result of amendments to the Human Fertilisation and Embryology Act and the Code of Practice that accompanies it. As mentioned earlier, a well-known case brought forward by Diane Blood resulted in her dead husband being named as the father of her children on their birth certificates (although they were conceived following his death). In California, as Amy Agigian (2004) and Laura Mamo (2007) describe, as long as donor semen is transferred to the inseminating woman by a physician, the donor's paternal rights and obligations to any child conceived are severed.[18]

The connections between the governance of assisted reproduction and the governance of parental recognition are evident throughout the history of cases in British Columbia, as well as situations which continue to emerge across Canada. For the women I interviewed, decisions about how to become a parent often involved working within the context of possibilities offered in the two areas – assisted reproduction and family law – and sometimes privileging one or the other, but often combining possibilities afforded by both in order to try to secure parental recognition. For example, one of the first public custody challenges in British Columbia to involve a decision following donor insemination related to the separation of two women (Agigian 2004). This case is cited as the BC physician's reason for refusing to inseminate women who state they have a female partner: in the court dispute he was called upon to confirm the women's intention to parent together (Agigian 2004, 62–3). The women turned to a discourse of reproductive intent (and norms of assisted reproduction) as a means of trying to secure recognition for their relationship to the children. In other cases discussed herein, the norms of donor insemination discourses and contractual relations were employed to combine conception with semen from a known donor with the new legal possibilities of completing second-parent adoptions. A number of the women interviewed had been at the forefront of making changes. Yet, in the situations that are described it is always necessary to wonder about the women who may not be aware or have the resources or the security to question current norms.

New Public Visibilities

Debates about queer women's uses of assisted conception technologies do not only take place within discussions about medical risk and resource scarcity. Nor are they contained to court room litigations or discourses of human rights. Throughout the 1990s new forms of public visibility emerged, placing queer families and new medical technologies, which would make possible so-called same-sex biological parenting, on the front pages of newspapers, magazines, and popular science journals. Images of pregnant lesbians and lesbian and gay parents appeared on television, in movies, bookstore windows, and local newspapers. From the popular television drama *NYPD Blue* to the sitcom *Friends* to more recent films, such as *Chutney Popcorn, French Twist, Everything Relative, The Object of My Affection,* and *The Next Best Thing,* queer parenting politics were being explored in mainstream and alternative visual media. In print, Lisa Saffron contributed a regular lesbian parenting column to *Diva,* a British-based magazine. American magazines, such as *Girlfriends, Curve, Genre,* and *The Advocate,* published feature articles on queer parents (see also Saffron 1994). The premiere issue of *And Baby* hit newsstands in July 2001, and *Proud Parenting* (previously *Alternative Family*), a glossy magazine marketed to a queer parenting audience, entered its third year of publication in 2002. Non-mainstream press, such as Canadian-based *Xtra!, Xtra! West, Siren,* and *Herizons,* published articles on alternative insemination and queer families, as well as birth notices posted by new parents. The parenting tales of Toni, Clarice, and son Raffi (characters in Alison Bechdel's *Dykes to Watch Out For*) and the attempted conception experiences of Kenneth Marie in Noreen Stevens' *The Chosen Family* offered two examples of weekly comic strip contributions to the visibility of queer parents and prospective parents.

Concurrent with the increasing visibility of lesbian parents in the alternative and sometimes mainstream media which contextualized the period of my fieldwork, lesbians and gay men came also to be depicted as natural consumers of assisted reproductive technologies within scientific, medical, popular culture, humanities, and social science literature. No longer are the stories of reproductive autonomy restricted to low-tech, at-home self-insemination, but rather reproductive technologies, which now include medically assisted insemination, egg donation, in vitro fertilization, and surrogacy arrangements, are represented as advancing opportunities for lesbians and gay men to become parents. Writing for various audiences, many authors emphasize the *asexuality* of conception engendered by technology. If sexuality is separated from reproduction, that is, if sex is no longer necessary to reproduce, then it follows, it seems, that new reproductive technologies create the possibility for lesbians and gay men to become parents. In Dion Farquhar's words, 'by facilitating conception through alternative insemination by anonymous donor, single women, hetero-sexual couples and both partnered and single lesbians can conceive without the onus of instrumental sexual intercourse engaged in solely for the purpose of conception' (1996, 35).

Ronald Green, author of a 1999 article on cloning in *Scientific American*, takes the association between lesbians choosing children and the new reproductive technologies a step further to predict that 'lesbians might be the most likely consumers of cloning technology.' He comments that cloning would enable lesbian couples to most closely approximate genetic reproduction and would undermine recent shifts in the legal status of gamete donors. In July 2001 newspapers reported that scientists in Australia had discovered a means of fertilizing eggs using any cell of the body, precluding the need for sperm. Newspaper headlines, and in this case one of the researchers herself, noted the benefits of this research for lesbian couples wishing to have children.[19] Such inclusion of the subversive potential of new technologies, which followed the early debates about mammalian cloning, and thus the potential of human cloning, have continued while research proceeds, especially in the field of stem cell and reproductive medicine. A licence was awarded to the UK's Newcastle Fertility Centre at Life in 2005 to conduct research involving the transfer of a nucleus from one woman's egg to the enucleated egg of another woman, one of the most recent strands of research to be noted for its potential use by lesbian women.[20]

Public representations of queer sexuality and assisted reproduction narrate both inclusive and exclusionary tales through the re-creation of images of lesbians, dyke moms, wannabe parents, and reproductive technologies. Medically assisted conception is represented as offering new opportunities by disengaging reproduction from canonical sexuality. Interestingly, the seeming availability of alternative insemination contributes to the construction of a normative discourse of 'appropriate' alternative insemination (that is, anonymous) or instrumentation of sexual intercourse between a woman and man. As discussed herein, the everyday meanings of such normativity render it possible to question one's lesbian identity following conception after sexual intercourse with a man, as well as facilitate the synonimization of sexual intercourse with a male ex-partner and donor insemination. The imagined ease with which lesbians and gay men slip into the world of technological reproduction, and the normativity of technologically assisted conception within these media, popular, and academic constructions of 'queer families,' lies in contrast to the prevailing absence of lesbians from social science studies of assisted reproduction or reproductive health (for exceptions see Mamo 2007; Walks 2007; Lewin 1998b).

Lesbian parenting is often identified within lesbian health literature as a health issue, yet when I began my research and continuing today, lesbian *reproductive* health issues were and are seldom the subjects of in-depth published research (Solarz 1999).[21] Early on in my fieldwork, Paula, a woman interviewed, explained that she had not involved her family doctor – a lesbian general practitioner who practised obstetrics – in her quest to become pregnant because it [getting pregnant] 'didn't seem like a health issue.' It was only after she had located a physician who was willing to inseminate lesbians that her general practitioner became involved in her care. Similarly, Rita remarked that she and her partner had never considered trying to get pregnant within the medical system, 'because it all seemed so easy': they had wanted to use a known donor, they located one easily, and her partner conceived on the first try. My attention to queer women's narratives of assisted reproduction as a health issue encompasses questions about seeking and locating health information and health providers and re-frames the experience of thinking about and trying to have children as one which influences queer women's well-being and is relevant to analyses of the politics of reproduction.

In this chapter I have provided images of the academic, political, medical, legislative, and popular contexts within which *Beyond Expectation* is embedded. As will be shown in the following three parts to this book, the meanings of the events, legislative changes, and shifts within social perceptions and articulations of the relationships between queer sexuality, identity, and parenting described in this chapter are in no way uniform. Rather, knowledge about and experiences with emerging forms of governance, new practices of assisted reproduction, and expectations of relationships and relatedness were mediated in varied ways and often re-negotiated over time.

PART I

Re-imagining Relations

'Spousal Rights Pass in BC' (*Xtra West* 1997)
'BC Gay Parents Gain Equality' (Matas 1998)
'BC Includes Queers in Family Law Act: Children Protected in
   Amendment' (Findlay 1998)

During the late 1990s British Columbia made headline news throughout North America and the world as one of the most progressive jurisdictions in which to be or become a queer parent (findlay 1998; Matas
1998; *Xtra!* 1997). As more than one lesbian mom or prospective parent
told me, 'We're lucky to live in BC.' However, changes at the level of
legislation do not always result in changes at the level of practice.
Formal recognition of parental rights and status held different meanings for the women I interviewed who were living in various regions
of British Columbia and who had differential access to important
resources such as financial support, health information, health care,
supportive (that is, non-discriminatory) social workers, and other
queer parents. Concurrent with women's more pragmatic and philo-
sophical quests for information about how to become a parent were
women's practices of strategically outing themselves and creating
environments in which they and their children would be recognized as
family. Legislation that supports and upholds the rights of lesbian and
gay men to adopt, and recognizes same-sex partners and parents in
spousal and custody disputes, promotes images of tolerance that
surpass acceptance. Yet, it is problematic to emphasize the rights
accorded to queer women by legislative shifts without paying attention
to queer women's everyday experiences. Homophobia and heteronormativity shape queer women's ideas and experiences of reproduc-

tion, reproductive health, and family. The ways in which the women I interviewed mediated positive and negative sites of 'difference' and made sense of their options, choices, and experiences within particular contexts highlights the multiple meanings of and connections between sexuality, kinship, family, and technology. Being queer; sleeping with women; identifying as lesbian, gay, bisexual, or transgender; being single or in a relationship; having sex with a man for pleasure or by force; coming-out experiences; and having lived in regions with or without community support were significant to the women's stories about their thoughts, expectations, and experiences of bringing children into their lives. Parents, or individuals who occupied significant roles in women's and men's childhoods, are often central to coming-out narratives, in some ways reproducing the privileged and expected relationship between parents and children. In the women's narratives about coming out as parents-to-be, women were often doing so in order to confirm kinship relations and the involvement of individuals in their expected children's lives. One's status as grandparent, uncle, or aunt was not restricted or even premised on biological relatedness but rather was characterized by action. Who claims kinship to children? Who actively establishes a relationship? The involvement of women's families was not dependent on who the biological mother was but rather on the meaning the women themselves attributed to that biological tie or to the broader scope in which relationships are recognized, rejected, or re-evaluated. In contrast to coming-out narratives that highlight fears of rejection, the narratives of those coming out as prospective parents highlight agency and strategy. Few women accepted practices of non-recognition or silence.

The chapters in this section address the changing and multiple strategies that women employed in order to address more pragmatic questions about becoming a queer parent (for example, where to find information about insemination, adoption, and medical assistance), as well as women's strategies for creating supportive living environments for themselves and their children.

2 Imagining Queer Parenthood

Nearly twenty-five years ago when her son was born, Rae felt like 'a pioneer, searching around for somebody to talk with about a similar experience.' Talking about the questions raised in becoming a parent, Rae reflected, 'I wasn't the dad; I wasn't the body mom. Who was I? That kind of thing, the identity thing.' Rae never found a role that fit. She stated: 'There's a sense of place more now, but not then. It was very confusing. At that particular time there were a lot of kids around in my life, which was good. I gravitated to women and kids, just to get some support – but not really. I felt alone – sort of like coming out as a lesbian, very similar.'

That sense of being pioneers has somewhat vanished. Queer women today know that there are other queer parents: the visibility of lesbian parenting in the news media and sitcoms, dramas, and films has established images of queer women as parents, in some cases even identifying their route to parenthood. In October 1997, the *Winnipeg Free Press* published a brief article on Ellen DeGeneres and Anne Heche's plans to have a baby.[1] The Mother's Day issue of the *Vancouver Sun* in 1999 featured an article by local Vancouver writer Karen Tulchinsky on the trials and tribulations of attempting to conceive (Tulchinsky 1999).[2] The story of David Crosby's contribution as a sperm donor to Julie Cypher and Melissa Etheridge's family made the cover of *Rolling Stone Magazine* in January 2000, hardly a medium that is out of the way or difficult to access.

By most estimates, there are many more self-identifying queer women actively trying to become parents these days than there were twenty years ago (Arnup 1995; Lewin 1993; Nelson 1996).[3] Women I interviewed in urban areas who were *already parenting* had as either friends or acquaintances at least five to ten other lesbian moms. Women in smaller communities often knew at least three to five other lesbian moms. Yet, in both large and small communities it was not uncommon for queer women *planning* to parent to tell me that they did not know another lesbian who had either tried to conceive or tried to adopt while identifying as queer. It seemed as though each woman I interviewed found herself in an information void, which she set about filling by using various strategies. Although the sense of being a pioneer, as Rae described, has somewhat diminished, many women I interviewed about their experiences still felt like they were breaking new ground in the mid- to late 1990s.

Comparing the experiences of women who were thinking about having children or who tried to get pregnant beginning in the mid-1990s to those that occurred between 1980 and 1995, there are significant differences in their approaches to acquiring information about becoming a parent. Whereas in earlier eras support groups formed to facilitate the exchange of knowledge and informed decision making, today queer women tend to navigate in greater isolation the questions surrounding the pursuit of parenthood. Women are more likely to read books about lesbians getting pregnant or to spend hours online reading the testimonials of queer parents, investigating the options at various clinics, or scrolling through donor profiles on sperm bank websites than to participate in real-time support groups for women considering parenthood or trying to conceive.[4] This chapter traces a number of the trajectories by which women sought and located information about becoming a parent.

Lesbian Conception Support Groups

The 1970s and 1980s were pivotal times for the women's health movement and for consciousness raising among women about the medicalization of women's bodies and, in particular, reproduction (cf. Boston Women's Health Book Collective 1994; Clarke and Olesen 1999; Terry 1999; Martin 1987). Sharing information, forming discussion groups, and learning collectively were means by which women acquired knowledge about their bodies. During the 1980s, and even into the 1990s, women I interviewed joined (or often formed) discussion and support groups comprising lesbians who were considering parenthood or trying to conceive.[5] Formed by women hoping to exchange information and share experiences, the groups facilitated discussions about the suitability of different donors, single parenting and shared parenting arrangements, and information regarding the legal status of donors and so-called non-biological mothers. As one woman explained, 'It was what we did in those days. If you wanted to learn something, you formed a group. If you wanted to stop smoking, you formed a group.' And, by extension, if you wanted to have children, you formed a group. Many of the women interviewed were the first of their friends to raise children who had been conceived (by themselves or, more often, their partner) in previous heterosexual relationships *and* were among the first to try to become pregnant as a self-identifying lesbian or attempt to become a parent within the context of a relationship with a woman. The support groups diminished women's sense of isolation and fostered the awareness that lesbian families by alternative insemination were being created. Yet, as the stories of women show, support groups could also increase women's sense of isolation and of not belonging.

A number of women interviewed had been pregnant and experienced miscarriages or abortions prior to exploring the alternative insemination route.[6] Whereas some queer women who formed or joined support groups were looking for information about the physiology of their bodies and the technical aspects of conception, other women were searching for information about and support for the act of creating families in alternative ways. Many women were seeking both. Yvonne was one of the women I interviewed who co-founded a support and discussion group for lesbians and straight women interested in alternative insemination. She had been pregnant and had an abortion before, but it was a second pregnancy in 1988 that marked the beginning of her story of assisted conception. Yvonne recalled:

> I was bisexual, and I was involved with men and I got pregnant. And I wasn't involved [that is, in a relationship] with him at all. I assumed I'd have an abortion, and then I started thinking, 'I could have kids; it would be amazing.' So I started talking to my friends, and it just sort of started becoming a great idea. I guess it was 1988. I would have been 32. So, that was sort of moving along, and then I had a miscarriage. But I knew, that's how I knew, I wanted to get pregnant and that I wanted kids.

Following her miscarriage Yvonne began exploring the option of alternative insemination and navigating the various issues involved. A friend of hers who was also trying to get pregnant passed on a contact

she had with a gay man who was interested in co-parenting. Although
Yvonne exchanged letters with the man, they did not pursue the relationship further.[7] Next, leaning toward not having the 'father'
involved, she was shocked when a gay friend expressed that he was
adamantly opposed to 'someone having a kid without a father
involved.' Yvonne recalled, 'I was pretty out about what I was up to,'
which ended up – I think if I were doing it again, I wouldn't talk to
everybody and broadcast everything.'

Women often encountered strong opinions from women and men
about the use of known and unknown donors, the significance of
genetic relations, the use of medical intervention, the importance of
gender role models, and the involvement of co-parents. Women
sought safe spaces in which they could explore different options and
have the support of other women working through similar questions.
The desire for such safe spaces was often the foundation of support
groups. Yvonne continued:

> [My friend] and I organized a bunch of women whom we knew that were
> trying to get pregnant, and organized ourselves into a little support
> group. There were about six or seven women. And I'm pretty sure, when
> we very first started, we were all trying to get pregnant, although one of
> them, I think, was pregnant for the first meeting and didn't know it. That
> group met a few times, and … one person got pregnant – and she and her
> partner were both in the group – very quickly. And then another woman
> who had been trying for a year on her own, and was having a kid on her
> own, really shortly after the group started got pregnant. And then [my
> friend's] partner got pregnant. Then [of two other women] – I guess
> maybe they'd just gotten together and they'd both been trying to get
> pregnant before they got together – [one] got pregnant. And then that
> affected the group because it was really hard to meet with people who
> were already pregnant when you were trying to get pregnant. It was too
> completely different a place to be, and it wasn't working for those of us
> who weren't pregnant. But the people who were pregnant belonged to
> this group. And we didn't split into two. We just kind of stopped.

By the time the group stopped meeting, Yvonne, having not yet
located a known donor, was 'headed toward clinics' and, living in
urban Ontario, decided to explore that option. In 1993 Yvonne inseminated for five cycles at a southern Ontario clinic and did not get
pregnant. Shortly thereafter, family obligations necessitated a move

and she 'put it aside.' In her early forties when we met, Yvonne commented:

Meanwhile I had kids in my life and I kind of focused my energies on those kids. And I have, since then, never been in a situation again where I thought I could do it. I haven't had any money, and, yes, the money stops me right there. I declared bankruptcy from the business, you know. I had very, very little money, and I couldn't afford it. And my life's been topsy-turvy. In the time where I made the decision I was in a job that I ultimately had had for seven years. I had maternity leave. I had the EI [employment insurance] pop-up plan.[8] It was almost all women at work. There was another woman who was trying to get pregnant at the same time with her partner. I was in a shared supportive environment. And that would be – you know, that was the setting for me.

Yvonne's decision to get pregnant was made at a point in her life when she felt that becoming a parent was quite plausible. The role that a supportive environment played in Yvonne's narrative was present in most other women's considerations of parenthood, although what constituted support varied. While some women made the point that there never would be a perfect time to have a child, most women felt that sometimes would be better than others.

Yvonne's experiences with the support group that she and her friend had organized were similar to those of other women who found that their needs changed quite quickly depending on whether or not they were able to conceive and whether or not other group members were getting pregnant. While in her early thirties Paula and her partner at the time decided they wanted to become parents and 'decided quite quickly that [Paula] would be the one who would become pregnant and who would have the child.' As Paula described it, they spent many unsuccessful months trying to find a sperm donor, talking to nearly all of the straight and gay men they knew over a six-month period.[9] Around this time Paula and her partner read an article in their local newspaper about a lesbian couple who had conceived two children and were 'working on their third' with the 'help' of a local physician. Paula commented:

The only reason we wanted a known donor was because we thought at some point in this child's life there would probably be reasons why they would want to be able to trace their medical history in order to make certain decisions or to figure out certain medical stuff. We wanted to be able to offer that child a medical history, and there wasn't any other reason. We wanted to not have the involvement of this guy in the parenting of the child. We didn't want to end up in court someday with this guy claiming parental rights. So, it was basically to avoid any involvement of anybody else. And the fear of losing ... At that time it seemed very real. I don't know how good it would be today. But it definitely seemed very real that we could lose [our sole parental status] in court. We would have immediately gone that route, but we didn't know there was anybody who would inseminate lesbians. We didn't even try that. That's why we were going to a trusted friend who would sign this piece of paper [releasing his parental claim]. It wasn't because we wanted a known donor; we thought that was the only way at that time that dykes could get pregnant.

The article in the newspaper, significantly, provided the impetus to begin a support group for lesbians who were trying to get pregnant. Paula said:

I don't remember if it was us or if it was another couple – because there was another couple who was trying to get pregnant at the same time as we were. One of us put a sign up at the Gay and Lesbian Centre, based on that article, because suddenly we knew there was somebody else out there, right. And in no time at all we must have had twelve couples in this 'lesbians trying to get pregnant' support group. It was very, very fast how it came together from that article. And then we stayed together. That group met probably once a month. And as we were all trying, we were all at the same place. Not all of us were trying to get pregnant, but all of us were thinking about it, asking questions, trying to create structures in our life that would facilitate that. I stayed with the group for about six months.

Paula sought out the doctor mentioned in the lesbian-conceptions news article and did intracervical inseminations at his practice for six months. She never became pregnant. Continuing with her description of the support group, she said:

That's mainly the body that I reported back to every month as a failure. And I also felt that I was letting down women who hadn't sort of started it yet. I didn't want to tell the truth about how I was feeling because I didn't want to discourage anybody who hadn't started yet.

Support groups were sometimes double edged as women sought support for their individual experiences but felt responsible for the well-being of others. Paula's feelings of failure were similar to those of other women who had difficulty conceiving. As she noted, when the group was founded, 'we were all at the same place.' Actively trying to conceive and not getting pregnant quickly marginalized Paula from what she understood to be the core objectives of the support group. She was not able to offer other women in the group a model of hope or to provide an example of how possible it was to become a lesbian parent – key reasons that women gave for wanting to share with each other the process to parenthood. Paula was also unable to get support for herself and to claim the space within which she could discuss her bodily experiences and her reactions each month to not getting pregnant. In support groups, pregnant bodies were symbols of success; non-pregnant women were reminders of failure. Even now, Paula stated during our interview, she does not feel comfortable sharing her experiences with women who are just beginning to try.

Queer women's narratives of conception are not only about a circumscribed act of 'getting pregnant'; conception stories are embedded in larger political discourses, reflecting both mainstream and counter-culture or alternative perspectives of the time. Support groups not only brought together women who were considering parenthood[10] to exchange information and build a sense of community but they were also sites of contestation; they were sites in which the politics and representations of the lesbian baby boom were discussed, debated, enforced, deconstructed, and recreated. Debates about various methods of conception, the role of medical intervention, and the politics of choosing known or anonymous donors or donors of differing ethnicities were at times heated (see also Hornstein 1984; Wolf 1982). As contrasting viewpoints emerged, members of support and discussion groups were required to reflect on the politics and ethics of the choices and decisions involved in having a child or children. Some groups had longer lifespans than others: the structure of the group remained the same while the members changed. Sometimes the members remained the same while the goals of the group changed to meet the needs of new contexts. In many of these groups, built upon the image of creating families, women drifted away when their bodies, choices, and/or experiences no longer fit.

Internet-Based Sites and Support

New communication technologies, especially the emergence of the Internet and its more widespread use by the late 1990s, re-spatialized information and redefined notions of connectivity (Rose and Novas 2005). Scholars have written about the changes that Internet technologies have made to notions of group organization, participation, and belonging with respect to several themes, be they political activism, health information access, or health experiences (Rapp, Heath, and Taussig 2001; Schaffer, Kuczynski, and Skinner 2008). A number of key websites devoted to queer-parenting issues provide information that ranges from lists of the fertility programs and sperm banks that provide services to single women and/or lesbians to samples of donor contracts.[11] There are also a number of electronic mailing lists and chat rooms for queer moms and prospective parents.[12] Although a few women I interviewed first approached their family physician in search of information about having children, after 1995 the Internet played a key role in providing to those women trying to get pregnant a sense of the number of queer women wanting to become parents or already parenting. For women who were 'connected,' the ability to interact with other lesbian parents and prospective parents transgressed the barriers of geography, privacy, and the ability to be out about their plans to get pregnant. For some women, especially lesbians living in regions with neither a large health services community nor a large queer community, the Internet was perceived as *the* gateway to information and knowledge. Just as some women might speak of going to a library, health clinic, or women's centre for information, Adele talked about going online. Her description highlights the non-ubiquity of Internet access during the period just prior to, and in fact during, my study. In contrast to current emphases on people's access to information, it is necessary to avoid presumptions about widespread knowledge of how to use and make the most of computer technologies. Adele commented:

> About a year ago I got on the Internet with a friend because I started thinking about [getting pregnant] again. Another of my friends had a baby, and that just kind of sets me off every once in a while. So I talked to

another friend who had the Internet, and we got on there together. She helped me kind of get through things and find different spots, and we got a bunch of information, just general kind of stuff. One was a chat room for lesbians – for even gay men, I think – that you could go and talk and tell how you had a baby. And so there were a lot of women saying, you know, they just found a friend. A lot of them were fathers already that didn't mind being a donor and doing it that way. And then I thought of the possibilities that, you know, there would be, maybe if I found the right person, a male influence, you know, in the child's life. And that's what a lot of people say: 'Wouldn't that be right (in their minds) for raising a child?' I don't agree with it myself; my mother was a single mother for a lot of years. You know, there's three of us, and I'm the only one that's gay, so ...[13]

For Adele, the Internet was not an everyday resource but rather it represented a site of key information to which she had only limited access, both in the sense of literal hook-up and in the know-how of navigating the information highway. For a number of other women interviewed who sought information a couple of years later than did Adele, the Internet was more familiar and accessible. Beth and Faye, a couple in their late twenties, did not know anyone who had tried to get pregnant by donor insemination; however, they were very familiar with the individual websites of commercial sperm banks, as well as websites directed toward queer parents. Their answers to many of the questions I asked about their plans to have children were based on information they had acquired online. For example, Beth and Faye relied on the Internet to develop their initial ideas about how to decide between a sperm bank donor and a known donor and, if the latter, whether or not to draw up a contract. Faye stated: 'From what I've read on different websites, it's not that [donor contracts are] not legal, but if somebody's going to fight for custody, they're not going to matter. So, I figured, there's no point. They might help you to sort of figure out some guidelines ... We found a site that had samples [of donor contracts]. I think it was that Alberta one.[14]

The Internet is often experienced as interactive or as a link to other women and men in similar circumstances. Yet, significantly, women were interacting with the information and not the individuals who provided the testimonials or advice. Adele's comment traced the links she made between women choosing known donors and the idea of having a male figure in her child's life to the discourse relating same-gender sexual orientation to the absence of a male figure, and then countered that with her own biography, stating that she was the only gay child out of three siblings sole-parented by her mother. Beth and Faye had read that donor contracts had not been tested in court and came to the conclusion that there was no point in having one, other than to assist in clarifying intended relations and roles. Although women like Adele, Beth, and Faye respond to the information posted on Internet sites by relating it to their own lives, they have limited access (limited by those inputting the information) to an in-depth understanding of the life history or biographical details that inform the online statements made regarding the choice of a known donor, the decisions not to enact donor contracts, and the practices of self-insemination. Also missing is often the access to the experiences of women who change their mind. The variety of choices women make and the multiple avenues women pursue are often missing from these representations.

As mentioned, other popular results of Internet technology are the emergence of online chat rooms and, perhaps even more commonly used, electronic mailing lists. Caroline and Pam participated on a dyke-mom LISTSERV for many years before they tried to have a child. With participants from potentially all over the world, but predominantly North America, one of the most common uses of such mailing lists was the receipt and distribution of information on legislation in different jurisdictions, particularly with respect to the legal status of children born to lesbian parents by donor insemination. The various perspectives of the website owners and LISTSERV participants constitute contemporary images of the lesbian baby boom on a much larger scale than that of the support groups previously described. Perhaps 'considering parenthood' support groups are not a thing of the past but rather have been relocated to cyberspace. Information and debates about known donors, anonymous donors, donor contracts, and so forth are now taking shape online.

Open Doors

We have participated in the lesbian baby boom because [of] almost everybody we know, and in every circle of friends, there are at least two to six couples that are parents. It's massive, don't you find that? In every one of our circles. Because we finally have a fertility clinic that [will inseminate lesbians]. It just takes money, and not that much money. It's very feasible. (Chandra)

The history of low-tech donor insemination in British Columbia is varied. For almost fifteen years women who identified themselves as lesbian to service providers did not have access to a sperm bank and donor insemination services in the province. Some women I interviewed told me about physicians in regions outside of Vancouver who, they believed, had access to donor sperm, but the most common narrative was that there was one physician in Vancouver who did 'AI' (artificial insemination); he was the 'only show in town.' Although women in my study knew lesbians who had been inseminated at this physician's clinic, common understanding was that, since the early 1980s, the physician had refused to provide insemination services to women identifying as lesbian.[15] Thus, some women I interviewed chose to use these local insemination services without discussing their sexuality or partnerships. Other women looked for information about assisted insemination and access to donor sperm elsewhere. Women who wanted to use semen from anonymous donors procured through a clinic were among the first women from British Columbia to travel to Washington State to use the services of a women's clinic or to pick up or have delivered semen from sperm banks based in California (see Luce 2009).[16]

The opening of a fertility clinic in Vancouver in 1995, which stated outright that services would be provided regardless of sexual orientation,[17] had multiple effects on both the collective narrative of assisted conception in British Columbia and the simultaneous segregation and conflation of issues related to trying to conceive as a self-identifying lesbian woman. Support groups, typical of the 1970s and 1980s, reflected a politics of engaged information gathering and sharing. One could say that they were contested sites of knowledge production and exchange as women debated and negotiated the politics of assisted conception. Within these sites the parameters of 'health' were significantly broader as women integrated their questions about creating supportive environments and families with their decisions about using particular donors and learning about their bodies in the process of attempting to get pregnant. Access to a local fertility centre offered solutions to problems of legal parental status and the perceived risks of HIV transmission – and trust, both in people and information. At the time of my interview with Beth and Faye they were both nearing thirty, had travelled extensively, owned a house, had been together for nearly ten years, and did not know any other lesbians who had conceived after coming out. Their co-workers and family expected them to have children, viewing parenthood as the next logical step in their relationship and lives. Yet, at the time of our interview Beth and Faye had made few decisions about how they would actually go about trying to get pregnant. Like Adele, they looked for information on the Internet. Unlike Adele, they were familiar with computer and Internet technology, which had advanced. They downloaded information about donor contracts and the cost of donor semen from a sperm bank and had already done a great amount of reading about the potential legal complications of using known donors. They were the only women interviewed who, in the late 1990s, were considering using an anonymous 'live' donor outside of the clinical system.[18] Today, most women choosing non-sperm-bank donors choose known donors in order to include the donor in the child's life. To contemplate using an anonymous live donor, women often find themselves assessing their understandings of heredity, genetics, and the means of HIV and other STI transmissions. They have to rely on their evaluations of risk and trust to a somewhat greater extent than do women who choose known donors with whom they have, or will develop, a relationship whereby certain forms of knowledge (or uncertainty) are supplanted by forms of knowing. Women must also assess the possible legal risks, in the absence of knowing a donor, in order to alleviate fears about potential custody disputes between the donor and the women. Thus, in contrast to the previous protection that anonymity seemed to afford, it is knowledge and knowing that are more prevalent in later narratives. Almost a year after the interview with Beth and Faye I received an email from them, enquiring about midwifery services in BC. They had decided to go through a local fertility centre. Beth was pregnant and Faye was still trying.

Contrasting in various ways to Beth and Faye's narrative, Jeanette and Katharine, both in their late thirties when they decided to have a child, had a number of friends who were already lesbian parents. They also had friends who had used the services of a fertility centre. Jeanette stated:

> Our friends who went through Creative Beginnings[19] had a really good experience ... And I also knew that I would probably need some fertility aid because I have a very irregular menstrual cycle. So I suspected, you know, that I'd probably need some help. So, our friends had a really good experience at Creative Beginnings. You know, not only did they have

really good results, they all say it was a really warm – they found it really a pleasant experience and helpful to them.

This narrative could have continued as a straightforward story in which the decision to go through Creative Beginnings was dissociated from the key questions most lesbians face when deciding between a known donor and an unknown donor. However, Katharine, who had been paying attention to their toddler (who was running around the table with my tape recorder), interjected:

> Did you talk about the fact that we debated about going with somebody that we knew?
> JEANETTE: Yeah, I guess we did think about that, didn't we?
> KATHARINE: We thought about it. We thought about different angles and got different people's opinions about how to do it. And there was a couple, a lesbian couple, that were thinking of – well, they actually had a donor that they knew to give them sperm, and it all fell through. And we sort of thought, before then, that no way were we going with someone that we knew because we want them as friends; we don't want them as dad. We do want them as part of Kyle's life.

Again, the fertility centre, and the severing of donor's rights through the normative practices of medically assisted insemination practice, in which the donor is presumed to have no parental rights, resolved the potential legal and social complications of using a known donor.[20] As well, Jeanette, referring to her irregular cycle, believed that she would need fertility aid, which for her raised the question of why she would start outside of the system only to move into it eventually. One of the unspoken dimensions to this logic is that the clinical practice policy at the time did not permit women to be inseminated with semen from an unrelated donor (that is, a man who was not the sexual partner of the woman to be inseminated) unless he was also anonymous or a participant in a directed donor program. The program involves testing the potential donor, freezing and quarantining the donor's semen sample for six months, and retesting the donor after this period has elapsed. If all test results are negative, the semen can be released. Until the implementation of the amended Semen Regulations in 2000 in Canada, gay men (formally, men with a 'history of homosexuality') were often prohibited from acting as donors within a clinical setting, based on practice guidelines. The implementation of the new Semen Regulations made it prohibitive for men who had had sex with a man to participate in sperm donor programs in Canada. Health Canada's Special Access Programme now facilitates access, through specific petition processes, to donor semen that would not otherwise be processed or released (Luce 2009).[21]

Jeanette and Katharine's awareness of their friends' experience with Creative Beginnings, and their knowledge of another friend's failed negotiations with a known donor, influenced their decision to begin the process of attempting to conceive at a fertility clinic. By using donor sperm made available through the fertility centre, the donor's rights have already been absolved, brokered through the norms of tissue and organ donation, thus alleviating the need to investigate the current (and future) legal standing of donor contracts. The sperm bank has already tested the donor and the semen for sexually transmissible infections and administered questionnaires regarding the donor's family-health history, hobbies, personality, and reasons for donating. A number of choices and decisions which could be made have already been narrowed down. Some women I interviewed spent years deciding on a known donor, discussing his involvement with the child, debating whether or not to develop legal contracts, and coordinating schedules so that both the donor and the woman who was inseminating would be in the same general vicinity at the time of ovulation. In comparison, choosing a donor from a catalogue, using frozen semen that can be thawed when one is about to ovulate, and knowing that the donor's paternity status has been absolved may seem significantly less complicated and time consuming.[22]

Real-Life Inspirations

In contrast to the iconic images of Melissa Etheridge and Julie Cypher or the chat room participants discussed earlier, lesbian mothers in reality still represent special sources of inspiration and information for queer women wanting to become parents. The number of queer parents whom women knew and included in their close circle of friends, or designated as 'families of the heart' (see below), varied according to shaping influences such as geographical region and leisure activities. Jenna and her partner had been together for thirteen years, and 'from the very beginning ... we both knew that we really wanted to be parents.' Being in the presence of lesbians who had children became quite significant once they had officially made the decision to go ahead with their plans to become parents. Jenna explained:

> We had lots of lesbian friends, and we had kind of heard and read about this lesbian baby boom, but we didn't actually know anyone … Actually that's not true. I did know one couple but only very, very peripherally, sort of an acquaintance level, who had had a daughter a long time ago, who's probably now thirteen years old or something. I can remember, sort of around that time when we were really seriously considering it, the few occasions when we went somewhere and there was a lesbian couple with a baby and what a huge impact that had on me. Just sort of: 'That could be us. What do you think that would feel like?' And talking to the women and just emotionally getting really close to the idea that we could do this. So then we sort of set about evaluating all the various options. And the other thing was, although we considered adoption, part of it for me was that I had always really wanted to actually get pregnant and experience childbirth and breastfeeding and all that. And although my partner also really wanted to be a mom, she didn't have that biological urge at all.

In the planning stages many women actively sought out other queer women and men who had children and could offer practical (and often 'technical') advice. Women themselves may not have known anyone else who was a queer parent, but someone they knew most likely knew someone who had conceived using reproductive assistance or had adopted. Even as the visibility of celebrity lesbian parents increased and the Internet became increasingly a site of information exchange, reading and surfing was often complemented by talking to a real-life lesbian mom.

The processes of imagining parenthood and literally setting out to find information that could make that possible have changed over time, informed by new communication technologies, transitions in usual modes of social networking or social engagement, and the emerging visibility and changing status of alternative family forms. As this chapter highlights, the context in which women's ideas about parenting, and specifically parenting as a queer woman, developed played a significant role in defining a so-called starting point and, ultimately, the decisions that were made. The narratives also show the diversity of experiences which can contribute to women's access to and use of support groups, online information, virtual communities, and interpretations of other people's advice and knowledge about existing health and legal services. The next chapter focuses more closely on how the women I interviewed actively created or rendered explicit specific relationships with children, expected children, partners, donors, co-workers, or other family members and friends as integral aspects of anticipating parenthood or parenting.

3 Strategic Outings

During my fieldwork two women told me a story that in my retelling always seems a slightly romanticized tale of transformation, but it is also perhaps indicative of the processes of recognition. The women live with their two children in the Okanagan Valley, a politically conservative region of British Columbia. Their neighbour had a bumper sticker on his car which identified him as a supporter of the right-wing Canadian Alliance political party. During the lead up to the Canadian federal election in 2000, members of the Canadian Alliance made several anti-gay remarks.[1] One afternoon the neighbour peeked over the fence to both introduce himself and inform the women that he would be removing the bumper sticker from his car. For the women I interviewed, symbolic refutations of homophobia, of which this is only one example, carried significant weight and were often tied to a realization and recognition of relatedness. In this case it was, perhaps, this man's recognition that his neighbours were included as targets of these anti-gay remarks or that such remarks affected his community. The everyday experiences of the women interviewed included celebrating public challenges to heteronormativity, as well as the smaller-scale, visible displays of non-discriminatory or changing attitudes such as the one described.

Although, politically, British Columbia, under the leadership of the New Democratic Party (NDP) from 1991 to 2001, introduced numerous legislative changes in support of lesbian and gay families, expressions of intolerance were very visible during the period of my fieldwork. In Surrey, just outside of Vancouver, the school board banned the use of three children's books in classrooms in 1997 – *Belinda's Bouquet*; *Asha's Mums*; and *One Dad, Two Dads, Brown Dad, Blue Dads*, which feature positive images of lesbian and gay parents.[2]

In 2002 the Supreme Court of Canada ordered that the books be reconsidered for use according to 'the broad principles of tolerance and non-sectarianism underlying the School Act' (as quoted by Egale 2002). At a restaurant in East Vancouver a flyer glued to the toilet-paper dispenser proclaimed the need to prohibit the adoption of children by lesbians and gay men. In the West End of Vancouver a similar posting glued to a newspaper box warned, 'Our kids are at risk if teachers are gay.' In Nelson, a small town in the West Kootenay Mountains, a flyer on a community bulletin board advertised a forthcoming 'Heterosexual Pride Day.'[3] Public homophobic utterances such as these re-produce and naturalize histories of homophobia and hate. They comprise a portion of the everyday contexts in which queer women think about becoming parents. Narratives of unexpected acceptance are thus recognized as unexpected interventions not only to the often much more dominant heteronormative culture but also to the homophobic and transphobic situations in which parents and children may find themselves.

Raising Questions

When we met, Bryn was twenty-nine years old, an artist, a student, and a lesbian, and she described herself as 'desperately' wanting to be a mom. She had been planning to 'enter motherhood' for nearly ten years and, with a slight laugh, remarked that she had thrown out six years' worth of temperature and ovulation charts just a few days before our interview. Bryn told a story that identified homophobia as a key reproductive health issue, an issue about which she expected her physician to have information. She had become pregnant and experienced a miscarriage in her late teens. Then, around the age of twenty-five, she had an arrangement with a known donor and spent nearly a year trying to get pregnant. Recently, she had approached her doctor, looking for information about the different options that might be available to her. Bryn was looking not only for knowledge about how to track her own fertility – which she was already doing – or how to access donor semen from a sperm bank but also for information that addressed the broader context in which as a lesbian mom she would be raising her child. She explained:

The other thing that I wondered about is more for the child's future. I wanted to meet other people or read on other people that had experienced family life as lesbian couples or gay couples. And, also, talking to children of gay parents – how did they handle it going through elementary school or junior high school when other kids knew that their parents were gay? That was a big concern for me because I wouldn't want my child to suffer because of myself being gay.

Queer women are often placed in a position of having to refute other people's questions about the impact of their sexual identity on any child or potential child. A woman's own questions about how children of LGBT parents will cope with homophobia are often not voiced. Until recently, the impact of homosexuality rather than homophobia was the focus of research on children raised by LGBT parents. The literature in this area predominantly focused on assessing children's development and the potential impact of a parent's sexual identity on children's gender and sex role behaviour.[4] Only recently have studies begun to emerge which address the experiences of children raised in queer family constellations (Wright 1998, 2001). The COLAGE (Children of Lesbians and Gays Everywhere) website notes the dearth of research about the broader everyday issues facing children of queer parents. Statements by children and teens of lesbian, gay, bisexual, or transgender parents (who choose to participate in research or organizations like COLAGE) identify the positive impact of their parent's gender and sexual identities. Young women and men state that they learned to challenge intolerance and cope with difference at an early age, which provided them with the tools to deal with change.[5] Maureen Sullivan, in a review of studies comparing lesbian families with heterosexual single-parent families,[6] states that the one marked difference is that 'children in lesbian households are often described as having more positive, tolerant attitudes towards unconventional lifestyles and social differences' (quoted in Arnup 1998, 67).[7]

As many queer health activists and queer scholars argue, the full impact of homophobia on children or adults is unknown. Research is now beginning to address the impact of systemic homophobia on children of queer parents (Gartrell, Hamilton, et al. 1996; Gartrell, Banks, et al. 2000; Wright 1998). Janet Wright (2001) found that more of the children in her study of lesbian stepfamilies expressed *fear* of teasing and discrimination than the number of children who related stories about actual events. As Wright points out, this fear that children experience points to the pervasiveness of homophobia within North American culture. It also indicates the cultural tolerance that still exists for

homophobic remarks, as well as the practices which maintain heterosexuality as normative. In Debra Chasnoff and Helen Cohen's 1999
acclaimed film, *It's Elementary*, a young girl comments that it is
common to hear students calling other students 'faggot' or 'gay.'
Teachers, she says, 'rarely say anything about the remarks and certainly don't stop them.' Like other types of discrimination, homophobia is not always identifiable or nameable, and, in Katherine Arnup's
words, 'It is not just the overt remarks that hurt our children. It is the
absences' (1998). There is a dire need for positive images of LGBT families that affirm children's relationships with parents and caregivers.[8]
Although these images exist to a certain extent in so-called queer
culture, the absence of visual non-derogatory images of queer families
in everyday spaces – school library books, grocery stores, television
programs, and so forth – marginalize queer families.

Queer women's wishes to become parents are often weighed against
the prevalence (and acceptance) of homophobia in our society and
people's complicit reproduction of heteronormativity. It is not uncommon to hear liberal expressions of tolerance such as 'It's okay by me if
you're gay,' or 'You're human beings, too,' or 'It doesn't matter to me
if you sleep with women or men.' There is a tendency for people to talk
about societal change but, to quote Kath Weston, 'put simply, it's still
a "big deal" to live a life of same-sex attraction because very little in
society is set up to acknowledge the family ties you propose to make'
(1997, xii). Throughout the course of my fieldwork, the fact that lesbians and gay men are allowed to marry in Canada was recounted to
me as a marker of progress and societal tolerance or greater acceptance
of lesbian and gay individuals and relationships. Seldom, though, was
it noted that although an increasing number of women and men were
holding public marriage or commitment ceremonies throughout the
1990s, Canadian court decisions had denied lesbians and gay men
the right to *legally* marry.[9] The same people did not seem to recall the
excitement over the possibility that Hawaii might legalize same-
gender marriage, and the swift introduction and adoption of the
Defense of Marriage Act in the United States in case that happened.[10]
Same-sex partners were not recognized by Canadian legislation until
2000 upon the introduction of Bill C-23, the Modernization of Benefits
and Obligations Act.[11] Same-sex marriage was legalized in British
Columbia in 2003, and then across Canada with the enshrinement of
Bill C-38, the Civil Marriage Act, in 2005. Many people I met seemed
unaware that until recently few men and women without significant

financial resources could contemplate launching a legal challenge that might ensure the continuation of a relationship to a child, recognition of parental status, or shared custody. A number of the women I interviewed 'lost' their parental status in relation to children they had co-parented. Some, who didn't lose their status, were initially advised to give up before starting because they would have no chance of obtaining even visitation rights. Listening to the stories of women who came out decades ago or the stories of women who are not 'out' at work, in their broader communities, or to their families, I found it difficult to know how to respond to people who, in response to my description of the focus of my project, declared, 'It's a good time to be gay.' Perhaps. Depending on where one lives, for whom one works, on whom one is dependent, or for whom one is responsible, the degree of societal change will be differently felt, experienced, and embodied. People who hold hands with girlfriends, boyfriends, or a partner whose gender is indeterminable, in public space – on street corners, in the grocery store, at a concert – are often considered to be 'pushing it' or being 'in your face.' Public participation in everyday life as a partner or parent – at work functions, school, hospital emergency rooms, or soccer practice – challenges everyone, straight or queer, to confront the pervasive expectation of normative heterosexuality.

Ontological Normativities

Public images of pregnant and parenting lesbians have increased over the years, with regular queer mom's columns, 'maybe baby' articles, and celebrity conception stories appearing in queer popular magazines, Hollywood and alternative films, and occasionally the mainstream press. However, many queer women must still mediate homophobic discourses that 'exile' (Weston 1991) lesbians, gay men, and bisexual and transgender individuals from heterosexually normative constructions of kinship and family. Kath Weston states, 'Babies conceived after a woman has come out demand a reconciliation of a nonprocreative lesbian identity with procreative practice' (Weston 1991, 169). This statement refers to the historically normative displacement of lesbians from the recognized institution of motherhood or, as noted by many, to the popular perception of *lesbian mother* as an oxymoron (Lewin 1993; Arnup 1995). However, there needs to be clarification of who needs to reconcile lesbian identity and procreative practice. In 1999 a Mother's Day article published in the *Vancouver Sun* by

Karen Tulchinsky about her and her partner's attempts to have a baby included a photograph of the two women taken at a children's playground (notably there are no children in the photograph). The caption under the photograph reads, 'Now that "lesbian mother" is no oxymoron, the writer and her partner Terrie Hamazaki are part of a trend' (Tulchinsky 1999, E5). In the mid-1990s it seemed odd to define sexuality in relation to reproduction and, furthermore, in a manner that upheld rather than destabilized ontological notions of sexual difference, gender, and biological bodies. Yet, the biologization of homosexuality (cf. Terry 1999) has left a legacy of scientific and popular essentialist discourses of the difference between queer and straight people and has situated a heterosexual romance narrative of procreation (Martin 1991) at the core of nature and all that is considered to be biologically 'natural.'

For many of the women in my study who came out before the 1990s, becoming a parent was not something they expected to do and, in fact, was more likely something they were expected not to do. In the early 1980s, Rae's partner at the time decided that she wanted to have a child, but Rae had never wanted to be a parent. Rae said: 'I can remember when I was a kid (because I knew I was a dyke when I was a kid), thinking, "Oh goodie, I don't have to have kids." I remember thinking that. And I must have been about twelve. "I don't have to do this trip" [she laughs].'

Both motherhood and queer identifications have acquired new meanings for women.[12] It is increasingly common for both straight and queer women to *choose* whether or not to become parents (Nelson 1996). As well, there are many lesbian and dyke moms today who visibly parent as queer women. Jenna stated: 'I think, coming out, it just had never occurred to me that this was going to mean that I couldn't be a mom, right. I was raised in an environment where I was encouraged to believe that I could be whatever I wanted to be and do whatever I wanted to do, and that included the luxury of being able to think for myself in those ways.'

Although many women themselves may not foreground the relationship between being with a woman and becoming a parent, for many women I interviewed the dominant relationship (or rather, non-relationship) between being a lesbian and having children was evident in the responses of their parents in coming-out narratives. Erica, a woman in her late twenties, had a difficult time coming out to her father. When she finally did, she was surprised and impressed by his composure. Like many parents, though, one of his first comments was to voice his disappointment about not becoming a grandfather. Erica recalled:

> He sort of paused and said, 'Well, you know, I guess the one thing that I'm a little disappointed about is that it means we won't have any grand-kids.' I have a brother, so it was kind of interesting that he said that, but I guess it's just because I always said I would have kids. But I also always said that I was never getting married and that I was going to have a kid by myself, and I'd never even met with any resistance. I said, 'It doesn't mean that at all. I plan to have a child.' 'Oh, you can't. What do you mean? You can't have children. That's drawing the line,' and, you know, 'I can deal with this and it's okay what you do and that you guys are together, but you can't, you can't raise a child – yeah, I know people do. I know every once in a while, you know, two women, or whatever, have – it's not right. It's not fair to the child.'

This was familiar terrain for many women. Parents, friends, and strangers could accept individualized queerness, and even the concept of same-gender couples, but having children was crossing a boundary or drawing the line. Erica ended the conversation with her father and declared to me that she will revisit the issue when she is six months pregnant: 'Certainly at this point I wouldn't feel comfortable broach-ing it when I was just in the thinking-about-it stages, because I think I'd meet with a lot of resistance and it would get me down, in particu-lar if it became a difficult process of not being able to find a donor, or having to go through artificial insemination, or that type of thing.'[13]

Lesbians and gay men have been represented as non-procreative beings. Although some women, like Erica, decided not to discuss their intentions to parent with individuals they felt might resist the idea, many women I interviewed worked to create environments in which queer parents were visible. This included talking about the possibility of parenting long before it seemed realistic to become a parent. Some women made concerted efforts to introduce the idea of having chil-dren into conversations with friends, family, and co-workers in order to contest the images that exclude lesbians from parenthood and to introduce images of lesbians with children.

Coming Out as a Parent-to-Be

Coming-out narratives and queer conception narratives follow similar trajectories and, in some ways, are closely entwined. Women whose children were in their late teens and early twenties, women who were pregnant at the time of our interview, and women who were years away from acting on their plans to become parents spoke about the relationship between coming out as a lesbian and coming out as a parent or potential parent. Being out was a strategy that many women I interviewed used to confront homophobia and actively facilitate their own and their family's health. Wanting and deciding to become a parent often resulted in redefining the parameters that defined how 'out' women were and to whom. Dawn highlighted the contextual and relational definitions of being *out*. She commented:

> Being *out* is a relative term. The partner that I was with was not, and as a result – this is hindsight, but the process of having a child moved me more 'out' into the community. But I operate from a place of, if I have too much information – and some people like to have all the information, but I don't operate that way; in fact, I deliberately will put up blinders and do one piece at a time so that I can thoroughly understand it in order to progress. I don't start worrying, 'Oh my God, am I going to have enough for their university education?' when I haven't even had the baby yet. Some people jump, and I don't do that. So my first step was to have to deal with kind of, like, the homophobia that my partner had, and the 'closetedness,' which was more closeted than I was.

One of the first steps that Dawn took in the process of becoming a parent was to address the homophobia that was a part of her life. As she noted, in hindsight she could see that 'having a child moved [them] more "out" into the community.' Although being out was considered a key aspect of planning to parent and parenting by most of the women in my study, the process and politics of disclosure, recognition, and identification varied according to individuals, communities, and broader contexts.

For many women, having a child did not just entail being out to their family or coming out beyond their immediate family members; becoming a parent meant being out in all aspects of their everyday worlds. Caroline and Pam faced a number of obstacles in their search for donors. They described the 'parallel course' they took in laying the foundations of a social structure for their child, while figuring out how to actually become parents. In the midst of navigating the emotional and practical roller coaster of deciding on a donor, they decided to have a commitment ceremony. Pam, who was pregnant at the time, said:

On kind of a parallel course at the same time, we were also talking about – in terms of becoming parents, of becoming a foundation for our kid – what we wanted to do in terms of the social structure. We decided to have a commitment ceremony. Part of that was to say to our families – my mom was great; I mean, she was hesitant, but she was great. My father's extremely homophobic. Caroline's family has been wonderfully welcoming, but we're not so sure how far they've gone with their own stuff. So, part of us wanting to have a ceremony was to say publicly, 'Ok, you need to acknowledge us as a couple.' And [it was a way] for them to meet our community. That felt like a really solid step to do in providing a base for the kid as well: to say, 'Look, this is part of who we are in that we've made this commitment to each other; we've made this commitment to you. This is the community that you're going to be welcomed into.' That was sort of on a parallel line, but it was something that we did talk about wanting to do before we had a child. And we talked about it a lot, because it's that whole – and challenging our families, well, challenging *my family*, like my father, saying, 'Look, you need to take this seriously.' He couldn't, but we had a couple of really important discussions that we've never ever had in over a decade. So it was good to have that, and it feels like it kind of paved the way.

Pam and Caroline chose to bring their parents and siblings closer to the core of their community by holding a commitment ceremony. Other women I interviewed also connected commitment ceremonies to their decision to become parents and to publicly announcing their family.

Whereas Dawn noted the ways in which having a child pushes women to be more out, other women I interviewed also described how becoming a queer parent pushed people around them – friends, families, and even strangers – to acknowledge their sexual identification and, in many cases, their girlfriends, boyfriends, lovers, and/or partners. This is significant. An articulation or clarification of sexual identity (that is, coming out) does not result in an integration of sexuality into straight-queer relations. It can sometimes be easy for straight individuals to displace an individual's queerness from the scope of their relations. Children, though, often make it more difficult to displace queerness from everyday reality. The presence of children often requires an explanation – whose children are they?

Following their commitment ceremony, and well into the process of pursuing parenthood, Caroline and Pam chose to write a letter to Caroline's parents.

We decided that it was important to us that my parents know that we were making this decision [to have children] as opposed to kind of springing it on them, sort of like, 'Pam's pregnant.' That just felt unfair for us. My parents live in town and, realistically, they will be the only grandparents that our child will know, so it was important to us to lay a supportive groundwork for them. They are very welcoming to [Pam]. They are very accepting of our life together, of me as their daughter as well, so that hasn't really been an issue. But at the same time, we know that they aren't out to most of their friends about me and our relationship. So, if they're not out about me, how are they going to deal with a grandchild? So we felt that it was important. We made some choices, you know. My mom has known for some time that we were thinking about doing this, but my dad, not in a really very sort of informed way that he really understood what we were thinking of doing. So, several months back we wrote a letter to them and also enclosed a description of the path that we just explained to you, so that they can appreciate that this was not an impulsive decision, that this was something that we'd really planned and which has taken a lot of energy and time and money and anxiety and sadness, and all that kind of stuff. We sent that to them, and you know, their initial reaction was distress, mostly because they experience the world as being a homophobic place where perhaps our child is going to have problems, and their anxiety was for the child – and, of course, for me as their daughter in terms of it bringing hardship for me in my life emotionally. So that, I think, was their initial anxiety, but to be quite honest with you, we haven't had much follow-up discussion on that. We had dinner with them earlier this week, and they were totally happy, friendly, everything was totally fine, and I'm really hopeful that things are going to be okay. And we have loads of friends who are, ironically, mostly straight, who think that this is the best thing ever.

Fiona and Melanie used a similar tactic and wrote letters to their parents and Fiona's sisters about their plans to have a child, when Fiona first started trying to get pregnant. They received letters back from both sisters, one of whom declared that, of course, she would support them but she believed a child needed a mother and a father. Melanie's parents were 'devastated.' Melanie stated: 'They didn't think this was a good idea. No. Especially my father whose reaction was, "How could you do that to a child? How could you ... You're more concerned with your needs."' A couple of weeks later, Melanie's mother called to say that the child, of course, would be treated equally, but she and Melanie's father did not think they could consider a child that Fiona gave birth to as their grandchild. Fiona's mother, on the other hand, seemed to have more difficulty with the practice of 'artificial' insemination than with Fiona and Melanie's raising a child together. The responses of Fiona's and Melanie's parents and Fiona's siblings demonstrate how queer families challenge the practices which render sexuality and sexual relationships invisible or at least unnamed. As Fiona articulated:

> Our whole analysis of this is that my parents have been great but they don't – They tell their friends, 'Fiona and Melanie moved to Vancouver. Fiona and Melanie bought a house. Fiona and Melanie got a dog,' but they would never use the *lesbian* word to their friends. So, our analysis was that this was going to be a huge coming-out thing for them if they ever wanted to say they have a grandchild. And, of course, I'm not comfortable talking to them and they're not comfortable talking to me about it. It was clear. We don't talk about it.

Fiona was not able to get pregnant. After sixteen cycles in which she attempted to conceive, combining inseminations at home with inseminations at a physician's office, they decided that Melanie would try to become pregnant with the remaining vials of semen that they had in storage. After four months, just before a trip to visit her parents, Melanie became pregnant. She said:

> I phoned a week before we were to arrive to tell them that they needed to know – and that was even before I knew I was going to be sick – 'I want you to know, I want you to have time to get your head around it before I show up on your doorstep, that I'm pregnant.' And then the initial reaction was, 'Oh.' Silence and tears. [Then,] 'I'm sure you know that this wasn't something we thought you should do. And, of course, we'll love the child that comes into your life.' But when we got there, it was kind of cute because it gave my mom an opportunity to share all these stories about when she was pregnant that I'd never heard about. And she was really sick for all three of her pregnancies.

As Fiona pointed out, they never found out how Melanie's parents would have treated a grandchild that was born to Fiona, because in the end Melanie was the one who got pregnant and gave birth to their son.

Getting pregnant was not something that Melanie's mother expected her to do once she had identified as lesbian. The reactions of Melanie's parents also point to another common experience in which mothers and their lesbian daughters share a new sense of bodily history. Surprisingly, given the beginning of the story, Melanie's mother decided to come to visit for her grandchild's birth. Melanie said:

> I'm thinking inside, 'No. First of all, I'd like to have a midwife. We [aren't] talking about having a home birth, but I want to be doing my labour at home, or as much of it as I can, and I don't want you around. I don't even feel comfortable, I don't feel comfortable being really affectionate with my partner when you are around, so why would I want you there when I need my partner to be right at my side?' So I was clear, 'Come after.' It was clear over the next number of months that she wanted to be there.

Melanie was due around the eighth of the month, depending on which insemination 'was the right one.' Her mother planned to arrive on the thirteenth. Women who know the reproductive history of the woman who gave birth to them often use their interpretations of that information to gauge their own expectations. Melanie's mother had her children well past their due dates. Thus, her plans to arrive five days after Melanie's due date would, in Melanie's view, most likely still place her at the scene in time for the birth.

> I was due, my due date – no baby. My mom came on the thirteenth. And my mom broke her arm the day before she came. She fell and knew her arm was really hurting, but had to fly. So she didn't actually go anywhere [to have it looked at]. She arrived on Friday, at night, and Saturday we took her to emergency and got her arm X-rayed, and sure enough she had a radial fracture on her arm. So that needed to be casted. And she was only staying for ten days. So we're counting down. 'Okay, how long are you going to be here?' And then my panic was that we knew that we wanted to do as much of the labour at home. We had it all planned. And our friends were joking about how they would come take her shopping, take her out of the house. At that point I was still nervous about having her see me in that state. And she kept saying that birth is a very personal thing, and how these people have all these people around in the birthing room, and 'I don't need to be there.' So we wait. Fourteenth, fifteenth, six-

teenth, nothing happens. And at one in the morning on the seventeenth I started cramping a bit and had my bloody show. I started getting contractions about three in the morning. My mom got up about six. She knew that we were up and that something was going down, and it just rolled into this hugely natural place. By the time the midwife got there – plus my water broke and there was meconium in it so the midwife needed to come over in a bit of a – earlier than she thought she might – it was totally natural. There's my mom timing contractions. There was no question that she was going to be part of it. And the midwife – pressure went up. It was clear that it was going to be good that I end up at the hospital ... By eleven o'clock in the morning we had to go to the hospital. I was hardly dilated. And then it was very natural at the hospital. My mom just was there for the duration ... By the time we got into the throes of labour, there was no question my mom was going to be a part of it. Fiona was on one side of me and my mom was on the other.

Clarifying Relationships

Many women I interviewed recognized having children as the time to expand the spheres in which they were out, by clarifying their relationship with another woman or explicitly defining their sexual identity. Women and men are invested to various degrees in providing particular people with clarity about their sexuality. Certain people are 'in' on the information, while other people are left in the 'suspect' sphere. Liz explained that her decision to become a parent with her partner clarified their relationship to people who might have suspected that she was gay:

My family wasn't much of a big deal except that it expanded my – like, my grandma and my aunt and uncles didn't even know I was gay, although I'm sure they suspected. My grandma didn't have a clue, but my aunt kind of figured it out. So it was time to let the whole family in because now there was going to be, you know, my partner and a baby. It was time to let everybody know. And nobody had any problems. My grandmother, she had the biggest problem. My aunt suspected, and my grandma I think was quite upset for about three days, but when she got input from family members she was fine. She's a great grandma [she laughs, realizing the pun]. She's a great grandma. [Liz turns to her partner, Amy.] And your mom and dad, we waited till the last minute to tell them.

Amy was out to her parents. Anticipating a negative response to her pregnancy, Amy waited to tell them until she was three months pregnant:

> My mom and dad, I knew, would discourage me from getting pregnant … and stress me out. So I waited until I was three months pregnant when the probability of having a miscarriage goes down. I drove to where they live and sat them down and – Mother Nature is just amazing because I think the pregnancy hormones are better than any tranquillizer – I was just so calm. I told them this just earth-shattering news and I was calm as a cucumber. And I said, 'Oh, Mom and Dad, it'll be fine. It's fine. We've got it all worked out. We've seen lawyers and we've seen doctors and we have a thirty-six-page [donor] agreement.' And Dad right away I could tell was happy, because [our daughter] is their only grandchild. They've got four kids, and I'm the third, so they were thinking they weren't going to have any. So Dad right away was very pleased, and when I told them that her last name would be my last name, you could just tell – he was, 'Oh, yeah, it'll work out,' to my mom. 'It'll be fine. Amy's a responsible person.' But mom was stressed and thought that this is a really selfish thing to bring a child into the world that's going to have – you know, like any kid has so much going against them, and to have an abnormal [family], that issue, that's adding insult to injury and not fair. So by the time [our daughter] was born she still wasn't … she wasn't okay.

Liz made certain that her parents and extended family understood that she and Amy were having a child *together*. Amy's mom, however, did not acknowledge Liz as a parent. Liz said, 'She didn't recognize me as anybody. It was like Amy was a single mom, and she would ask, "Are you sure you're getting enough help?"' Parents' reactions to women's announcements that they were planning to parent or that they, or their partner, were pregnant struck a familiar chord with some of the women I interviewed. Amy stated:

> I felt bad for [my mom], but we went through the same thing when I told her I was gay. So it was my second go-around. Then, when [our daughter] was born, I wanted to send birth announcements to her siblings, and she kind of vetoed that. I went along with her and I didn't send out birth announcements, but then I started getting calls from cousins who'd found out, and they're just so happy, and there's gifts coming in the mail from cousins that I haven't see in ten, fifteen years. I think they really

helped her, too, to accept that this is okay and I'm still a part of the family and [our daughter] is certainly part of the big family. So, eventually – [our daughter] was colicky, and I had to go stay with mom and dad for a while because it was just too much, and Liz was writing exams … So I had to go out there to stay, and I think that's when they finally realized that this was their granddaughter. [My mom] just loved her to death. They just love her. Nobody dotes on our child like my parents.

Timing is seen to be a key factor in coming-out narratives, whether they are about being queer, becoming a parent, or both. Amy, like Erica, felt that letting her parents in on the news that she was trying to get pregnant would be stressful and, thus, held off telling them until she was into the second trimester of her pregnancy. Parents-to-be, people who are already 'in the know,' and people in the larger spheres in which a woman's family will be visible are confronted by normative discourses of 'family' and challenged by the particularities of varia-tions in queer families. Women who announced they were planning to have a child sometimes evoked voiced intolerance and stories of social unacceptability. Queer families necessitate a renegotiation of the parameters and boundaries that people place on sexuality and family and demand an acknowledgment of the relationship between queer sexuality and family. As Amy noted, 'I felt bad for [my mom], but we went through the same thing when I told her I was gay. So it was my second go-around.'

Many women in my study actively 'outed' themselves while trying to get pregnant or to adopt. Others came out to family, co-workers, and strangers once they, or their partner, were pregnant. Rita and her then partner, Celine, were living and working in a small BC community when they decided to have a child in the mid-1980s. Celine conceived after the first time they tried. I asked Rita what it was like when she realized that they were going to have a child. She replied:

Well, it was a constant challenge because my partner was much more out than I was. She'd always been out and was sort of a butch type who was fairly visible, whereas I wasn't. But once we decided to have a child, I knew that I didn't want to raise a child unless I was out. Like, I didn't feel I could not be out and have a child. So part of the process was me coming out. And my job is fairly visible, you know. I remember the first person outside of our immediate circle that I told it to. It was a secretary in one of the schools that I [worked at], Catholic and fairly, you know, rigid, I would think – fairly traditional, let's put it that way. I was just in the staff room that particular day, and there were only three or four of us, and the conversation just happened to turn on who in the town, and this was a fairly small town, was pregnant. So, there were different people. And then the two other people in the room got up and left somewhere. So, just to carry on a conversation, I decided this was it. So I said to this woman, 'So, guess who else is pregnant?' And she said, 'Oh, who? Who?' And I said, 'Celine.' And she looked at me and she said, 'You mean, Celine who lives with you?' And I said, 'Yes.' And she said, 'Oh, I thought she didn't have a partner, that she wasn't into men.' And I said, 'Well, she isn't. She has a partner. Her partner is me. And, you're right, she's not into men.' 'Well, how did she get pregnant?' [she asked.] I said, 'Artificial insemination.' There was this silence, and I could see, you know, that it was very touch and go as to how she would react. And finally she said, 'Well, I think that's just great.' And so it went from there. It was an endless hassle in some ways because once it got around the community, there were people who, of course, thought this was totally immoral and inappropriate, and others who were very supportive. And as the time approached, I applied to have a few days off, you know, to be there for the birth and that. And as luck would have it, somehow the permission – I did receive permission, but it got sent to the wrong school, not in an envelope or anything, you know. And things like that that just happened. And, I think, that's partly why it was better to be out because at least when it happened, it was easier to cope with.

Women who didn't feel visible made explicit statements in order to identify themselves as lesbians and to gain recognition as a partner and/or a parent. Discussing the inadequacies of the concept of non-biological or social motherhood for capturing the experiences of co-mothers, and the possibility of their lesbian sexuality being effaced by their mother status, Maureen Sullivan writes:

In fact, it is exactly through nonbirthmothers' sexual identities that their maternal status eventually becomes intelligible: in spontaneous and discrete interactions with individuals, a comother is confronted with inquiries about her particular relationship with a particular child with whom she appears to be so close and for whom she appears to be responsible. *The truth is that she is the mother of a child who has two mothers.* (2001, 234, italics in the original)

The significance of Liz's and Rita's experiences, as well as the experiences of most other (to use Sullivan's term) nonbirth mothers I interviewed, is that they actively identified themselves as parents-to-be in relation to a child that did not yet exist. The lesbian identity of the birth mother could not be effaced, and rather, needed to be made explicit, because it was through *planned* encounters and clarifications about a woman's relationship to her pregnant lesbian partner that her own relationship to a fetus or imagined future child was identified. Rita felt that her partner's 'butchness' made her more visible as a lesbian. Thus, in order to identify *herself* as a lesbian, and as a parent-to-be, Rita made it clear that she was Celine's partner.

This chapter began with illustrations of the pervasive and tolerated forms of homophobia that children and parents encounter within their everyday life. I then looked at how the women I interviewed strategically outed themselves – as queer or as planning to parent – in order to create an environment in which the connection between being queer and being a parent was made explicit. Many women who came out in extended spheres of their life, whether to co-workers, family, friends, health service providers, or strangers, often felt like they were taking a risk but described it as a necessary risk in order to receive recognition for the parent-child relationship they were creating.[14] The narratives in this chapter explore what women imagined to be necessary while they were planning to parent. The next chapter turns to look more closely at women's stories about their child's or children's experiences.

4 Out for the Children, or Childhood Outings?

Women who were parenting children and thinking about getting pregnant or adopting had already witnessed some of the homophobia that children of queer parents are exposed to. When I met Adele, she seemed enthusiastic to share her thoughts about getting pregnant. However, when I arrived at her home for a scheduled interview, she told me that her partner, Vivian, was concerned that participation in the project might hurt her sons. Vivian's reservations were based on an incident at her son's school a few weeks earlier, during which a classmate had confronted him, declaring that Vivian was gay. He replied that she wasn't, but then came home quite upset about having lied. Adele explained:

> He thought that he should lie and say that it wasn't true. That's what the real problem was, not that somebody said something and somebody else found out. It was that he thought that he had to say no, that it wasn't true. And then he knew he had lied and he was all upset, right. He knew he lied, but he thought it was the right thing, and then he was really kind of confused I think ... I think that's what it was. He thought it was going to hurt his mom if he lied and said it wasn't true when it was. But he thought he should lie and say that it wasn't true.

A number of women commented that their mother had a difficult time when they came out because they thought their daughter would face additional barriers in life as a lesbian. Similarly, many queer moms and prospective parents worried about the additional hardships their children might face because of their mother's (or mothers') sexuality. The experience of Vivian's son illustrates how children try to protect themselves and their parent(s). Adele's story also highlights the dilemmas that children face when called upon to decide how 'out' they want to be about their families.

Adele and Vivian's story points to a particular distinction between, and coexistence of, the concerns of women considering becoming moms as lesbians, the concerns of parents who become lesbians, and the concerns of women who begin lesbian and parenting relationships simultaneously. As discussed in the previous chapter, queer women contemplating parenthood often outed themselves to family, co-workers, and friends. Many spent years setting the stage and building a supportive foundation and community for their children. Although Adele plans to get pregnant and have a child in the context of her relationship with Vivian, she began parenting Vivian's sons shortly after she came out.[1] Vivian had been married to her sons' father until shortly before beginning her relationship with Adele. Both have had to deal with gossip about their sexuality, a difficult custody case, and concerns about how their decision to be out will affect Vivian's children. Given their worries, Adele and Vivian mediate the everyday politics of being out in various ways. Adele and Vivian's eldest son negotiated their public relationship after experiencing numerous uncomfortable moments at his school. Adele stated:

> The kids [at school] would start to say, 'Who are you? Are you the babysitter?' And the oldest, he kind of didn't know what to say. And at first, I didn't know what to say, either. We both were very uncomfortable at school for a couple of days, and finally I sat down with him and I said, 'What should we say?' Because I didn't want to say anything and have him have to go, 'Okay, I guess that's it,' you know? So we decided that we would say that we were room-mates because I live here, and people that live together are room-mates. So that's what we decided we would do with it. I live at the same house so we … You know, we didn't have to lie to anybody. We live at the same house, and I said we don't have to tell anybody.

Adele and her stepson call each other room-mates at school, and she often uses the term *room-mate* when talking about her partner at work. However, she states, not being out raises a number of issues.

> It's a double standard because you want to teach them what's right. And what's right is that I love this person and that's okay. And they can stay in my bed and that's okay. And we love each other just like any mom and

dad does and that's okay. And that we love them and that we're bringing them up in a family. But then, in the other instance, a friend will come over, and right away we're different, we've got distance, right? We talk differently, we use different words, we're different. It kind of makes the kids different, you know, and it kind of just changes everything. And we don't do it because ... Like this woman [at a meeting of queer parents with children] was saying, 'And I don't do it because I'm embarrassed to be gay; I do it because I'm trying to protect my children from being discriminated against because I am gay. It's one thing for me to be out; it's another thing for me to force my children to be out.' So it was kind of a double standard to try and teach them everything that you believe is right, and then, on the other hand, when you're in public, your roles change and you change. And it's kind of almost like you're teaching them how to be fake around people and only be yourself when you're at home alone – which is not right either, but what do you do? You're only doing it to try and protect them.

Vivian and Adele both ended up participating in the interview. At the time, they were both trying to balance wanting to be out and active in the local lesbian and gay community with wanting to shelter their children from the perceived stigma associated with having a lesbian mom. As a compromise, Vivian participated in 'behind the scenes' activities. Commenting on Vivian's activism, Adele stated: 'But she won't go on [an AIDS] walk, because she's got the kids. Or what if somebody takes a picture and sees her in a gay parade, and her kids see it? She won't do any of that stuff, not if it's going to be out in public during the day.'[2]

Whereas Adele and Vivian were figuring out how to be out and trying to cope with the harassment they and their children experienced at school and in the community, other women were concerned about the decisions their children had made to be closeted. Rae had described herself and her ex-partner as 'pioneers' in the lesbian baby boom, her partner having given birth to their son, Jason, in the early 1980s. Although Rae and her partner ended their relationship when Jason was a year and a half, Rae remained a part of his life. When he was nine, Jason and her ex-partner, whom Rae described as Jason's 'body-mom,' moved away from the community in which he had spent the early part of his childhood. In the area where he grew up, and where he continues to spend vacations with his donor-dad and Rae, Jason's family is known within the community. In his new home Jason has chosen not to be out about the configuration of his parental relationships. When I asked Rae if there was anything that she felt was integral to my study that we had not yet talked about, she stated:

Well, the whole thing around homophobia. Jason is very homophobic. He was brought up by lesbians, he's got mothers, but he doesn't bring his friends home. So he's hooked in with that ... That has to work out in his life. I don't know how it's going to work out in his life. He's definitely, I think, right now, heterosexual. He's very much open here [in the community where he was born]. When he comes here, he's very – this is where he feels comfortable having lesbian parents or gay parents. Because when he is with his dad, he's with all the gay boys. And then he's got all, he's got the best – he's got quite the life. He's got all the gay boys and all the dykes. But when he's in [the other city], it's sort of like he's living incognito. And it's not doing him any good. And he doesn't acknowledge who he is there. And he comes here and he's much freer. So, that's an issue. That's a huge issue when the kids ... with a teenager and adolescent stuff – Jason has asked for and wanted to know if there are any other kids like him. He knows he is an AI [assisted/artificial insemination] baby; he knows how he was conceived. And he has found a couple of people here, so he doesn't feel alone, that much alone, in the AI department. Definitely it's very important, I think, to be very honest with the kid about where he comes from and what it's all about – what he's stepping into. He's not coming from your regular family.

Many of the women in my study, and it seemed their children as well, felt that seeing and knowing other children of LGBT parents was important. Women wanted to provide children with the opportunity to see a diversity of family configurations, as well as families with similar compositions to their own. For example, Rita was aware of other children who were being raised by lesbians, but their parents were not out within the community and the children were not out about their family. When her son was twelve years old, he participated in a new, and short-lasting, program for children of lesbian and gay parents. Rita stated:

That was the first time that there was anything really visible and available. And for years, and this was really hard, my son used to say, 'Am I the only one?' And, you know, for a long time ... Although we heard of a couple near [here] who were very closeted, who had had a son(I think he's about a year younger than my son), and I knew that he was in the same school as my son, I didn't feel I could say anything because they weren't women I knew. But it was very hard for my son, because when he was seven, eight, nine, he was asking, 'Am I the only one like this?' And it was hard to say, 'Well, no, you're not.' We'd say that, and then he'd say, 'Well, where are they? Who are they?' We could read him books like *Heather has Two Mommies* and that, but he did not know anybody, really, who was in the same situation as he was. And I think that was very isolating for him. So when this group came and he could see there were other kids having more or less the same experience, I think that was good.

Jenna also stated the significance of being able to provide her daughter with the opportunity to meet other children who also had two moms. She and her partner had moved to a rural community in the central interior shortly before Jenna became pregnant. They returned to a more urban environment when their daughter was two years old, wanting to provide her with opportunities to interact with other queer families. Jenna commented:

We did start to feel really isolated. Like, we had lots of – well, I mean, for me, I had lots of queer friends there, and we had lots of supportive friends, but we did not know any other lesbian moms. There were none [where we were living], and that started weighing on us. And [our daughter] was then starting to talk and she was doing all this kind of imaginative play, and everything was like, 'Here's the mommy, and here's the daddy, and here's the little kid.' And we were thinking, well, of course, you know, because she's never seen another family like her own family. So we definitely started thinking about moving away, and one of the reasons was because we didn't want her to grow up there. We didn't want her to grow up in an environment where she never saw another family like her own and where – I just felt like there was not enough opportunity there for her to develop a good solid kind of positive self-identity, and although the daycare provider was good and we were friends of other parents in the daycare and we had lots of support from our friends, the reality was she did not know any other kids in families like her own, and we felt ... So then, obviously, a whole chain of events occurred, with us applying for jobs and deciding to move to [the city] and stuff. And I remember feeling so happy, about four months after we moved back, you know, when we had been able to start socializing with other lesbian moms and stuff. [My partner] and I overheard [our daughter] in her room playing, and she's like, 'Here's the mommy and here's the mama and here's the little girl.' And we were, like, 'Yay!' And I do really think it was because finally she was seeing her own family structure reflected around her a little bit. So, that was definitely a contributing factor in us deciding that we didn't want to stay there. It wasn't the only reason, but it was one of them. And, you know, there was some sadness in that. There were things about – I mean the sadness being that we shouldn't have to make those kinds of choices. If we want to live in a small community, that's just a really – that's too bad. [This city] definitely would not have been my first choice of a place to move to, but the knowledge that we had friends here who were queer moms, and there was a community that we could be a part of and stuff, was one of the things that made us decide that we wanted to come here. The next generation will be a little different, no doubt.

Queer Parenting Communities and Families of the Heart

Creating a sense of community and providing children access to reflections of their own family configurations was, as illustrated above, a key goal expressed by the women I interviewed. However, when queer parents, or the lesbian moms whom the women noticed around town, were not part of their usual circle of friends, the difference between being a parent and wanting to be a parent appeared to be significant. Pam, who was ten weeks pregnant at the time of our interview, noted, 'It was great when we could talk about our choices and our hopes,' but there is 'definitely a difference between being and not being.' She stated:

I'm in touch with a couple of other couples who want to be moms as well. So that feels good. It's sort of been in limbo because we've met some dyke moms, and yet we're not. We want to be, but we're not. So it's sort of that, What's our connection? It's our interest in being parents. So I feel it's neat that we'll be able to have more of a concrete connection now that we're sort of further along the road that way. So, that's helpful. And we're really committed to having a good community of gay and lesbian parents so that, even though we may not meet all the time, we may not necessarily be friends in other aspects of our lives, but sharing parenting concerns and sharing a community [where] our child can see that it's common to have gay dads or lesbian moms, that that reflects his or her reality as well – we're very committed to that.

Pam anticipated that being 'further along the road,' that is, being pregnant, would allow her and her partner, Caroline, to cross the line between being and not being parents. Interestingly, this sense of a division between parents and not parents was not a part of Caroline and Pam's everyday lives with respect to their relationships to children. It did seem, though, to be a border that they felt in terms of developing relationships with other *queer* parents. Pam stated:

> Definitely I want to have a community of gays and lesbians, but, also, we have a good network of straight friends who have kids, who are very supportive of us. And we're like, great, because both of us feel very committed to the idea of adults, different adults, in our kid's life. Seeing that, it's not just what your primary caregivers choose that is all of what life's about. Both of us feel quite strongly that it's important for kids to understand that you have different choices about things, and you do things differently. And I know, for me, growing up not having that and being in that nuclear family model, it was so constricting. So we look forward to that. And, also, we play a big part in our friend's kids' lives. We have two godchildren who we see quite a bit of, and so they're already getting that from us. Both of those kids came to our commitment ceremony and talk about it. One of them is five and he says to his mom, 'Well, you know girls can get married and boys can get married. Because Auntie C ...' That's just his life, that's just reality, which is great. He doesn't question it at all. So we already play that part in their kids' lives, so they too will play that in ours as well, which is great.

Dyke-mom groups were not very visible (especially to non-parents) and often, like earlier support groups, had short lifespans. Until lesbians become lesbian parents, their relationship to what might be imagined as a larger community of queer parents and children is limited.[3]

Caroline and Pam's story was not the only time the recognition of boundaries between being and not being a parent was evident during my fieldwork. One particular example was a set of workshops for queer families organized by the Centre[4] in Vancouver. In October 1999 an 'Adventures in Queer Parenting' workshop was organized to provide community members with information about becoming queer parents. The workshop featured expert-parent speakers who had taken significantly different routes to parenthood, as well as lawyers and social workers who work with LGBT clients. The feedback from participants indicated a desire for a workshop focusing on parenting itself rather than on the journey to parenting. A second workshop, held in the spring of 2000, responded to the request and reached out to queer parents and their children. This 'family day' featured a family brunch at Harry's, a local Vancouver café, with an opportunity to view the *Love Makes a Family* exhibit;[5] an afternoon of parenting workshops; and a family picnic and dance in the park. The women I knew who attended both workshops had recently transitioned in status from planning to parent to being pregnant, or were already parents at the first workshop. The attempt to meet the needs of the community inadvertently reproduced the distinction between two communities: queer parents and children; and queer prospective parents.

For the women who were not the first among their queer friends to become parents, and certainly for the women planning their second pregnancy or adoption, the separation of these two worlds was not as defined. Most often these women were already part of a community or family that included queer parents and children. Like Caroline and Pam, Jeanette and Katharine played active roles in the lives of their friends and their children. In contrast to Caroline and Pam, Jeanette and Katharine 'were surrounded by lesbian couples who had kids.' Talking about the decision to become parents, Katharine noted, 'What society would think – that had a small part of it for me as well, you know.' But Jeanette quickly added, 'Having friends that already had kids was really helpful. It was comforting to know that not only were they doing okay, their kids were great.' Although Jeanette and Katharine faced similar questions to those of other women regarding the anticipated changes in their social life, namely the perceived loss of freedom and the sense of immense responsibility that comes with having a child, they knew that their child's family would be affirmed and reflected by families close to them. These relationships comprised, in Jeanette's term, their 'family of the heart.'

In terms of our friends and stuff, when you talk about kinship, [our son's] got this *circle of aunties that are like his mothers*. There's a friend of ours who comes every Tuesday night to take care of him, and has, since he was five weeks old. She takes care of him one night a week because I work evenings. And, so, ever since the very beginning she's been there. She just adores him. And she doesn't have children. And other friends that have three kids, he's as welcome in their house as their own children. And they're his aunties. So he has this circle of aunties that are his family, outside of us, that we couldn't manage without. We couldn't manage without that support system. I don't know how – I know that lots of people have grandparents that take care of things ... So, they have these grandparents who do all this babysitting and all this kind of stuff. So people have their ways around it, but without our friends that are like our family we couldn't function – I mean, not in the way that we do. There's no way I could be going to school. And besides from that, they'll call us up and say, 'You know, I'll come over and sit with Kyle tonight,' or, 'Bring Kyle over, and you guys go to the movies.' He's stayed overnight at our friends and does just fine there and he's comfortable and he loves the kids. And it just gives us an opportunity to breathe. I know people who've created those types of connection ... We go to the community centre, and that's been a great experience, but, you know, you cultivate those things as well. We go over and take care of – they have three kids, and we stayed there for a weekend, and they came and stayed in our house for the weekend. Because you have to help each other out. Because the cost of babysitting, I mean, you barely have enough money to go to a movie as it is, you know, when you've got a mortgage and you're going to school and you're working part-time. And then on top of that to pay for childcare? It's so nice to go out, just the two of us, to go to a movie once in a while. And if you don't do that, you just get lost. You don't actually get lost, but he becomes our entire focus. And we had good advice from friends, really good advice. They said, 'You've got to go out. Leave your kid here. He'll be fine. You've got to go out.'

Caroline, Pam, Jeanette, and Katharine were members of larger sets of relations, which included being a part of children's lives before becoming parents, throwing into question a 'naturalized' distinction between being and becoming a parent. Pam's answer to her own question ('What's our connection?'), 'It's our interest in being parents,' also replicates a normative understanding of caring relationships with children. This common interest in being parents or, in other cases, perhaps like Zoe and Rebecca (below), in supporting parents, children, and the act of parenting, cannot always overcome a privileging of particular forms of experience. As shown in a number of narratives throughout this book, many women's specific experiences of wanting to parent or be involved in a child's life are displaced by divisions between being a parent or not being a parent, which do not include the possibilities for other forms of relating.

Three couples I interviewed, and their children, were connected to each other by Zoe and Rebecca, a couple in their late forties to early fifties. In Chandra's words, Zoe and Rebecca, are the 'hub of the wheel ... [They] are kind of like the grandparents of everybody, grandparents of the kids.' Zoe and Rebecca introduced the six women to each other. The children of the three couples celebrate their birthdays together and are growing up with the chance to know each other. Curious, I asked if Zoe and Rebecca also had children. Chandra replied:

> No ... You know what, Zoe and Rebecca, if they were our age, they'd be definitely having kids. They love kids and they're really good together. They've been together for over twenty years. And that's what I mean: they're like a stabilizing force. They were the first gay couple that I knew as a young gay woman coming out. And they'd been together for like four or five years then, right? And so I knew of them. It's kind of like the role models that all these people are kind of looking at. And there's more people, not all the ones that have kids, but there's more people that kind of look to them in that role.

The relationships that are narrated here are interesting both in the sense of how Zoe and Rebecca are positioned as non-parents in relation to their biological age – 'If they were our age, they'd be definitely having kids' – and the representation of the current societal age in which it is more common for women with women partners to have children. They are positioned as grandparents to the children of the six women, but as role models (not mothers) to the women themselves. The image of the children celebrating their birthdays together is one that resonates with images of cousins (the children of siblings) of the same generation, yet the women (mothers of the children) do not share a longer history. Jeanette Edwards and Marilyn Strathern (2000) explore the ways in which relatives may either drop out of the family or get dropped. They write: 'Blood ties might theoretically allow connections through genealogy and procreation to be traced in ever widening circles, but if it comes to *recognizing* persons as relatives, then in the English experience social exhaustion prevails' (2000, 159–60; italics added).

The stories here are not about *forgetting* relatives but about creating relationships which are at times familiar and yet also novel. Along similar lines, Jeanette's story identifies the work involved in maintaining and cultivating relationships with members of your 'families of the heart' – including women who are parents, women who are not parents, and, significantly, people *whom you already consider to be family*. Chandra's description of Zoe and Rebecca as a stabilizing force captures the impact that they have had on creating and sustaining this constellation of families as family. She added: 'I think that as far as family's concerned, I mean, sure, there's your biological family, but with this situation these friends of ours, they're the people that we kind of go to for guidance and just for a role model. I mean holy shit, you know, they've gone through stuff together – everything you can kind of throw at them – and survived and are doing well. And, like I said, *they foster the children in their lives.'*

Here, yet another form of language connoting particular relationships is used in Chandra's statement that Zoe and Rebecca 'foster the children in their lives.' Fostering is a contested relationship concept, which historically has been associated with time-limited or even distant caring or support for children, often in situations where parental resources (of care, time, ability, or finances) are not able to meet the needs of the children. However, as Wozniak shows in her ethnography, *They're All My Children*, assumptions about fostering relationships are produced through normative understandings of what the term refers to, which may differ significantly from the meanings given to these relationships by the foster parents and children involved (2001).

American magazines such as *Proud Parenting* (previously *Alternative Family*) and *And Baby*, which were available at the time of my fieldwork,[6] advertised chapters of national organizations such as COLAGE and programs for children coordinated by LGBT community and health centres. However, organized programs such as these did not exist in the communities where the women I interviewed live, and even if they had, they may not have met the needs of, or been accessible by, women and children living in various familial constellations and socio-economic contexts.[7] Although the Pride events I attended across British Columbia were inclusive of children, ongoing formal opportunities for children to interact with other children from similar family compositions were rare. Events geared toward children that could provide images of diverse families happened on a much more ad hoc or time-limited basis. Parents relied on meeting and getting to know other parents or individuals who would take on the roles which were conducive to their child's or children's well-being and who supported and validated queer families.

In this chapter I have explored the ways (in contrast to but also sometimes parallel with the strategic outings discussed in chapter 3) in which women were confronted by their children's homophobia or absorption of normative understandings of what constitutes family. Many women sought the possibility to provide their child or children with experiences in which their family form was valued and simply visible in what they encountered around them. This was much less possible for the women I interviewed whose children were born in the early 1980s, and as Jenna pointed out, it was much more possible in urban centres. The chapters in part I thus far address stories which relate to the clarification of ambiguous relationships or identifications and means of actively trying to shape the environment in which a child or children will live. The final chapter of this section draws on a few narratives which highlight the powerful impact of so-called misreadings, situations in which there seems to be no room for clarification.

5 Misreadings

Queer studies and, more generally, gender and sexuality studies celebrate ambiguity and countercultural performances of gender and sexuality, predominantly relying on demarcated 'queer' subjects and spaces to produce comments, theories, and performances of 'queerness' (Butler 1990; Morris 1995; Bell and Valentine 1995). Although an emphasis on discursively constituted bodies within contemporary social theory has questioned definitive relations between sex, gender, and sexuality, bodies appear to only be transgressive when they visibly contest these relations and manifest dissonance on and through bodily performances. Lesbian bodies in fertility clinics, pregnant lesbians, and queer moms do not immediately conjure images of transgression, unlike male or female bodies in drag, analyses of bar culture, or pride parades; instead these women's bodies are more often, in theory, normalized rather than 'queered.' Pregnancy is so concretely linked to biology that queer women – claiming genders and sexualities that subvert biology in the abstract – are unable to contest (and thus displace) the heteronormativity of biology in the concrete and tangible materialities of cervical mucus, developing (or non-developing) follicles, and huge bellies. Even as the number of lesbian, gay, bisexual, and transgender parents increases, pregnancy and parenthood are still read as markers of heterosexuality. As one lesbian mother of a three-year-old exclaimed, 'There is nothing like having a child to send you kicking and screaming back into the closet.' As Kara elaborated:

> I feel like in the street people automatically assume that I'm married or, you know, I'm straight, whatever. That's the automatic assumption. And when I go to [lesbian and gay] dances and stuff, I think that people –

people who know me know, but – I don't know – it's like when you come out, you have to prove yourself, you know, that you're out. And then, being pregnant and having Avery, I have to prove that I'm out, or something. And I guess I think that if other people want to take the time to know, then those are the people that I'm interested in, and not people who just assume other things.

Kara's sense that one has to prove oneself when one comes out and then again when one is pregnant highlights the disassociation of reproduction and parenting from lesbian bodies. Pregnant and parenting women are often ascribed heterosexual status, necessitating explicit articulations and performances of queerness in order to counter the straightness that is assumed. Janine, a single mother of two, points to the difference between being recognized as a lesbian and having to come out as one: 'Just being out in the community as a single mother, I have to *really* come out as a lesbian. If I was with another woman, it would be more obvious, or I could talk about my partner ... So I have to come out – which I've done quite a bit because I really want to talk about alternative insemination and choosing a different kind of way of starting a family.'

Heather also encountered varied responses to her pregnant body and her co-parenting relationship with her close male friend, Brian. When we met, Brian and I talked about the fact that he and Heather do not face many of the issues regarding adoption, legal parental rights, or the right to include both parents' names on the child's birth certificate;[1] although neither of them is heterosexual, their genders match the boxes on government forms. The image of their family, though, results in different types of misreadings. Heather commented:

[During my labour, they got the] OB guy [obstetrician] to examine me. And he said, 'I know that name from somewhere.' I said, 'Well, I'm a teacher.' He goes, 'No, that's not it.' So I said, 'I used to be on a local committee.' 'Oh yeah.' Then he gets this quizzical look on his face and he looks at me and says, 'Can I ask you a question? Aren't you a lesbian?' And I said, 'Yes.' And then he points to Brian, who actually was curled up in a corner with a sheet over him, and he goes, 'Well, who's that?' And I said, 'Well, that's the father.' And then I said, 'I'm a lesbian, and he's a gay man.' And then he goes, 'Oh. I'm a gay man, too!' And then, you know, everybody in the room kind of came out or didn't come out.

Heather's partner has teenage children and is not expected to take on the responsibility of parenting Heather and Brian's daughter. However, she and her children, Brian and his family, Heather, Heather's step-daughter, and Heather's parents are all intimately involved in the toddler's life. Heather often finds herself explaining their family configurations and confronting 'the assumption of straightness' that people have. While the story about the coming-out episode during her labour is humorous, queer people reading a queer pregnant body, a child, or children as cues to heterosexuality was also cited as disturbing. Heather stated:

> Everywhere you go you have to explain. Sometimes it's hard on [my partner] because she's the person who stops the picture from being a little nuclear family. The other problem is being mistaken as heterosexual, which can be very upsetting. I find it very upsetting. We went to this parenting class, and there were these lesbians in the parenting class, and they thought we were straight. That really bothered me. Like, a number of people we knew were in the class, and they knew that we were a gay man and a lesbian, but I think something weird happened the very first night, kind of when everybody was introducing themselves. There was a daycare for our daughter, and with either me or Brian checking on her, we never got to fully explain our situation the first night. So these two women thought that I was straight, and I've never had this problem before. Nobody ever thought I was straight before, and it's like you suddenly become 'unlesbian.'

The possibility of becoming 'unlesbian' by virtue of the configuration of their family was an uncomfortable position for many of the women I interviewed. Popular readings of lesbian pregnancies and lesbian families as processes of normalization (Aird 1998), or readings of access to the status of womanhood (Lewin 1993;1998b), do not address the discomfort that many interviewees had experienced as a result of the straightness imposed on them or of their assumed new access to mainstream status. Although contemporary notions of queer politics foreground the issue of visibility, meanings and experiences of 'being visible' are contextual and relational. People who do not, or choose not, to 'see' or recognize queer moms or queer families often impose invisibility. The complexities and dynamics of being out in heteronormative spaces (family gatherings, broader community events, and, for most women I interviewed, prenatal classes and maternity units) are most evident when this state of invisibility becomes visible to queer women and men.

As the stories of many women I interviewed show, deciding to become a parent often rendered their queerness visible. Parents, friends, siblings, employers, co-workers, and strangers were often challenged to acknowledge a woman's queer sexuality when confronted with the presence of a child in their midst. At the same time, however, a number of women who anticipated potential homophobic or hostile responses chose not to disclose their plans to parent to people outside of their immediate 'families of the heart' until they were pregnant, or had finalized adoptions, or until their baby was born. Thus, silence governed many queer women's thoughts about having children and their experiences of trying to conceive. Getting pregnant or becoming a parent perhaps made it easier to come out about the choice to parent: the pregnancy or the child already existed. This silence, though, had a particular impact on the women who did not get pregnant or were unable to adopt. Paula, whose story was discussed earlier, had informed her family about her decision to have a child.

> They sort of knew but they never asked again, ever. To this day, they've never asked, 'Did you even try? Did you get pregnant and it didn't happen? Like, what happened with that decision?' I told them I was going to do it. I wanted to know, 'Are you interested in aunting? Are you interested in uncle-ing? Are you interested in grandparenting? If you are, I want to know now.' I got their answers to all of that, but never once did they ask me if I had gone ahead and tried.

Women who were not able to get pregnant or to carry a pregnancy to term and who had not shared their experiences of trying to get pregnant did not have a sanctioned space in which their sadness about not having children could be acknowledged.

Talia tried to get pregnant for approximately a year and a half in her mid-thirties. She was new to the west coast, did not have a strong support network, and, for a significant portion of that time, was accessing fertility services provided by a physician who had declared he would not inseminate lesbians, and she was concerned about being outed. Talia said:

It's not something that I really share a whole lot with other lesbians. And I feel sad about saying that. Yeah. I mean, there are people in my life that I do share that with, and I can think of, even in the last couple of weeks, naming that as one of the things I feel grief about in my life. And it's also bound with the death of my partner, too, in the sense that that was the context within which I could see that possibility. Even in terms of peers, my age group, I think one of the things that [my partner] and I often experienced was our peers did not have children and we had children. And sometimes that worked and sometimes it didn't. Sometimes it was a barrier in terms of bringing our kids into our community. Other times it was a barrier because people didn't understand the kinds of issues that we were experiencing. And I see that still, now, in terms of my own peer group, in that there are very few among my peer group who've had children from whatever stories. So the life issues that we deal with are different.

For women who were unable to conceive, women who miscarried, and women who terminated pregnancies, the silence that surrounded their experiences became louder at particular times of their life. Talia continued:

I realized that there would be people who I hadn't come out to – that if I was pregnant, I would be coming out in a whole different way. So I think that affected me. I think the fact that I came from a working class background where it would not have been accepted – I never told my mother. I didn't share with my mother and my father that I was wanting to be pregnant or attempting to be. They were not very supportive of who I was and would not have been supportive – even though, you know, when I came out to my mother, one of the first things was, 'Oh, I'll never be a grandmother,' you know. And I wanted to be able to tell her that that's a possibility.

In 1999 the Supreme Court of Canada decision in the widely covered case of *M. v. H.*, in which the former woman partner of another woman challenged a lower court's denial of her right to spousal support upon the end of the relationship, ruled that the definition of *spouse* as pertaining only to opposite sex partners is unconstitutional. The court ordered the Government of Ontario to change the restrictive definition of *spouse* within the Family Law Act. Bill 5 was passed by the Ontario government. Bill C-23 was then passed by the federal government of

Canada in July 2000, implementing two categories of spouse and common-law partner, the first reserved for married couples (with *marriage* defined as between members of the opposite sex) and the second encompassing couples of either same or opposite sex.[2] Both prior to and following the implementation of Bill C-23, debates ensued regarding its impact on the meaning of *marriage* (which, at the time, was still restricted to two individuals of the opposite sex) and the sanctity of *the family* in Canada. Talia has two children, in their early twenties at the time of our interview, whom she had co-parented with her partner since they were six and eight years old. Following her partner's death, Talia remained in contact with her partner's father. They exchanged emails about the proposed legislation. She commented:

> He's been very supportive over the years and he's also got some areas where he just can't quite move into. And one of the things that he emailed back to me about the Bill [was], 'I'm really glad they reserved the word *marriage* for procreation.' [We laugh.] So I laughed and I also thought, 'Ohhhh.' So my email back to him is – I'm going to tell him that I tried to get pregnant, and, you know, so the word is not so sacred that it has to be held only for the act of procreation and that lesbian and gay people have – I'm also going to tell him that, in fact, there's a baby boom in the queer communities now.

Bill C-23, known as the Modernization of Benefits and Obligations Act, allocates benefits to same-sex common-law partners in areas which are within the jurisdiction of the federal government (including taxes and social security benefits). However, the Act did not change marriage legislation at the federal level, which continued to stipulate that marriage is between a man and a woman. One of the strong arguments put forward was that this distinction was, and needed to be, maintained because marriage is tied to the act of procreation; and procreation is deemed to be an outcome of an opposite-sex relationship. In the representation of this exchange, the father of Talia's late partner made a distinction between parenting (which his daughter did while partnered with a woman) and procreation (the active bringing into the world of a child). Talia's planned response was aimed at making visible 'procreation' which was taking place regardless of state-sanctioned status. By drawing on the example of her own experience (with his daughter), she would render the discussion, perhaps, more immediately relevant to him. A prevailing discontinuity in the connection between marriage and procreation and the allocation of rights according to particular sets of logics is evident in a case reported in 2007 whereby a married female couple in Nova Scotia who were expecting a child discovered that both women would not automatically be the legal parents of their child (Bourassa and Varnell 2007).[3]

The stories in this last chapter of part I highlight the very systemic manners in which assumptions about the relationship between queerness and parenting are reproduced. It is not always possible to challenge stereotypes, nor is there the energy to do so. The categories of 'straight' and 'queer' that are at times employed to differentiate between the spaces and contexts in which queer families or queer parents might be recognized break down as women are confronted by the normative assumptions which may prevail across the board. Certain developments, in Canada especially in discussions around the legal recognition of same-sex relationships, opened up the opportunity for previously undisclosed experiences to be shared. In many situations, though, the perceived stakes of sharing sad or traumatic experiences, which were not shared in the first place due to expectations of confrontation, are too high. The thoughts remain unstated.

PART II

Negotiating Relatedness

In May 1998 the *Vancouver Sun* ran a two-page story about lesbian and gay families in Vancouver. Under the headline 'Gay and Lesbian Parents: We Are Family' the subtitle explained: 'Same-sex couples are raising children successfully and happily as society's new openness encourages gays and lesbians to explore such avenues as foster-parenting, adoption and artificial insemination to build families' (Aird 1998, C10).

The article draws on the experiences of a gay dad raising his teenage daughter and a lesbian couple parenting their infant son. The slogan 'We are family' was (and still is) used to represent imagined and real communities of queer people in the LGBT rights movement (cf. Weston 1991; Arnup 1991). In this article the statement 'We are family' simultaneously invokes the history of a broader community engaged in a struggle for rights and appears as a more matter of fact representation of reality: queer women and men are parents. In Elizabeth Aird's words, 'while the Supreme Court of Canada rules on issues of equality for gays and lesbians, while some Canadians wring their hands about the collapse of the family, gay and lesbian parents are changing diapers and wiping tears and doing laundry' (1998; C11). Following this statement and based on her interviews, Aird concludes, 'Parenting is the one place where being gay is not an issue' (1998, C11). Conclusions such as this cloak the concerns of LGBT parents and their children, rendering invisible and silent the very real issues that 'being gay' presents to both parents and prospective parents. Given 'society's new openness,' I would propose that it should then seem surprising that articles such as this one, which depict lesbian and gay families, continue to enact a normalizing discourse. The article refers to the

Adoption Act amendments in 1996, which facilitated adoptions by lesbians and gay men, and dialogue about the Surrey school board's decision to ban the use of *Asha's Mums*, *Belinda's Bouquet*, and *One Dad, Two
Dads, Brown Dad, Blue Dads* in school classrooms because the three
picture books depict same-sex parents. (The decision was later overturned.) Many straight and queer women and men employ strategies
to normalize families comprising queer members, and indeed, the
inclusion of the picture books above in the school curriculum is
viewed as threatening because they do just that; they normalize queer
parenting. The suggestion, however, that 'society's new openness' is
'encouraging' more lesbians and gay men to explore parenting options
is both true and limiting. I would suggest that the perception of
society's new openness stems from the *legal* recognition of same-sex
partners as spouses and the recognition of same-sex partners in relationships as (potential) parents. In the discussion of both families represented in this article, adults who figured prominently in the route to
parenting and the parenting structure are displaced from the every-
dayness of parenting. In the case of the gay dad and his teenage
daughter, his partner is displaced from a discussion of parenting and
family. In the case of the two women parenting their infant son, the
known donor (who is also a close friend) is displaced from the sphere
of family. While the 'new openness' of society alludes to a new recognition of social kinship, this new recognition of queer families, especially in the dominant mainstream media, is perhaps dependant on the
shifting legal relationships between LGBT individuals and children.
The 'dad' is the biological father of the teenage girl and, thus, legally
related to her. The two women used sperm from a known donor and
then filed for a second-parent adoption. Thus, they are now both legal
parents of their son.

Queer women's locations as single prospective parents, step-
parents, or adoptive parents, and their previous histories of parenting,
are significant to the process of negotiating kinship. I interviewed a
few women who felt that the law had no place in defining the relationship we have to our children and to each other. Yet, although queer
women's parental status has seldom been included within the protec-
tive facets of the law, we live in a society governed by laws. Few
women I met during my research established their families outside of
the law (if that could be possible), relying instead on the legal absolu-
tion of donor's paternity rights when the semen donation or the
insemination was brokered through medical practice; the legal sym-

bolic weight of donor contracts; as well as the impact of guardianship papers, wills, health care directives, pre-conception custody agreements, and adoptions. Today women look to the changes in the Family Relations Act, the implementation of the Adoption Act, and, more recently, federal legislation recognizing same-sex partners in the definition of *spouse*, to support their claims for social and legal recognition as parents.

Both before and following the legislative changes in British Columbia, which are introduced in chapter 1, women articulated numerous perspectives on the status of their relationships to donors, possible partners, and potential children. Part II of this book examines the complexities defining not only the legislation that exists but also women's attempts to understand the apparent gaps in which their experiences might fit. The narratives that are shared in the following chapters reflect a tension between women's and men's ideas about biological and legal relationships and the privileges accorded to each.

6 Legal (Re)Framings

The 1980s and 1990s, the period during which the women in this study attempted to get pregnant or become a parent, brought about significant shifts in court interpretations of the 'best interests of the child' and witnessed the precedent-setting inclusion of sexual orientation as a protected status under the Human Rights Code in various Canadian provinces. In 1996 the Canadian Human Rights Act was amended to explicitly prohibit discrimination on the basis of sexual orientation, based on a 1995 Supreme Court ruling. In 1998, in the Supreme Court judgment of *Vriend v. Alberta*, sexual orientation was 'read into' the Canadian Charter of Rights and Freedoms: the exclusion of lesbians and gay men from provincial human-rights-protection legislation countered the Charter.[1] Although a parent's sexual orientation may be used by former spouses and, as noted in Gavigan (2000) and Arnup and Boyd (1995), by children's grandparents as a means of citing women's unfitness to parent,[2] in many situations, being lesbian or gay no longer represents *the* reason for determining custody and access in favour of a heterosexual party. Gavigan writes that although women's sexual orientation may be raised as an issue, 'litigating husbands [and others] can no longer be supremely confident of winning' (2000, 111). For most of the women I interviewed, their awareness of custody disputes between lesbians and sperm donors, as well as between lesbian co-parents, overshadowed their knowledge of the continuing cases between straight and queer ex-partners or other family members. The experiences of queer women who become pregnant by having sex with a man with whom they do not have a spousal relationship, but who are also not considered donors, are not very prominent in discussions, although, as Kara's comments below illustrate, they are a concern. Until very recently, an emphasis had been placed on lobbying for legal parental recognition and status according to a model that accepted a maximum of two legal parents, even if the social practice differed. A 2007 case in Ontario in which a judge authorized three legal parents may be an indicator of possible future configurations of legal families in which former partners, co-parents, and donors are not displaced via existing normative legal frameworks (CBC News 2007; Hilborn 2007).

The complexity of legal relations and the strategies that women employed to gain recognition and signify relatedness is significant to readings and representations of narratives of queer conceptions and queer families. Gavigan suggests that lesbians have contradictory relationships to the law. She states: 'It seems to me that we can no longer assert generally or with confidence that lesbians are in or out of the law or on the wrong side of the legal tracks; it is important to identify, illustrate, and analyse the varied and changing, indeed, contradictory ways in which the law relates to lesbians and lesbians to the law' (Gavigan 2000, 102). Queer women's (and donor's) rights and abilities to define relationships and to determine kinship outside of legal parameters are only possible when all parties involved are committed to recognizing non-legal relatedness. In the following pages I focus on the ways in which personal and public histories of family status and custody disputes informed women's decisions about donors. Women's narratives highlighted not only the often-discussed status of their relationship to the child with regard to the donor but also, for women in a relationship with a partner, their stratified relationship to the child they were parenting or intending to parent.

Concerning Custody

During the 1970s and 1980s many women lost custody of their child or children to a male ex-partner (who was also a parent of their child or children) when courts deemed women who identified as lesbian, and expressed their sexuality,[3] unfit to parent (Lewin 1981; Robson 1995). The rulings in these early custody cases often set perceptions of heterosexual normalcy and stability in opposition to presumed lesbian abnormality and instability (Lewin 1981; Robson 1995). Stereotypes of lesbians and lesbian sexuality excluded women who were attracted to women, or shared their life with a woman, from the frame of publicly (socially and legally) validated parenthood. In this sense, *lesbian mother* was an oxymoron (Lewin 1993): by virtue of attraction to another woman, a woman's access to recognition as a mother was challenged and often denied (cf. Arnup 1995; Lewin 1993).

A number of feminist scholars have examined the legal discourses by which lesbians were denied custody of their children (Arnup and Boyd 1995; Gavigan 2000; Millbank 2003). Sociologists and anthropologists focused their ethnographic gaze on lesbian motherhood in order to provide data that would support the claim that lesbian mothers are just like other mothers (cf. Lewin 1993, introduction). Ellen Lewin's ethnography, *Lesbian Mothers*, published in 1993, provides a rich account of gender and motherhood, based on research she conducted in the early 1980s. Social science research sometimes inadvertently reproduces the very same categorical normativity that it wishes to challenge; the women at the focus of Lewin's early ethnographic study of lesbian motherhood were women who could biologically or legally assert their identity as mother and who sought continued social and legal recognition of their parental status.[4] Women who occupied the positions often referred to as non-biological mother, co-parent, co-mother, step-parent, or other mother seldom shared equal access to the category of 'mother' or 'parent' in legal or family contexts (Gavigan 2000), nor did they achieve mother status within the frame of lesbian mother research at the time. This stratification of parenthood along the lines of biological, genetic, or legal norms (minimized, perhaps, within the context of a relationship) has carried significant weight in situations involving custody of and visitation with children, as well as the public visibility of parenting relationships.

The institutionalized exile of lesbians from legal motherhood (Gavigan 2000; Dalton 2001) was and is supported by legislation, as well as informal practices, which prohibit adoption by single or partnered lesbians, deny full parental status to lesbian non-legal parents, and perpetuate heteronormative representations of family in most sectors of society. Recognized parental status facilitates everyday parenting activities, including making health care decisions, authorizing children's participation in daycare or school activities and field trips, and being mobile. It also legally secures one's rights and obligations to continue parenting a child. Robyn, who was in her mid-twenties when we met, commented that she was not very concerned about the legal status she and her partner would have to the child: 'I don't think about it too much. I feel like you take your rights one way or another. You sort of force your way in and you just do what you want to do. And wait until they drag you right down before you give up. I'm not too concerned about that.' In many ways, Robyn's life experiences supported this perception that she would be able to 'take' her rights. She had very little income, an unstable job, and questionable working conditions and was very visibly out within a small community. On the other hand, as Robyn stated next, she was not currently in a situation in which the stakes of being institutionally recognized – rather than publicly visible – were of great importance. 'But, I'm also not actively trying to get pregnant. And I'm not in those situations where, you know, I've just been in a car accident, and [my partner's] the only one to make decisions, and they won't let her. So until you really face those situations, it's hard to say how you'd feel about them because we can't even imagine what they could all be. And I know that British Columbia is the most progressive place for [lesbians] right now.'

One difficulty to which Robyn's comment points for queer parents is the awareness of differential potentialities for recognition. Throughout the 1980s and 1990s local decisions were made and changes (and challenges) took place through which women achieved varying degrees of recognition as parents. Rita was granted parental leave with respect to the child to whom her partner gave birth. However, she was told by hospital staff just after her son's birth that only parents were allowed to remain, and therefore, she drove the hour home before returning as a parent. Two women who adopted a child were both named as parents at the time of adoption and subsequently on their son's birth certificate, but another couple were advised at the last moment, on the basis of a social worker's experience with a particular judge, to proceed with the adoption by one of the women as a single parent and then to file for joint parental status in another jurisdiction. Changes to employee policy, or informal readings of same-sex partners into the definition of *spouse* or *domestic partner*, took place fairly quietly and often applied only within certain jurisdictions. Challenges to legal practices of spousal and family recognition took place across Canada at different points in time and via different forms of policy and legislation. This resulted in varying degrees of access to legal status and, consequently, uncertainty regarding the mobility of recognition, and thus families, across provincial and Territorial borders.

In the opening paragraphs of 'Mothers, Other Mothers, and Others,' Shelley Gavigan notes the historical shift that has born witness to lesbians and gay men 'taking their lives to court to challenge and resist homophobic discrimination' (2000, 100). Just as Jennifer Terry (1999) identifies the challenges facing lesbians who are struggling for appropriate health care information and services within a medical system which has historically pathologized same-sex attractions, Gavigan writes: 'A community of people who scarcely, if ever, experienced the law as a shield has taken it up as a sword to advance and vindicate equality claims. To even the most casual observer, the successes and near misses of lesbian and gay litigants and law reformers illustrate that a significant social and political shift has been achieved over the last decade' (2000, 100).[5] Queer women who are parenting or thinking about becoming parents do so within the context of legislative changes and court decisions. The narratives of women I interviewed were informed and historicized by challenges to the legal governance of 'family.' Aird, the author of the article discussed in the introduction to part II, invokes an image of queer parenting as a normal, ongoing, everyday occurrence, framing court decisions about the status of queer men and women as peripheral to their existence; the legal status of the families featured in her article is obscured. However, I would suggest that the legal status of these families is extremely significant.

Women who were actively trying to get pregnant or adopt were often aware of the limitations and benefits of legal parenthood or were made aware of them by developing a consciousness of their legal relationship to their child. Kara, a single mother in her late twenties shares childcare responsibilities with her daughter's father. Her vision of having children had included a 'turkey baster' and donor sperm. Instead, she unexpectedly became pregnant after having sex with her ex-boyfriend. From Kara's perspective, she and her ex-boyfriend are now in a lifelong relationship because of their daughter. As their lives unfold, their shared parenting experiences have been, for the most part, positive. Yet, the fact that Kara dates women does come into play when she considers the legal status of their individual relationships to their daughter. Kara explained:

> I worry that [my daughter's father] may get married one day and decide that he wants to have Avery and that he'd be better for her than me because he's married and he's a man and he'll make more money than me, you know. He'll be more settled and he's heterosexual, you know. I worry about that. So I thought about going and applying for custody. And then I thought, 'Why should I apply for custody of *my daughter* – who I gave birth to, who I care for every day of her life since she was born and before she was born – because of this man who decided that he

wanted to be part of her life?' I don't know. I really resent the fact that people have to, that women have to do that.

Over the course of my fieldwork I met women who did not feel the need to have their relationship recognized by law, who did not feel the need to adopt their child whom their partner had given birth to or adopted, or who did not go through the courts to determine custody arrangements following the dissolution of a relationship. Some of these women did not want their life and their relationship to their child to be determined or governed by the legal system. Other women did not have the social or financial resources to enact (or circumscribe) legal relationships. Just as Kara views applying for custody of her own daughter as absurd, other women explained that they might choose *not* to adopt a child to whom their partner gave birth, because of the absurdity of having to adopt their own child. The time, energy, and money that it takes to establish the legal status of an individual's relationship to children are discriminatory. On principle, queer women may refuse to participate in a system that will now allow them the right of legal parental status but makes them pay for the privilege.

'We Are Family' Revisited: Contesting Parental Status

The beginning of the lesbian baby boom is often attributed to the early 1970s, coinciding with second-wave feminist consciousness, the women's health movement, and the emergence of alternative perspectives on what makes a family. During this same period, lesbian mothers who became parents in the context of heterosexual relationships and marriages faced considerable barriers in family court systems, which viewed being lesbian as counter-intuitive to ensuring the 'best interests of the child' (Lewin 1981). A significant amount of the rhetoric at the time, which affected single heterosexual mothers as well, revolved around the damaging effects to the development of children when they were being raised in a household without a male role model. In light of these struggles that played the normative heterosexuality of fathers against the deviant visible lesbianism of mothers, many women who were trying to become parents while identifying as lesbian wanted a sperm donor who was anonymous and, often, gay. If anonymity was compromised, or if the donor was to be known, gay men were viewed as a 'category of males most likely to recognize the lover of the biological mother as a full-fledged parent, and to abide by any parenting and custody agreements reached in advance of a child's birth' (Weston 1991, 177).

A statement that I heard in my research, which echoed many of the sentiments and fears of women I interviewed, was, 'We didn't want to end up in court some day with this guy claiming parental rights.' The possibility that a sperm donor could be awarded parental status was perceived to be a real threat. Most often, thoughts regarding the choice of a donor were tied to the role that women wanted the donor to have in the child's life, their imagined constellation of parents, and analyses of possible contestation to the parental status of the woman who would *not* be recognized as the child's legal parent from birth. The women I interviewed offered various readings of their thoughts and decisions regarding asking straight and gay men to be donors. While gay men might be viewed as most likely to abide by custody agreements, women also speculated that they might be less likely than straight men to have other opportunities to have children and, thus, might be more likely to change their mind about the level of involvement they would want to have with the child once the child was born. However, one woman I interviewed stated somewhat matter-of-factly that a judge was probably less likely to award custody to a gay man, even if the other option were to award custody to a lesbian. Straight men, on the other hand, hold heterosexual privilege and, if they are with a partner, can be seen to provide a stable heterosexual environment. However, straight men would potentially also have the possibilities to become fathers in other ways and thus may not likely view this child as their only parenting possibility. One of the difficulties in imagining potential scenarios is the decontextualization of analysis from the embodied experiences of individuals and the transference of normative assumptions over time. As both research and the experiential narratives of the women in my study show, shifts in perceptions of families, father's rights, gender roles, donor anonymity, and so forth may introduce unanticipated and previously untenable combinations of justification for various decisions and actions.

In contrast to the image of gay men 'helping' lesbian women to become parents, as well as the romanticized vision of queer women and men unified as family, Arnup and Boyd (1995) describe the 1993 U.S. case of *Thomas S. v. Robin Y.*, in which a gay man who had been a sperm donor to a lesbian couple sought a declaration of paternity and visitation rights in relation to a child born in the early 1980s. The judge who denied the order stated: 'Ry [the child in question] does not now and has never viewed Thomas S. as a functional third parent. To Ry, a parent is a person who a child depends on to care for her needs. To Ry, Thomas S. has never been a parent since he never took care of her on a daily basis' (quoted in Arnup and Boyd 1995, 77). In 1994 the appellate division of the New York Supreme Court overturned this judgment, with the three-to-two majority observing, 'The notion that a *lesbian* mother should enjoy a parental relationship with her daughter but a *gay* father should not is so innately discriminatory as to be unworthy of comment' (quoted in Arnup and Boyd 1995, 96, italics added). Whereas the original decision conveyed the potential for two women parents to challenge the definition of parenthood based in biology, according to Arnup and Boyd '[overturning the decision] invokes biology as the key determinant of legal paternity, demonstrating that it may be some time before it is possible to eliminate the long-standing judicial determination to "find fathers" for children, even where lesbian families are concerned' (Arnup and Boyd 1995, 96).

Rereading the brief explanatory sentence selected from the appeal decision which overturned the original judgment, I have italicized the adjectives ascribed to the so-called biological parents in order to question the determinants of legal parenthood invoked. In the first judgment the possibility for three parents, presumably the two mothers and the petitioning sperm donor, is put forward in the reasoning that the child has never viewed the sperm donor as a functional third parent. The definition of parenthood then rested on functionality: the role in the child's life, which presumably, if the donor is potential parent number three, the other mother (unnamed in the case) fulfils. The statement in the second judgment discursively reduces the potential contenders for parental status to two: a lesbian mother and a gay father. The second lesbian mother is already rendered invisible, but I am uncertain as to whether this then stabilizes biology as the basis of parenthood. Instead, I am drawn to consider how a discourse of father's rights combines with a discourse of equal opportunities for lesbians and gay men to participate in the socially sanctioned and valued practice of parenting. The petitioning sperm donor, who had had a varied relationship with the two children (Ry and her sibling) who are parented by the two women, eventually withdrew his paternity claim. However, the case, heard in the early 1990s, as well as the emergence of new media narratives which have positioned sperm donors both as 'victims' and 'fathers' are examples of the possible contestations to parenting roles and family composition that can take place. While much of the literature and previous narratives linked such contestations to known donors, recent challenges by sperm donors, recipient mothers, and children conceived by donor insemination have reconfigured the normative anonymity of the so-called anonymous donors whose sperm was distributed through fertility treatment programs and sperm banks. Teenage children's use of Internet and genealogy-tracing technologies to identify anonymous sperm-bank donors; the proliferation of Internet-based registries of donors, donor-insemination offspring, and siblings; and the decisions of sperm donors to contact offspring have multiple effects. These activities demonstrate sound contestations of the initial practices of donor anonymity but also reveal the inadequacy of practices at times to ensure anonymity, thus raising the risk of contestation to a family's status by not only known but also unknown donors.

The difficulty with the case outlined by Arnup and Boyd, and women's speculations about similar scenarios, is that it throws into question queer women's abilities to define lesbian families as inclusive of 'fathers' and for both women and men to experience the meanings of fathering outside of a framework of potential contestation to the parental status or authority of one party. The perspectives on the relationships between queer women, donors, and children developed in this book are based on interviews with queer women and on publicly available narratives. In my study, donors' ideas about relationships with and obligations to children conceived by donor insemination were accessible only through the narratives of the women I interviewed, a few of the donors I met over the course of fieldwork, and emerging public stories. The men who became sperm donors occupied defined relationships to children and women within preconceptualized 'families,' relationships that then may have been redefined through time and lived experience. Yet, the donors were also often marginalized through the discursive performance of 'family' and 'parenthood,' a strategy supported by a legal framework which, until the recent 2007 decision noted above, had worked within a limited two-parent model. Whereas it is increasingly common for children to have more than two parental figures in their lives, a system of records and recognition of parental authority (rather than role) has required the factual displacement of additional figures, enacted through a relinquishing of legal parental status. This logic of factual displacement governed women's decision regarding donors as well as the records of donors that were made, purchased, or avoided. Corinne Hayden

(1995) discusses practices of 'kinetic' kinship in which biology is mobilized for different purposes and effects. I propose that the relationships between donors, children, and women are also demobilized, with distance enacted through various technologies (Luce 1998, 2003) including the use of 'paper tools' (Landecker 2003).

A number of women's stories about the arrangements that they had made with donors involved contracting a relationship with them. However, until 1996 when the Adoption Act was amended, permitting second-parent adoptions by women partners of women, there was no tested means by which to dissolve the legal parental status of a sperm donor. Single women felt that they were in a more precarious position. A number of the women interviewed in my study described both their own relief and the donor's relief once second-parent adoptions became an option in British Columbia. However, it is important to note that many potential donors were not chosen as donors because they expressed a desire to be central to the family being created; they wanted to be fathers, not donors and not 'uncles.' Seldom did women consider that they themselves might contradict the terms of a donor agreement or contract. Even less frequently did queer women apply this same discourse of legal risk to discussions about their relationship with a girlfriend or partner. Yet, decisions about donors very often reflected strategic means by which women would be linked via the donor or adoption practice to a child or children, regardless of who gave birth to the child, in whose name the adoption was processed, or, more recently, whose eggs were fertilized.

Changing Lesbian-Mother Relations

Custody cases involving women ex-partners are more common, or more visible, now than they were fifteen to twenty years ago. One possible reason for this shift is the increasing number of queer women who become mothers or raise children together. A discourse of reproductive intent (Dalton 2000; Cussins 1998b), which is activated most commonly in the field of assisted reproduction in order to determine parental status in the light of the new ambiguity presented by, for example, egg donation and surrogacy, is also mobilized by woman-woman couples as a means of solidifying the claims to mother status by mothers who did not give birth to the child. Although situations certainly existed during the 1970s and 1980s in which lesbians were denied access to children whom they had co-parented with other women or couples in alternative family arrangements, these cases were seldom mitigated via the legal system. Most mothers who had not given birth to their children and did not have legal status as an adoptive parent did not view the legal system as an avenue by which to assert their parental status. Given the paucity of social recognition of their role and the relatively non-existent avenues by which they could have established legal standing in relation to the child in the context of the relationship, non-biological or non-legal parents relied on their ability to make arrangements with the child's biological or, more importantly, legal parent. Women who become parents in partnerships with other women are perhaps more likely now to seek court recognition of a parenting role that has been inscribed as such through everyday life practices, conception narratives, and documentation.

In contrast to the cases emerging between lesbians and straight ex-partners (who were most often the biological and legal parent of the child), in which male ex-partners could no longer be assured that a mother's lesbian identity would be used against her, the cases involving two lesbian co-parents often simultaneously invoked, reproduced, and challenged heteronormative images of family and parent. Two parents of the same gender were often unthinkable, such that dichotomous (male-female) gender norms and related parenting roles were inscribed in the bodies and narratives of the two individuals in question. In many of these cases, one lesbian's status as mother was recognized, while the other lesbian's status as either a mother or a parent was denied (Dalton 2000). The explicit use of heterosexist law by lesbians and gay men against lesbians and gay men made it clear that taking custody and access issues to court would be a struggle and presented challenges to a collective 'we are family' narrative. In court cases, evidence was presented regarding the ways in which finances were organized, contributions to care were made, and so forth. The arguments seldom accounted for the different economic status of women, their different career and education opportunities, and so forth. In many earlier decisions, the discreetness with which a woman expressed her sexuality or her status as a single lesbian was often cited in her favour. In contrast, in other cases, a paradoxical emphasis was placed on whether the woman had been visible as a partner and joint parent, an emphasis that does not pay attention to the negative effects that such visibility may have on a woman's job security or location within a community.

A number of the women I interviewed were unable to continue parenting a child as a result of a relationship ending. The stratification of legal parental status (often along the lines of biology) and the lack of public and legal recognition of parental status played a significant role in women's perceptions of their ability and right to continue a relationship with a child. Many women who were non-biological parents or step-parents without legal status did not view the legal system as one that would affirm their right to continue a relationship with the child they had been parenting. The end of their relationship to the child or children was in fact normalized and naturalized by the friends and family who rendered unnatural a woman's expectation that the relationship would or could continue. After all, the connection to the child was by affiliation,[6] a result of the relationship to the child's 'mother'; it was neither biological nor legal. One woman I interviewed sought legal advice when, upon the end of her relationship, her ex-partner denied her access to the children whom they had been parenting together. Describing her conversation with the lawyer, she explained: 'He listened to my whole story and said, "Walk away. You don't have a hope in hell of getting access to these kids, so just walk away and start your life again."' The next years were spent in court before it became possible to continue a parenting role, but only one to the child conceived during the relationship.

Lesbians, whose lives are governed by heterosexist laws but who have differential access to protection from these laws, are, as one woman in my study stated, expected to behave 'ethically' in the event of a break-up or the dissolution of separation or custody understandings. However, as the experiences of women I interviewed and the cases reported in other studies demonstrate, this is not always the case. Women who had had experiences similar to the cases above were sometimes more likely to emphasize the need for women who are in co-parenting relationships with women to clearly define their relationships to their child or children and to secure a legal relationship to the child in the absence of a legal tie between the women, a tie which in heterosexual couples automatically confers legal status to children born within the context of that relationship. Other women found ways by which to subvert the possibility of being denied recognition as a mother at any point, often relying on multiple perspectives on parental relationships to do so. In most cases, however, women expressed concerns about custody with respect to the rights that a sperm donor would have.

The visibility of cases involving sperm donors and lesbian co-parents, or perhaps the weight they carry in discourses of queer kinship, has to do with their out-of-place status within North American 'cultures of relatedness' (Carsten 2000) and within discourses of chosen families. Whereas the custody disputes which were typical of the earlier days of visible lesbian parenting mustered support from lesbian activists to fight against a heterosexual family imperative, newly visible cases featuring lesbians and sperm donors and lesbian co-parents provoke ethical dilemmas (see Arnup and Boyd 1995). The lesbian, gay, bisexual, and transgender movement that was built on the foundations of chosen family, and identified with the slogan (and theme song) 'We are family,' constructed queer kinship in relation to and in contrast with dominant heteronormative kinship narratives. The breakdown of so-called relations of choice, and disputes involving children, in many ways challenge the nature of chosen families: many lesbians and gay men use the rhetoric and reality of legally and socially recognized biogenetic relations to contest other lesbians' and gay men's claims for recognition. On the other hand, perhaps the kinship contestations between queer women and queer women, or queer women and queer or straight sperm donors, are reminders that, no matter the political debates regarding the role of the law in our lives, we live in a society that determines by law the place of children and the issues of support and access.

This chapter traces the trajectories of legal custody disputes and normative judgments, which have informed women's decisions about sperm donors and their use of the law. It is not possible to employ reductive reasoning in order to frame women's co-parenting relationships or choices about sperm donors along fixed lines. Rather, the multiple forms of sense-making must be considered alongside invocations of experiential knowledge as a base from which to make decisions. The next chapter addresses the fluctuations in notions of anonymity, which can be read in tandem with the shifts discussed here.

7 Figuring Anonymity

In *The Ultimate Guide to Pregnancy for Lesbians* Rachel Pepper states, 'One of the biggest decisions you will make in trying to get pregnant is whether to use a known or an unknown donor' (1999, 32). In her discussion of the pros and cons of using known or unknown donors, Pepper quotes Kate Kendall, director of the U.S. National Centre for Lesbian Rights, who states, 'Using a known donor is a minefield of risk' (1999, 36). In a similar vein, at a discussion of same-sex rights and family status which I attended in 1998 in Vancouver, shortly following the amendments to the Family Relations Act,[1] a prominent lawyer and activist within the BC LGBT community warned prospective parents about the legal implications of using a known donor. Simply put, she argued, if a body can be related to the sperm, that person will be considered the father, whether or not heterosexual sex is involved. As a recognized father, the donor would have full parental rights. 'Authoritative knowledge' about queer families advocates that, in order to avoid a potential custody dispute with a sperm donor, the 'safest' route to parenthood involves the use of an anonymous or unknown donor. For the women I interviewed, the decision to use a known or unknown donor was most often tied to women's perspectives on the amount of involvement they wanted the donor to have in the child's life, and, correspondingly, their fears regarding potential custody disputes. Interwoven with these concerns were women's perspectives on 'natural' methods of assisted conception. The combination of these factors shaped the choices and compromises women made in their selection of sperm donors, as well as the decisions about the place and the method of attempting conception.

In the past, *anonymous donors* were unknown to the recipients, and the term referred to both anonymous 'live' donors (fresh semen) and anonymous donors from sperm banks (fresh or frozen semen). Today, few women choose to use anonymous live donors. Instead, most women choose between what are referred to as known, unknown, and willing-to-be-known donors. Reference to a *known* donor as anonymous means that the donor is known to the inseminating woman or intended parents and possibly the child, friends, and family, but his role as a sperm donor is only known to a select few. *Unknown* donors are anonymous, their anonymity having been arranged by the sperm bank with which they are affiliated. *Willing-to-be-known* donors are anonymous only until the child turns eighteen (or until another arranged or sometimes legislated time).[2] At that time, some sperm banks will release the identity of the donor to the adult offspring so that she or he may contact the donor, and other sperm banks will facilitate a meeting between the donor and the offspring.

The distinction between known and unknown donors is culturally and politically embedded in multiple discourses of expectation, regulation, health, and the very conceptual framings of such notions (and technologies) of *knowing* and *anonymity*. The meanings of both knowing and anonymity were mediated by women I interviewed in relation to, for example, individuals, bodily fluids, genetic histories, and information and communication technologies. Along with the growing range of options available from sperm banks with respect to the information one can receive about a donor, or the potential contact that one's child might be allowed in the future, numerous societal shifts in what it means to know someone or something have also occurred. Over the course of my research I interviewed women who had anticipated making an arrangement with a man who would agree to be a known donor, or an anonymous live donor, and yet they ended up purchasing semen from a sperm bank. I also interviewed women who expected to use a sperm-bank donor and then decided to use a known donor. Deciding between a known or an unknown donor was very often neither the beginning nor the ending to women's narratives.

Local and Live

The use of an anonymous donor who was known to a friend or an acquaintance – sometimes referred to as a *local* donor or a *live*[3] donor – was quite common during the 1970s and even the late 1980s (Achilles

1993; Nelson 1996; Wilkes 1985). An intermediary – also known as a *sperm runner* (Nelson 1996; Wilkes 1985) or a *bumblebee* (Weston 1991) – couriered requests, sperm, and sometimes donor contracts,[4] between the two parties and was responsible for maintaining the anonymity of the donor and the recipient. This practice, and the fact that sperm runners were often mutual acquaintances of both the donor and the recipient, meant that the anonymity associated with local donors did not carry the sense of permanence conveyed by the use of donors affiliated with sperm-bank and fertility-treatment programs. For the women in this study who chose anonymous donors from outside of a sperm-bank context, the distance – both literal and figurative – between the local donor and the recipient was significantly less than the distance between sperm-bank donors and clients.[5] For many of the women I interviewed, it was important that the donor agree to be contacted, if necessary or desired, at a later point in a child's life. Locating a sperm donor outside of the medical system offered the ability to negotiate such arrangements with sperm runners who, as mutual acquaintances, provided a route back to the donor. This stood in contrast to the practices of many sperm banks and fertility clinics at the time that claimed, and still claim, that they did not keep records of a donor's identity and, therefore, would be unable to provide such information at any point in the future.

Sperm banks such as the Sperm Bank of California and Pacific Reproductive Services came into being in the early 1980s to meet the demands of lesbians and single heterosexual women for both 'anonymous' and 'screened' semen (see Tober 2001, Agigian 2004, and Mamo 2005 for histories of the sperm banks). Since inception, these two programs have provided women with willing-to-be-known donors. For some Canadian women, these U.S. services were unknown, involved additional stress around coordinating deliveries, and/or were economically inaccessible. For other women, the time lag of eighteen years before the identity of the donor would be released did not address their concerns. How likely were these sperm banks to be in operation that far in the future? What would happen to their records if they went out of business? According to best-practice guidelines, sperm banks today keep records of the donors and the children conceived using their sperm.[6] In contrast to the recommendation of Health Canada's Standing Committee on Health,[7] Bill C-6, when passed, did not implement a definitive process of donor identification, opting for a structure which would facilitate the release of identifying information only with the consent of the donor. Thereby, an emphasis was placed on the indefinite maintenance of records and the consistent collection of health reporting information.

Concerns about running into the donor in your community or having someone recognize physical features of the donor manifested in your child are also implicit in marketing statements. During my fieldwork the promotional material of one Vancouver clinic advertised that donors were from outside of British Columbia. Countering this, another clinic emphasized that the sperm donors were from British Columbia. The women I interviewed negotiated these different meanings and practices of anonymity alongside their perceptions of, and past experiences with, custody issues, interpretations of queer women's and straight and queer men's relationship to the law, their ability to find local donors or known donors, and their access to medically assisted insemination programs or sperm banks.

New Relationalities

Nadine was involved in an alternative family arrangement with a straight couple during the 1970s. When the adult relationships deteriorated, her parenting relationship to her son was compromised. Friends who were familiar with her experience suggested that she speak with another woman they knew who had just gone through something similar. This woman, Maureen, was the mother to a child whom she and her ex-partner had intended to parent and to whom her ex-partner had given birth. Nadine recalled: 'I actually avoided talking to her because I thought, "What am I going to tell her? It's hopeless? It's not going to work?" So we met and ended up becoming lovers. Right from the outset, it was really clear that we both wanted to have children, and – it seems ironic to me now – we started planning it almost within months of starting to be in a relationship. [She laughs] I do things a little more slowly now.' The fact that both women were coping with the experience of losing a child to whom they were not biologically related factored into their discussions about how they would have children.

I guess we spent quite a bit of time just talking about the whole range of things, and I realized that it was really important to me, and I think she did the same, that we have some biological connection to the child. So we talked about getting our brothers to be the donors, or having one of our eggs taken out and implanted in the other's uterus so we'd both be the biological parent. But it came to us one day that we could just have two kids. And then it felt really important to me, once we made that decision, that they'd be with the same donor so that they would be siblings, so that the link would be there, and, no matter what happened, there would be biological blood connections. You know, even though we were sure that would never happen, we'd never split up. I just felt like, having lost [my son] because there was no biological connection, I needed some assurance that that was built in.

Nadine and Maureen approached the physician who had inseminated Maureen's ex-partner a couple of years earlier. He refused to provide them with services – 'He didn't think Maureen was a good mother if she was not continuing to parent the kid that had already been conceived' – but he also could not guarantee donor continuity. With that option closed, Nadine and Maureen sought a local, anonymous donor. The first donor they chose was located through a men's group in their community.

I went to one of the men that I knew who was in a men's group and asked him if he would be willing to facilitate this. He said, yes, he would go to his men's group ... I made up a questionnaire, which had three sections – family history (kind of basic health stuff), lifestyle questions (like what do you eat and drink and smoke?), and then kind of a description of who you are (you know, I think things like what you're good at and what you like). But the first part was just physical, hereditary stuff. He took the questionnaire to his group and asked people if they were willing to become a donor. He was going to be the only one who knew. And there were three guys who said yes. They each filled in the questionnaire, and they just put A, B, or C on it, and then we read them all and just picked one. We picked the donor and we got the sperm, and Maureen got pregnant ... And then she had a miscarriage.

During the three-month period between Maureen's miscarriage and the cycle during which she was going to inseminate again, each of the three men who had volunteered to be donors changed their mind. The men's partners, all women, had informed them that acting as a donor was inappropriate. Frustrated, Nadine exclaimed: 'The women were saying that "this is not taking responsibility; you can't just go around fathering children and walking away from them." But that was what we wanted.'

Nadine's narrative about attempts to locate an anonymous donor is similar to those of other women. Donor anonymity was viewed as a means of obtaining semen without the risk of the donor deciding that he wanted to be a parent. Yet, objections to men being donors often came from straight women who emphasized the need for men to take on the responsibilities of parenthood.[8] Many women who were unable to make an arrangement with a live, anonymous – and later, known – donor outside of the medical system sought sperm-bank or donor insemination services that they could access either as lesbians or by representing themselves as straight women. Other women, like Nadine and Maureen, were faced with an opportunity that was quite different from the scenario they had imagined as necessary to create a family in which they would be recognized as the sole parents. Nadine explained:

We lived in a housing co-op, so there were a lot of men there. I remember being at this one meeting, and one of the women – who was in a relationship and had three kids already, a pretty young woman – was pregnant again. She wasn't too thrilled about it. And I just started to cry because I thought, you know, it's so easy for her; she keeps getting pregnant and she doesn't want to be, and we still don't know how to find a donor. So, there was a guy at the meeting who, afterwards, asked me a lot of questions. And I outlined what we were looking for: an anonymous donor and an intermediary and all that. Then, I think it must have been a couple of months later, he knocked on our door and said, 'I'd like to volunteer.' We had been pretty clear we didn't want to know who it was, and there he was.

This man acted as Nadine's and Maureen's sperm donor for the next two years. Following popular advice at the time, they did not have a donor agreement or a donor contract drawn up to define their own and the donor's parental relationship to the child. It was believed that any acknowledgment of paternity in writing, even in the form of a statement relinquishing parental rights, could later be used to assert parental rights. 'We kind of had to just trust our intuition that this guy wasn't going to turn around and say, "I've changed my mind. I want custody of these kids," down the road. But in some way we felt like, we have to do that. And we both had a really good feeling about him, and he seemed to be a very genuine guy, and we really questioned him a lot on his motivation.'

Both Nadine and Maureen gave birth to children conceived using his sperm. Thus, as originally hoped, their children have the biological blood connection that Nadine had wanted as built-in assurance that each woman's claim for recognition as a parent to both children would be recognized. Perhaps, though, as Nadine speculated, the experience of losing a child on the basis of the absence of a biological tie had had a greater influence on her own and Maureen's commitment to shared parenting than did the establishment of a biological connection between the two children.

> We didn't have a contract or anything. I think we both really felt [what] the other one had been through, losing a non-biological child, and that we wouldn't do that again. We could never do that to someone else, because it had been so painful for each of us. So, even though nothing was in writing, I think we both just believed deep down that that would never happen because of our shared experiences, and it has proved to be true. We have continued to co-parent through the worst, all of the worst of it. I think that's the direct result of each of us having had that experience. It's interesting, because each of us gave birth to the other gender than the child we had been parenting, and continued to have the non-biological child of the same gender as the one we'd lost. Because she had lost a girl and now is Katrina's other mother, and I had lost a boy and now have Dylan.

The would-have-been-anonymous donor has not asserted any parental claim over the children, and, Nadine commented, in their early teens her children are active producers of the cultural meanings of assisted conception and understandings of biological connections and family:

> I think things have shifted in our world so much, even in the last ten years, that [being conceived by donor insemination] is not as deviant as it would have been. They don't want him referred to as a donor any more though. They think that sounds weird. But they never met him. I mean they met him when they were babies, but they don't know him. But they're thinking about it now. My daughter actually is ready to meet him, and her brother's willing to go along with it. It's not his choice. He's

never been at all interested ... Being inseminated is normal for them, and being in a world where everybody's gay and lesbian, but hippy guys are different. They haven't wanted to meet him, but now Katrina is thinking that she does.

Nadine and Maureen's decision to attempt to conceive with semen from an anonymous donor was coupled with their wish to both have children using the same donor. They were denied access to clinical donor-insemination services, yet using the clinical services would not have enabled them to ensure the use of sperm from the same donor for both children. Nadine framed the desire for this connection in terms of a built-in assurance that the relationships would endure – if not between the women, then between the children and, by relation, each individual mother. Many women in a relationship with a woman viewed this same practice as a means of diminishing the asymmetry of relations between the non-biological and the biological mother. In this scenario, each woman becomes both non-biological and biological mother to their children who are biologically related to each other. The imagining of connections in this way also serves to symbolically distance the donor's biological claim to recognition as a parent. The child already has two parents, a formation that is recognized even when it falls outside of the heterosexual norm. What is integral in Nadine's narrative is that biology was the basis on which she and her partner had each been denied recognition and a claim to the child they had parented in a previous relationship. Thus, mobilizing biology (Hayden 1995) was viewed as necessary to ensure recognition of parental status to the children they had had together. Invoking biology in this situation is about laying claim to the continuity of relationships. It is not definitive of the women's definition of family but, rather, represents an awareness of how dominant definitions of 'real' family can disrupt women's relationships to children.

Catalogue Options

As suggested above, the anonymity of sperm-bank donors carries with it a permanence that is less than common when using anonymous local donors. For women who obtained semen from a sperm bank, the donor's anonymity was already mediated by the sperm bank and ensured by the policies and protocols regulating the use of donor gametes. These policies and protocols, and in some places legislation, are informed, as Erica Haimes (1990) argues, by presumptions of 'family.' The secrecy that surrounds the use of donor eggs and donor sperm works to preserve the image of natural reproduction. The practice and perpetuation of donor anonymity, she states, 'can therefore be regarded, perhaps, as an exercise in damage limitation, by those who wish both to accept gamete donation and to resolve some of the problems it represents to notions of the "ordinary family." It helps to preserve as many as possible of the conventional features of the family by setting a barrier around the unit. No routes exist to provide a way through that barrier: the donor has no way back into the family, post-donation, and no member of the family has a route back out, to reach the donor. Each remains anonymous to the other' (1990, 169).

It is often assumed within the dominant discourse of gamete donation that the donor will be anonymous and will remain anonymous.[9] The use of a known sperm donor by heterosexual couples appears to be the exception to the rule (Becker 2000, 144; Gallop 2007). Acknowledgment of the use of a sperm donor at all by heterosexual couples seems to be exceptional as well.[10] Donor insemination is widely regarded as a private endeavour, a taboo subject, and may be perceived as a third-party sexual threat to the heterosexual relationship (Becker 2000). Although donor insemination is a low-tech, non-invasive, and relatively inexpensive treatment for male-factor infertility, Becker notes that heterosexual couples often only consider the use of donor sperm as a last resort. Becker writes:

> Typically, men and their partners learn about donor insemination in a roundabout way. With the exception of those who happened to consult an urologist or an infertility specialist who was an advocate for donor insemination, men in this study reported that urologists often did not mention donor insemination in discussing their infertility. Physicians thus are in the position of gatekeepers, with the ability to limit their patients' knowledge of available medical procedures. All physicians have opinions and are more favourably disposed toward some treatments than others. But donor insemination stands out as a procedure about which physicians may be particularly diffident, and their attitudes limit people's access to the procedure. (2000, 139)

As technologies develop, new techniques such as intracytoplasmic sperm injection (ICSI) – a technique in which 'a single sperm is injected into a mature egg' (Villarosa 2002) and which requires that the woman undergo egg-collection surgery – is being used where possible in lieu of donor insemination.[11] The use of a donor in the case of heterosexual couples disrupts the assumed normative continuity between biological and social or legal parent. The couple intending to parent envision themselves as parents, often expecting to become parents with minimal consideration of the meaning attributed to *biological* connections. When this seemingly natural method of biological reproduction is rendered visible by means of charted ovulation, diagnostic testing, and planned sexual intercourse, women and men are required to negotiate the meanings of *biology, genetic relatedness,* and *bodily connection.* A number of Becker's respondents believed that 'an adopted child would belong more equally to both parents than a child conceived through donor insemination (2000, 136). Yet, many women 'stated they would prefer the use of a donor to adoption because they could experience pregnancy and childbirth' (2000, 136). Becker's finding that men in heterosexual couples are more likely to pursue adoption than use donor sperm demonstrates that there is more at work here than feelings of biological displacement.[12] Becker proposes that sperm and eggs are 'cultural icons of gender and fertility, symbols that epitomize cultural ideals of manhood and womanhood ... The proposal that a couple use an egg or sperm donor strikes at the cultural meanings women and men attach to gender' (2000, 133).

The anonymity of a sperm donor in the case of heterosexual couples' use of donor sperm is seldom discussed in terms of legal concerns regarding parental status. As Becker points out in *The Elusive Embryo,* straight couples' narratives about the possibility of using donor sperm do not typically raise the question of whether or not the donor will have more legal rights than will the non-biological male parent (2000). Men who are the partners of women who conceive a child within the context of their relationship are presumed to be the father in every sense – social, biological, and legal. These questions are not perceived as pressing and have often already been rendered non-issues through the implementation of assisted-reproduction legislation. As Cannell (1990) and Haimes (1990) demonstrate, the goal of legislation and policies that regulate the use of donor sperm and donor eggs has been to render technology 'natural' and to minimize disruptions to the appearance of the 'natural' family, which is normatively defined as the two-parent heterosexual family. Furthermore, Cannell points out, legislation implemented in the UK allows the non-biological father to name himself as 'father' on the birth certificate, only adding 'by donor insemination' at his discretion (1990). Individuals named on birth certificates are recognized as a child's legal parents and have the authority to make decisions regarding the child's welfare. In British Columbia, practitioners acknowledge that male partners of women who have a child by donor insemination are required to adopt their child in order to become the child's legal father. However, as testified in a BC Human Rights Tribunal case, this is seldom the situation. The name of a male partner (or social father) is simply entered on the birth certificate, which presumes a biological relationship and confers legal recognition. The male partner's legal relationship to his female spouse, whether married or common-law, enables the child to access benefit services through him. The use of a donor is rendered invisible on documents and in social practice by the pervasive recognition of the heterosexual two-parent family structure and assumptions regarding the biological or genetic continuity between parents and children.

Queer women's use of donor insemination is governed by the practices, protocols, and in some places legislation, which for the most part were developed on the basis of heteronormative definitions of family and understandings of sexuality. These policies and protocols have a significant impact on lesbians' health and well-being and the ways in which queer women choose to create their families. As illustrated above, donor anonymity was not desired by the women I interviewed in order to conceal the use of a donor but rather to provide women with a sense of security and protection from potential custody disputes. Familiar with stories about the legal nightmares of known-donor scenarios, fears of HIV transmission, and other concerns presented by the possibility of another individual who might want to take on parenting responsibilities and who could possibly be legally recognized as a parent, many queer women I interviewed sought sperm-bank donors.

Information, Anonymity, and Knowing

For nearly ten years Hilary had talked about having a child with her gay, male best friend. When she and her partner moved out to the west coast and her best friend did not follow, they began to reconsider their options. Hilary explained: 'Justin and I decided that unless we were living together, or living in the same city, then we wouldn't have a family together. It would be too hard on both of us.' For Hilary, the difference between a known donor and an anonymous donor was the difference between the man involved being their child's father and there being a 'genetic material donor.' New to British Columbia, Hilary and her partner attended an information session for lesbians thinking about having children. Afterwards, they decided to use the services provided by a fertility centre. From Hilary's perspective, 'timing was an issue.' They did not have any close male friends on the west coast, and they felt there was a real possibility that a new government might revoke the legislation brought in under the NDP government which both recognized lesbians and gay men as spouses and enabled them to file for adoption.[13] Hilary reflected:

> That made timing an issue. And the legal side was a big one, and knowing the donor was also another one, because looking at the fact that the father could move away – and, if we did use a known donor, they would be the father, not just the donor. We were clear on that. Because we didn't know someone and we didn't want a father in our life, we decided to go with an unknown donor. That was the first step, which was fairly easy to come to after that information session. Where we had problems after that [and which] wasn't introduced in our information session was [the choice between] identity or no identity. We didn't know that that was even an option. We thought if you go to a sperm bank, and that's what we thought they were called at the time, then we didn't know the identity of the person. They were a number, and that was it. But, of course, [the] fertility clinic is much more progressive, and everywhere in the United States is much more progressive now, and you have all these options again. So, once we went to [the] clinic, they told us we had the right to photos, baby photos: for some [donors], baby photos and current photos; for some, one or the other. And some gave a right for the child to establish contact after the age of eighteen.

Hilary alludes to her misperceptions about the world of assisted reproductive technologies in her comment, 'We thought if you go to a sperm bank, *and that's what we thought they were called at the time*, then we didn't know the identity of the person. They were a number, and that was it.' Now the mother of a two-year-old conceived by donor insemination at a fertility centre, Hilary distinguishes between fertility clinics and sperm banks, making it seem as though it was her inexperience or naivety that led her to believe that she would literally go to a sperm bank. The two are distinct, yet they are contemporaneous. Women I interviewed sought donor insemination or IVF services at the local fertility clinics, which often ordered and received their donor semen from commercial sperm banks. Women I interviewed also accessed commercial and non-profit sperm banks on their own and had the semen couriered to their home, to a physician, or to a northern U.S. courier depot for pick-up.

Typically, women in this study who tried to get pregnant using donor sperm within the context of fertility services (which used a commercial sperm bank or the fertility clinic's own anonymous-donor program) during the 1980s, and even early 1990s, did not choose their donor. The physician chose for them, most often matching their own physical characteristics (or their partner's) with a donor's. Since the early 1990s, women who make the decision to use an unknown donor rather than a known donor are faced with further choices regarding the degree and duration of the anonymity they desire. Hilary's reference to the difference between a donor as a 'number' and a donor with an identity reflects both shifting perspectives regarding an offspring's rights to know the identity of her or his genetic father and the contemporary commodification of health, behavioural, personal, and genetic information. Whereas some women I interviewed knew nothing about the donor other than, perhaps, the colour of his skin, eyes, and hair, women today have access to a great deal of information about sperm-bank donors. Donor profiles describe in detail the donor's family history, including health information and occupation and education backgrounds. The profiles often include a statement or an essay by the donor explaining who he is and why he decided to become a sperm donor. More recently, baby photographs, adult photographs, and videotapes of the donor may also be purchased in conjunction with the vials of semen.

Hilary's expanded explanation of how she and her partner chose the donor demonstrates that their decision provides yet another reading of the relationship between anonymity and recognition as a child's parent. In this situation, their legal relationship to the child, or rather the donor's non-legal relationship to their child, is secured by the practices governing gamete donation.[14] Hilary stated that, on the plus side, she thought a photograph of the donor might allow her child to connect with a history of physical continuity. Her child could say, 'Oh, I've got my father's nose,' or, 'I have (this trait or that trait).' She also seemed to lean toward creating a structure in her son's life that would allow him to choose whether or not he was out about having two moms. She thought that having a photograph of the donor might help her child to 'pass' at school: 'If he wants, he can put the picture up when he's in school, and nobody has to know. His father and his mother are no longer together.' She and her partner were concerned, however, that their child might invest a significant amount of energy in the literal image of the donor, imagining him as an absent, yet ideal, father. The child might rebel against his mothers and use his 'father' as way of escape. Her partner's teenage experience of discovering a photograph of her biological father, who had left her and her mother when she was young, was also a factor in their decision:

> That was just devastating because then she had to go through the whole [experience of] grief and loss for someone that, before she had pictures, didn't even exist. When she brought that up, I thought, that is so true. If he knows us as the only parents he's ever known, since before he was born, and that he was very planned ... And Bridget pointed out an important note that, with her, her father had 'abandoned' her. It's very different for a child that's been adopted. Fundamentally, if the child's been adopted, then that natural curiosity you have to help promote as much as you can. But a child who has been planned, not abandoned from the parent, for a very good reason is not going to have that dire need, I don't think. Time will tell us.

After weighing the options, Hilary and Bridget decided to choose a donor who did not give consent to be contacted when the child reached eighteen.

> So that was no longer a fear, but we still didn't want a picture. If we went with a donor that had a picture available and we didn't take that option, then we'd feel guilty because then our child could hold it against us. So we wanted to go where we had no choice. The donor that we would select didn't have a picture and had no interest in meeting the child after the age of eighteen. That way, we wouldn't be withholding ... because we'd never withhold something from our child.

Although donors who provide photographs and videotapes are still anonymous donors, the photograph challenged Hilary's and Bridget's ideas about the purpose of anonymity. While their first reason for choosing a sperm-bank donor was based on concerns about legal connections to the child, their final decision about a donor was shaped more by concerns about recognition as the child's true parents *by the child*. Like other women in this study, Hilary and Bridget drew a comparison between adopted children and children conceived by donor insemination. Many women referred to the lessons learned throughout the history of adoption policies and decided that they want their child to have access to the donor's identity at some point later in life. Hilary and Bridget decided that donor-insemination children are significantly different because they are wanted children. Whereas they relied on the information provided by the donor to give them the sense that he was a wonderful man and gay friendly, without a photo that would embody the donor they would be 'the only parents [their child] has ever known.'

Limiting Anonymity

Most of the women I interviewed were clear about wanting to be socially and legally recognized as their child's parent(s). However, many women also wanted to be able to provide their child with answers to questions about her or his biological and genetic history. In contrast to Hilary's belief that children born with the use of anonymous-donor sperm will not have a dire need which she believed adopted children might have to know the identity of their biological or genetic parent, many of the women I interviewed who chose to conceive by donor insemination wanted to provide their child with the *option* to know.

Most of the women in this study who chose to use a donor from a sperm bank used donor semen provided by The Sperm Bank of California (TSBC), Pacific Reproductive Services (PRS), California Cryobank (CCB), ReproMed, or Xytex Corporation. Based in California, TSBC and PRS are committed to providing accessible sperm-bank services to women and have a significantly high percentage of lesbian clients. Both sperm-bank facilities provide women with direct access to donor semen, enabling them to choose to inseminate either at home or in a clinical setting. Since 1982 and 1984, respectively, TSBC and PRS have offered clients the option to choose willing-to-be-known donors (also known as 'yes' donors). These donors have agreed to have their identity, not simply their non-identifying information, released to any offspring that petition for the release of the donor's identity upon reaching the age of eighteen. According to the TSBC identity-release program, donor offspring will be provided with the first, middle, and last names of the donor, the last known address, and the donor's driver's licence number.[15] According to the PRS program, the donor will be contacted, and a one-time meeting between the donor and the offspring will be arranged.[16] The California Cryobank takes another position altogether on the issue of complete anonymity versus identity-release programs. Their website states that they question the appropriateness of asking women and donors 'today how they might feel about such a sensitive and complex issue 15-30 years from now … We do believe the issues are real. Our task is to maintain our records and prepare ourselves so that we can appropriately respond to individual needs.'[17] Rather than an identity-release protocol, the California Cryobank has developed an openness policy whereby requests for information will be reviewed on an individual case basis.

At the time of my fieldwork there was no donor registry in place to keep a record of donors and offspring, nor was there any legislation governing record keeping related to the use of donor gametes, or an offspring's access to the identity of her or his genetic father.[18] Women who actively sought and were unable to locate known sperm donors were likely to choose willing-to-be-known donors or 'yes' donors from sperm-bank selections. Women in my study who voiced concern about the potential legal or health risks of using a known donor, yet who wanted their child to have the option to know who her or his genetic father was, were also among those women who chose to 'mail-order' donor semen from TSBC or PRS in order to use willing-to-be-known donors.[19] In May 2002, Bill C-13, intended to regulate assisted reproduction in Canada, was introduced into Parliament. The bill called for a 'mandatory sperm donor registry' and 'provides for the voluntary release of donors' identities' (Villarosa 2002). When reintroduced and proclaimed as Bill C-6, the Assisted Human Reproduction Act, in 2004, the legislation provided for a registry with access to health information. The release of donor information will only be considered with the consent of the donor. The issue is still debated considerably, and, at the time of writing, the registry had not yet been implemented.

Information on the website for TSBC states that participant requests were the impetus behind developing a willing-to-be-known-donor program. Similarly, PRS is committed to meeting the needs of their clients, which often is done by offering a combination of screened semen, legal protection of parental status, and the potential for offspring to meet their genetic father. As discussed in the next chapter, the recent history of contractual relations, and the court decisions upholding these contracts on the basis of proven reproductive intent, perhaps shifts the climate in which women and men develop known-donor contracts with confidence. Furthermore, access to second-parent adoptions in British Columbia in many ways reduced the perception of risk associated with the use of known donors for many lesbian couples. Second-parent adoption paved a way for a donor to relinquish his parental rights to the child so that a non-biological mother could adopt the child, acquiring full legal parental status. These shifts, however, displace one genetic parent, making the social parent a second legal parent. Unlike women in relationships, who both have the potential to be recognized as legal parents through practices such as second-parent or step-parent adoption, single women worry about the possible issues regarding parental status that might arise. The continued preference in society for two-parent families was evident in women's narratives. Janine, a single mom of two young children, explained:

> I chose [a sperm bank in California] because, ideally, I would have liked to have a known donor, who could be sort of in an uncle capacity for the kids. But I was very worried about paternity issues – maybe more so because I was on my own. I was quite concerned about that. Because I knew that I didn't want to 50-50 co-parent with somebody. So I chose an anonymous donor. But I chose [this particular sperm bank] because they are owned and exist for the lesbian community, and they have willing-to-be-known donors, which means that when my kids are eighteen, they can find out the name and residence of the donor.

Finding a donor who would agree to the amount of participation that women envisioned the donor having in their child's life was often difficult. While many of the men who were asked to be donors were amenable to playing an *uncle* role (however defined) in the child's life, just as many were not comfortable with the notion of segregating the roles of genetic and social father (that is, as genetic father and social uncle or friend). Although Janine chose an anonymous donor, her children will be able to find out his identity when they turn eighteen. The act of choosing a donor and deciding to order semen from a California sperm bank was not a large component of Janine's narrative. Using donor sperm from a sperm bank that would ship semen to women's homes gave Janine the flexibility to inseminate in the place of her choice and to have children without worrying about negotiating a co-parenting relationship. The availability of willing-to-be-known donors and access to a sperm bank, which was aligned with her own sense of community, made her experience from the moment of deciding to parent to the moment of insemination streamlined and relatively uneventful.

Other women's routes to the donors they eventually chose were significantly more complex. Like many women, Pam and Caroline developed a shortlist of potential donors, drawing from the men they knew. Although they knew women who had had successful known-donor arrangements with men whom they did not know very well, an immense sense of trust in the individual was one of the key criteria that Pam and Caroline used to create their shortlist. Pam said:

> We wanted to go with someone we knew, and ask him to be a donor but not to be a custodial parent: to be a donor, to be willing to be identified as the baby's biological father, but not be dad ... We also felt that there had to be a huge amount of trust because I do think that there is enormous risk that you take when you sort of trust that the guy's not going to take a look at that baby once he or she is born and say, 'Wow, you know what, I didn't know I was going to feel this way. And now that I'm feeling this about this child, my decisions have changed.' And that's a huge risk to take, especially if you're going to be asking a gay man. This may be his only chance. So, that was a huge thing for us.

Asking men to be donors and waiting for their response could be time consuming and emotionally draining. For some men the timing was not right, while others were not comfortable with the idea of being a donor. One man whom they would have liked to be a donor was HIV-positive. Each time they asked someone new to be a donor, there was time involved in waiting for his answer. 'I mean, some [men] immediately said no, and others took longer. We ultimately approached this final friend [who previously had jokingly offered to be a donor], and he immediately said yes. And we thought, 'Great. Problem solved.' We started talking about the logistics of it and what that would mean, and knew that, of course, that would extend it by a few more months, having to talk out all the logistics and be really realistic about it with him, and then giving him a chance to explore how that felt.' After many discussions with Pam and Caroline, his partner, and family, a few months later this donor-to-be decided that he was not comfortable acting as a donor due to his concerns about the prevalence of alcoholism and drug use in his extended family and the possibility that it might be hereditary. Pam and Caroline respected his decision but were exhausted by their efforts to find a known donor whom they trusted and who would agree to the parental arrangement they were seeking. Caroline stated:

> That left us in a place where we never anticipated we'd be, quite frankly. We'd assumed that with one of these men it would work out, or we'd find a guy we felt comfortable with, or whatever. That put us in a place of having to assess our remaining options and, ultimately, what we decided that we wanted to do – because at that time we felt that it was really critical that we went with a donor that could be known to the child – we were under the impression that that was really critical at that time. The second best option we figured was to use a willing-to-be-known donor, a 'yes' donor. We contacted the few U.S. clinics that offered that option and got their information and chose the clinic that we were going to work with and paid our big U.S. bucks – big [currency] exchange [rates], 50 per cent at the time – and registered with a clinic and did all the intake appointments over the telephone – ka-ching, ka-ching, ka-ching, as the weeks and days go by. And, ultimately, we find a donor. I'm sure talking to people, you know that that's such a weird experience and also just very stressful. The competition for donors sometimes is really high, and then willing-to-be-known donors, it is ruthless in terms of getting those guys. Our first pick was gone, sold out within twenty-four hours.

The frustration over the amount of time, emotion, and energy that had been spent to reach the point of finding a donor was evident in Caroline's tone of voice. She and Pam went from having a difficult time finding a known donor to facing 'ruthless' competition for vials of semen emitted from a donor who was willing to be identified nineteen years in the future.

> It was literally twenty-four, forty-eight, hours later. He had been in full supply and went down to zero supply in that amount of time. It became clear to us that people are so desperate for willing-to-be-known donors that they'll pretty much take him regardless of who he is. That was frustrating, but we did find a guy that we could get the number of vials that we wanted, and we purchased. Of course, with the deal that it's completely non-refundable, under no circumstances, et cetera, et cetera. We put that on the Visa card and laughed hysterically and thought, 'Oh my God, it's going to happen, it's going to be so great!'

Vials of semen from willing-to-be-known donors are slightly more expensive than vials of semen from anonymous donors and are in high demand. Some of the women I interviewed stated that they 'retired' the donor of their choice, buying his remaining stock to ensure they would have enough vials of that particular donor's semen to last them through their attempts to conceive and, if possible, to store for future attempts to have another child. Many women that I interviewed about trying to get pregnant during the 1980s and 1990s by using donor sperm from a donor insemination program or a sperm bank did not have a choice of donor. Today, donor traits, the amount of available information, and the donor's consent to identification at a later date are all commodities and part of the industry of low-tech assisted reproduction. As consumers, women choosing donors and purchasing vials of semen[20] at a cost of between US$165 and US$250 or between C$300 and C$500 at the time are often heavily invested, emotionally and financially, in the donor they end up choosing. Pam and Caroline decided to combine their use of the U.S.-based sperm bank with the storage and insemination services offered by a fertility centre in Vancouver in order to maximize the chance of Pam conceiving in the quickest and least stressful way. After so much time spent searching for a donor and choosing donor sperm, they were more than ready to move forward with their plans to have a child.

Unfortunately Pam and Caroline were one of several couples I interviewed whose plans were disrupted by a quarantine placed by Health Canada on donor semen stored at facilities across Canada and by a ban on the importation of semen that did not meet newly introduced donor-screening regulations.[21] Xytex Corporation, the sperm bank used by many Creative Beginnings' clients, met the testing requirements laid out by the new guidelines.[22] The majority of Xytex donors are what one of the women I interviewed referred to as 'willing-to-be-contacted' donors. A statement on the Xytex website explains their policy: 'Xytex follows the recommendations of the American Society for Reproductive Medicine (ASRM) regarding the privacy of donors. If the offspring of a Xytex donor contacts us after turning 18 years of age and inquires about the identity of his or her biological father, we will try to contact the donor and determine his interest in arranging a meeting. However, we do not release names, addresses or other personal information without the donor's express authorization.'[23]

Willing-to-be-contacted is significantly different from *willing-to-be-known*.[24] With yet another donor option foreclosed, Pam and Caroline faced difficult decisions, which required them to question many of the beliefs underpinning their experiences thus far:

> There was a time that we thought that we would not have a child because we felt it was so important that they have access to this male person who helped to create them. We went through a period of saying, 'Well, maybe this isn't going to happen after all.' You know, we felt so strong in our conviction about that at the time. And then we realized that it would make us very sad not to have explored all the options. In hindsight now, I think what also was happening in a really big way is this sort of (which I now believe was misguided) comparison of unknown-donor children with adopted children, this idea that a child conceived using an unknown donor would have all of the same sort of issues that many adopted children have – the abandonment issues, the rejection issues, all that kind of stuff. And we kind of realized in talking with a lot of people who had chosen to use unknown donors – we found out in talking to psychologists who do this kind of work and other people that, really, you can't make those kinds of comparisons. I think that that was very liberating for us, to realize that it's not the same thing at all. I think in society, generally, we often attribute the same stuff to both of those kinds of children, and I think that they're two very different groups. That our child is going to know his or her birth story, his or her conception story – he or she may or may not have the opportunity to meet the donor that we ultimately chose, and that doesn't have to be a bad thing. It doesn't have to be something in the way of some children's adoption story. Ultimately what we decided to do was link up with Creative Beginnings, and we ultimately went with them, getting the donor from [a large U.S. commercial sperm bank], of course.

Pam became pregnant following the first insemination and was ten weeks pregnant at the time of our interview. Pam and Caroline's narrative began with an emphasis on the amount of trust they needed to have in the man whom they would choose to be the donor in order to ensure his recognition of them as the parents. Constrained by the options available to them, they came to emphasize the reality of *their* parental status as two women intending to have and parent a child. The issue of whether or not the donor will ever be known is minimized and made peripheral to their narrative. Their legal relationship to their child is no longer a defining feature of the narrative, because by their using an anonymous donor from a sperm bank, the donor's parental rights have already been severed.

As illustrated by the narratives presented in this chapter, decisions about donors were made by navigating the interconnected and disconnected social, legal, and medical discourses, practices, policies, and norms which govern the ideas about family. The legal issues and normative constraints that have an impact on women's abilities to autonomously construct families of choice by incorporating a pregnancy experience directly influence women's ability to choose where and how they attempt to conceive. Women who planned to use semen from an anonymous donor developed unexpected relationships with men who volunteered to be a part of their plans to have children. Women who had originally expected to use the most minimal intervention, by choosing a known donor and inseminating at home, instead underwent diagnostic fertility testing (hormonal tests and hysterosalpingograms were standard protocol) and did intrauterine inseminations.

The decision that queer women face when planning to become pregnant is very often presented as a choice between an anonymous or a known semen donor. The meaning of *anonymity* figured prominently within women's narratives, a concept that within the context of gamete donation, narratives of adoption, and the emerging digitalizations of identity (in the form of online donor catalogues, photographs, and videotapes, et cetera) was not fixed but rather was mediated by many other (at times, competing) occurrences. In the next chapter the second part of this construction is addressed by looking at how women talked about the meanings of not only knowing a donor but also their own sense of knowing themselves as mothers and parents. In contrast to representations of the decision between known or unknown sperm donors as a means of defining relationships with a donor, the next chapter looks at the ways in which various discourses of reproduction and assisted reproduction – and, correspondingly, decisions about donors – factor in relationships between women and between a woman and her child or children.

8 Mediating Knowing

Everybody in that room, except me, wanted to have an anonymous donor. I was the only one that didn't. And I didn't because I didn't want my child to have that blank, to really have absolutely no idea of who his or her father, or donor, or whatever you want to say, was.

(Cynthia)

Cheri Pies, author of *Considering Parenthood: A Workbook for Lesbians* (1988) – a book that was sometimes visible on a bookshelf or under the coffee table in the homes of the women I interviewed – notes that in the short period of time between 1979 and 1985 lesbians seemed to shift from choosing completely anonymous donors to choosing donors that could potentially be known to the child at some time in the future. Maureen Sullivan (2004), for example, notes that in her study involving thirty-four couples, only five couples chose known donors and twenty-nine chose anonymous donors from sperm banks, of which twenty-eight were so-called 'yes' donors, that is, donors who were part of iden-tity-release programs, as Pam and Caroline discuss in chapter 7.[1] Anonymity in the present alleviates concerns about potential custody issues, yet leaves open a route back to the donor (see Haimes 1990) in order to facilitate the future revelation of the donor's identity to the child.

A second shift in the history of the lesbian baby boom occurred during the early 1980s when HIV/AIDS emerged as a devastating syndrome, especially visible at the time among communities of queer women and men (Weston 1991). One woman I interviewed described her experiences with known donors in the early 1980s as belonging to a 'pre-AIDS' era. However, other women in my study who talked about experiences during the same time period included references to AIDS tests. As discussed more fully in part III, many women planning to parent needed to make decisions about donors in the face of a paucity of available information about AIDS at the time. A familiar narrative suggests that the advent of HIV/AIDS led an increasing number of lesbians and single women to seek donor semen from sperm banks and to access medically assisted insemination (see Weston 1991). The potential risk of HIV transmission with the use of a known donor and fresh semen continues to be highlighted as a reason for women responsibly choosing to use a donor from a sperm bank (see Hayden 1995; Kahn 2000), and at the same time as an argument in support of permitting lesbians and single women to have access to fertility treatment services. Yet, other than the few U.S. sperm banks that offered willing-to-be-known donors and would ship semen directly to women, choosing a donor from a sperm bank meant that women began using completely anonymous sperm-bank donors and inseminating in clinical settings. Women often weighed their perceptions of the risk associated with known donors (HIV transmission and custody issues) against their desire to know the identity of the donor and to inseminate outside of a clinical setting.

A third historical shift shaping queer women's narratives of assisted conception is an increasing acceptance of, and belief in, the potential to contract relations with respect to reproduction (see chapter 9). The increase in commercial surrogacy, contracts governing non-commercial surrogacy, egg-donation programs, and embryo adoption has normalized the performance of various reproductive activities and the exchange of substance, as being transactions regulated by binding contracts (see Hartouni 1997; Grayson 2000). Although known-donor contracts have not yet been tested in a Canadian court, many women I interviewed considered them useful and necessary.[2] In contrast to the advice against acknowledging paternity in writing which was most popular in the 1970s and 1980s, most of the women I interviewed who had tried to get pregnant during the 1990s felt more comfortable drawing up a known-donor contract than not doing so. As women across the U.S. and Canada challenged courts for the right to make second-parent adoptions, additional weight was given to the practice of outlining the reproductive intentions and parenting responsibilities in pre-conception contracts in order to refer to them, and (potentially) have them recognized, in court.

Donor anonymity was, and still is, a key factor in an individual's negotiations of and claims for social and legal recognition as a child's parent. However, as discussed in the previous chapter, the concept, practice, and meanings of *anonymity* are contextually defined and often mediated. Known donors are known to inseminating women and have varied roles in the child's life. Some known donors remain 'anonymous' to people in the child's life, and possibly to the child, with regards to their role as donor. Others occupy defined roles in the child's life as friend, 'uncle,' biological father, or 'dad.' Their visible presence and acknowledged status as an embodied donor situates them in a position of power in a society that privileges male-female gendered narratives of conception and parenting. However, instead of distancing or displacing genetic fathers, genetic-material donors, or sperm donors via the mechanism of anonymity, many women I interviewed negotiated their relationships to each other, children, donors, and other family members on the basis of the meaning given to biological and contractual relations. In this chapter I look at women's stories with a focus on practices of knowing. In contrast to distinguishing between known donors and unknown donors, I focus more on the ways in which women's stories about knowing a donor were embedded in their narratives. Furthermore, I address the ways in which knowledge and practices of knowing were engaged as a means of enacting various possibilities.

Biology

One of the most common known-donor scenarios considered by women in relationships with women involves asking a brother of the non-inseminating woman to be a donor. I was at a café on College Street in Toronto, reading *Lesbian Mothers* (Lewin 1993), the first time I heard someone suggest this scenario. A woman sitting at the next table was explaining to a friend that her partner really wanted to have a child. From the perspective of the woman telling the story, the most logical and least risky choice of a donor would be her brother. As she explained, 'That way, if anything ever happened between us, I would be biologically related to the child.' Considering the use of a brother's semen in order to have a biological connection to the child can be read in terms of adherence to the 'code of substance' by which, along with the 'code of law,' David Schneider proposed that American kinship is defined (1980). To do so, though, would continue to reproduce a version of kinship derived from normative exclusions. Although Schneider is best remembered for his emphasis on blood ties as the ties that endure, the production of blood ties was regulated by law. Configurations of kinship outside the law would not constitute kinship.[3] In order to examine this common 'brother as donor' scenario, I turn to the argument of opaque and transparent kinship status put forth by Charis Cussins (1998b). In her analysis of kinship configurations in the context of infertility treatment procedures, Cussins argues 'against a fixed or unique natural base for the relevant categories of kinship' (1998b, 40). Furthermore, she states: 'One can map out what is rendered relevant to kinship (what I call an "opaque" stage in the process of conceiving and bearing a child) and what [is rendered] irrelevant (what I call a "transparent" – perhaps "transparent" would be better – stage where kinship is not affected by a certain stage of the procedure). From this mapping exercise one can suggest some things that underlie ways of using biology to configure kinship' (1998b, 41).

The concept of opaque and transparent stages of procedures facilitates the recognition of the intended mother or parents. Cussins' analysis of family relationships in the case of donor-egg IVF or gestational surrogacy is particularly useful to a discussion of the ways in which the women I interviewed represented their decisions to use, or not use, donor sperm from a family member. However, in contrast to Cussins' work, in which two women (gestational and genetic mothers) actively negotiated kinship in order to, for the most part, define one woman as mother, many of the women in my study who had discussed using a family member as a sperm donor hoped to facilitate recognition of both women as mothers (social-gestational-genetic and social-genetic).[4] One of the key differences is, of course, that queer women most often make their claim to a genetic link to the child through a male body. In order for dual-mother status to be recognized, the brother-donor needs to be positioned as an intermediary; his kinship status must be transparent. To use Cussins' words, the brother is imagined as 'completely transparent to kinship – kin passes straight through [him] without involving [him].' He does not become the father by donating sperm, but rather is, as he would have been, the child's uncle.

The notion of opaque and transparent kinship in the context of woman-woman couples and sperm donors who are family members is more complex in the absence of normative legal practices that enable intended parents to be recognized as the social and legal parents, as is standard in the case of surrogacy arrangements and clinical procedures involving heterosexual couples' use of donor gametes.[5] In the situation above, the non-inseminating partner's contribution to the genetic make-up of her child would be facilitated through her brother's sperm/genes, rendering the child genetically related to both mothers. In order for both mothers to be recognized as mothers, the donor's role must be simply as an intermediary, 'a step in a procedure' (Cussins 1998b, 49) for the two women. The discussion I overheard between the woman considering parenthood and her friend, however, highlights the fact that her brother's transparent kinship could, if necessary, be rendered opaque 'if anything should happen' between her and her partner. If the relationship between the two women were to end, the biological mother, in this case the woman's partner who plans to become pregnant, would not be the only mother understood to have a biogenetic relationship to the child. The woman telling the story would be the child's biological aunt and non-biological mother, but her brother would be the child's social uncle and legally recognized biological father. Her story suggests that by using her brother as a donor she could assert her biological-genetic relationship to the child through her brother's body – a body whose genes link her own to her child. In the absence of legally viable (and tested) contracts by which a known donor's paternal rights could be alleviated, her brother's opaque kinship status could provide a means of negotiating a continuing relationship to her child. Establishing a biological relationship between the child and the 'non-biological' mother and her entire family, through her brother who acted as the donor, could be used to counter the privileged location of biological mothers within dominant narratives of kinship and family. By emphasizing bilateral kinship, and the child's biological tie to both women (through the donor-brother) and, by extension, to both families, non-biological mothers may rely less on legal recognition (after all, the court's recognition of the donor's biological status as father would not translate to recognition of her as a legal mother-parent) and more on the powerful influence of dominant discourses of genealogy and the idea that shared biological connections and heritage are enduring and meaningful.[6]

Sybil, who plans to be the 'body-mom' of the child whom she and her partner plan to have, expressed concern about the relationship connections and thus the potential implications that trying to conceive with semen from her partner's brother might present – a scenario that her partner would be interested in pursuing. Sybil stated: 'I guess, in this great book, *Lesbians Considering Parenthood*, it says, don't do it! It's in big black and white: "Don't let your siblings be the parents." I know that's something [my partner] really wants. You know, we always say, "Oh, our relationship's great, you know; nothing will happen if we break up." You never know. I've seen it in my job. I've seen the horrible custody battles that occur. Who knows?' For women who perceive themselves to be in a legally disadvantaged position, the above-described scenario of a brother acting as the donor seems to be a good option: their relationship to the child would be supported by numerous other people's (family members') relationships to the child. However, given that Sybil plans to resolve the legal asymmetry that arises via the asymmetrical biological relationship that she and her partner would have to the child, by having her partner adopt their child, the messiness she envisions is more likely linked to the broader family dynamics that would be involved if they were to break up. The visible donor, who in this case would be the biogenetic father and social uncle, would act as a reminder that this child is tied by blood (a tie that is very often normatively and culturally valued) to both women and, more specifically, both women's families. It might then be much more difficult to rely on the belief in the two women's ongoing mode of relating to each other and a child – 'Our relationship's great, you know; nothing will happen *if we break up*' – because even if their relationship were to end, they will not be the only ones invested in defining ongoing relationships.

One of the women I interviewed, Sara, had always thought about having children, but as she said, 'I guess I ruled it out – not ruled it out, but I didn't know how I was going to go about it once I sort of "came out" to myself and realized that I wasn't going to have a male partner to do it. It wasn't going to be that easy.' When she and Kim first started dating, having children was not something that Kim thought she really wanted, but she was 'open to talking about it.' Four years later, Sara and Kim made the decision to go ahead with plans to become parents. Kim had always been interested in adoption, but Sara, who is adopted, explained, 'I'm fascinated when I look at families and see the genetic links between families. I have a desire to have my own child and see the genetic traits passed down.' A few women I interviewed considered the possibility of donor-egg IVF, or what Hayden calls the 'fantasy of distributed maternity' (1995) in which two women becoming mothers together would contribute to either the genetic or gestational dimension of pregnancy.[7] Thinking along similar lines, Kim recalled:

> We sort of talked about impossible scenarios that would be really nice, like combining our genetic material somehow and that kind of stuff. But we decided a good way to go about it was that we would have two children, and I would have one and Sara would raise it – like, she would be the primary caregiver – and then she would have one and I would be the primary caregiver, to establish those bonds. And so that would be one way. And the other way, too, is to have the same father so they really would be siblings.[8]

'Because of her biological clock' (Kim is older than Sara), they decided that Kim would try to get pregnant and give birth to their first child. In a variation of the brother-as-donor narrative, Sara and Kim considered the possibility of asking the husband of Kim's sister (Kim's brother-in-law), Lyle, to be the donor. It seems that her sister, Sally, had already thought about it but then decided, 'It would just be too weird.' Sara's and Kim's analysis of why it would be too weird and why it would not work is interesting. Sara clarified that Lyle, Sally's husband, 'would be the father *and* the uncle – well, not the father, but he would be, I guess, the biological father.' Kim recognized the complexity of the relationships on another level, adding, 'And Cherise, my niece – *our* niece, and our child would be, yeah ...' Her voice trailed off without finishing the sentence. Social cousins would be biological half-siblings. Although the overlap in kinship roles seemed complex, Sara and Kim pointed out that they also suspected that Lyle being the donor might contradict their expectations of how involved the donor would be in their child's life. They couldn't imagine Lyle staying on the periphery. Sara confirmed: 'Yeah, that's what we decided. He, and his parents as well, would want to play a bigger role in the child's life than we would be willing to let them, and that's, for me anyways, more crucial than the whole sibling, cousin, uncle, father thing.' Kim added: 'In terms of a donor and what role a donor would play, I think something we'd agreed upon is that "uncle" is about as much involvement as we want from our donor. And, in fact, for quite a while we were convinced that we really only wanted sperm and we didn't want anyone involved. But I think we sort of changed our mind because of the person that we decided upon, and, of course, this is all contingent on him agreeing.'

Like many women, Kim and Sara described wanting to find a donor who would agree to be an uncle to the child. In this scenario, an uncle (Lyle) might, as a biological father, not be willing to be an uncle. Women who considered using a family member as a donor and chose not to pursue that option often decided that a biological relationship of, for example, a sibling, nephew, or cousin could potentially be used to subvert the co-parent status of the two women. The donor might want more involvement in parenting the child, and other family members might support his wishes, given that the child 'is really his' even more so (biologically) than one of the child's mothers. Women recognize that a family member as a sperm donor may in fact further displace the non-biological mother, or both mothers, from the position of parent.[9]

Parental Certainty

The women I interviewed who chose anonymous, unknown, or willing-to-be-known donors had a relationship to the characteristics of the donor as described in the donor profile or essay that was available through the sperm bank. These women had no need to negotiate a relationship with the donor, and his role was clearly defined. The women who chose known donors had questioned their past, present, and future relationships with potential donors. Thinking about the many scenarios, good and bad, that could arise in a known-donor scenario was integral to the process of becoming a parent.

Kim and Sara decided to ask a close friend to be the donor, but as both women concurred (for different reasons), asking a man to be a sperm donor was 'a scary thing to do.' In Sara's view, once they asked and if he agreed, it would mean moving ahead with their plans. For Kim, what they were planning to ask of the donor was the scary part:

> You're asking the donor to do something that is both intimate and distant, you know? It's just a really sort of weird paradox. I think that's part of it, too, because it's a whole lot to ask for them to give their – I don't know, anything I say is going to sound goofy – their life essence or something, you know? But to do that and with the intent – the intent is obvious. It's not like just sort of asking him to sleep with me so that we would get off or whatever. This is, I'm asking him to give up his sperm, and he's going to have a partial genetic copy of himself running around. And that's an awesome thing to ask.

Many women expressed surprise by the attachment that men seemed to have to their sperm. Reflecting on the frustration that they had experienced in trying to find men who were willing to be donors, Pam had commented, 'We've made jokes for years about what a shame it was that the morning wank of so many men got wasted. You just think, oh my God, we could use that.' Kim's perspective on the donor's relationship to the child – as a donor – differed significantly from the views of many women who were amazed at how difficult it was to find a man who was willing to act as a donor. Kim clearly distinguished between 'getting off' and a man 'giving up his sperm' for the intention of reproducing a child. Asking a man to provide semen to women for the purpose of procreation – in other words, to be a donor who will know the 'partial genetic copy of himself running around' – was, in her view, profound.

Women who chose to ask a man whom they knew to be a donor expressed a variety of ideas about the concept of a donor. This was, perhaps, based on the different relationships that women often had with known donors who would be involved to varying degrees in their (the woman's or the women's, but also the donor's) child's life. In contrast to the commodification of sperm – 'clean' semen, genetic information, and identity-release practices – that was evident in the jokes about 'visa card babies' made by women who purchased vials of semen from sperm banks, the women's stories about known donors often emphasized gift-giving and altruism. Jenna, whose daughter was almost four, stated:

> We have this kind of lifelong bond with [the donor]. I cannot really express how I feel about him. I mean, I like him as a friend, but also I feel, not indebted (it's not the right word), but I just am so thankful. Like, it's been one of those things in my life that that – I can't describe it, how it makes me feel, you know, the fact that for nothing – because it really does seem to him like there's almost no emotional hook for him there. He has not wanted to be a father and he really did this as a totally selfless act because he likes us and he wanted to help us be parents. It just seems like such a gift.

Sperm-donor, egg-donor, embryo-adoption and surrogacy programs employ a business transaction model in order to define kinship. The individuals seeking treatment and paying for treatment are the 'designated parents' (Cussins 1998b, 43). As opposed to the donor, who was compensated for his time, the women purchasing donor semen from a sperm bank are recognized as the intended parents. The absence of the sperm donor, combined with the act of paying fees associated with the use of donor semen from a sperm bank, serves to erase any doubt that the woman or women are the parents. Negotiating parent-type relationships with sperm-bank donors is not an issue.[10] The difference in the relationship between women and known donors and between women and donor semen from a sperm bank is similar in many ways to the characteristics defining the properties of open and closed adoptions (Modell 1999). Known donors take on very different roles in children's lives, some as family friends, others as uncles, and still others as dads. Some known donors are absent from children's lives, while others are a significant presence. The necessity of negotiating these roles, and defining relationships, facilitates ongoing revisions to definitions of parenting, family, and kinship.

'Truths'

Women negotiate the powerful discourses of biological relatedness in many different ways and at different times in their relationships with partners and children. At the time of our interview, Paula described herself as having 'started menopause' six months earlier. She had tried to get pregnant by donor insemination during two separate time periods. Now she imagined she would only become a parent if she were with a partner who had a child or if she adopted. I asked Paula if she thought her relationship to a child to whom her partner might give birth would be different or similar to the relationship she imagined she would have had with a child if she had conceived. She paused.

It's interesting, because there's this whole biological truth thing that happens inside. I want to say it would be the same, but when I imagine that this child came from my body, I see myself never ever being willing to part with that child if the relationship ended. Like, no matter what. Even though I say all these things like, 'I don't think I'd stay home with the child or be a primary parent,' I can't imagine separating from that child. But when I think that my partner had [the baby], I feel distant already from it. And, as hard as it would be, I don't think there is anything that could ever make me take her to court and try to take that child from her. I would always know that that was her child and I was basically an assistant parent as opposed to ... I don't even know, if I was like a guy and I had sperm, if I would feel that I had the same relationship with that child in the same way as if I were – I don't think it's just about whose genes are in that kid; I think it's about, whose body did that kid come from?

One logic of motherhood advocates that a child's mother is the woman who gave birth to the child.[11] Adoptive mothers and gestational surrogate mothers, in general, contest this view (see Ragoné 1994; Grayson 2000; Crews 2005). Women who conceive by donor-egg IVF or embryo adoption, in general, uphold it. Still other women advocate the potential for shared-mother status. Paula clearly identifies that the connection to the child would be mediated through her body, not her genes. From Paula's perspective, if she gave birth to a child, she could see herself 'never ever being willing to part with that child if the relationship ended.' Yet, she imagines, she would 'feel distant already' from a child to whom her partner gave birth. Given this logic, a logic which separates biology and nurturance from genes in Paula's view, she would be an 'assistant parent.' Furthermore, given her status as an assistant parent, she would be in no position ethically to 'take [her ex-partner] to court and try to take that child from her.'

This so-called logic of motherhood, whether based on genetic or bodily relatedness, challenges many women's attempts to maintain relationships with children they have parented. Women become parents not only to children conceived or adopted in the context of a relationship, but also to children who were conceived or adopted prior to the relationship. Heather encountered this type of logic when she and her partner of ten years separated. When they began their relationship, her partner's daughter was a toddler. Throughout the relationship they agreed that if they ever split up they would share parenting. This did not prove to be the case. The stratification of access to parent status is even more normative in relation to women who parent children conceived and birthed, or adopted by, another woman prior to the commencement of the relationship. When the relationship ended, a friend challenged Heather's attempts to establish and co-ordinate a shared parenting relationship.

I found that people said things to me that shocked me. I felt that they were revealing some level of homophobia, and that surprised me. [My partner and I] had agreed just shortly after the separation that, of course, we would alternate weeks and, of course, that's very difficult at first to do. [My stepdaughter] was acting out and she was unhappy wherever she was. I think it's pretty standard for when parents separate. Then I had one friend phone me up and say that she thought a child ought to be with its mother. Would she say that about her and her husband, that her child should be with her full time and not with the other parent? I'd been in this child's life for ten years, acting as a parent. All this legal – you can have a legal agreement, but if people treat each other badly, it's going to be a mess anyway. So I had to really consider at that time whether I should pursue some legal avenue, and I just didn't.

Heather and her close friend Brian decided to become parents and raise a child together. Their situation, for the most part, conforms to questions such as those asked on birth registration forms, and both have acknowledged status as biological and legal parents from birth. Conception was achieved by self-insemination with the use of sperm from a known donor, but the donor is the father, and Heather, as the recipient and inseminating woman, is the mother. Unlike the situation that occurred with her stepdaughter, Heather perceives her relationship to the daughter to whom she gave birth as solid: she and Brian are committed to recognizing each other as parents. Heather stated: 'I just see that we have to work together to be parents. And we're going to have that connection for a long time, so whatever else changes in our lives, we have to accommodate that and see that we have taken this parenting on together.'

This situation is significant because, given Heather's experience raising her stepdaughter, she knows that a biological relationship is not the foundation of parenting. Yet, given her experience, biological relationships are the ones that are recognized as legitimate. The structure of the family that she and Brian have created is different: it was a close friendship and is now also a parenting relationship. Now in her early twenties, Heather's stepdaughter is once again a strong presence in her life, spending time with Heather's toddler. Heather's partner, who has teenage children of her own, is not a parent to Heather and Brian's daughter. Yet, she may over time find herself acting as a parent. Given the complexities of the relationships that Heather and Brian are defining by and beyond biology, they may find themselves redefining the meanings of *biology*, *parent*, and, of course, *family* throughout the course of their lives.

Women who are co-parenting, who are fighting for child support, or who seek legal recognition of their status as mother in order to acquire custody, visitation, and access rights, point to their intentions to co-parent, their participation in choosing a donor, the kinship terminology by which the child refers to them, and their presence (indeed, participation) in the insemination process as proof of their mother-parent status (Dalton 2001; Gavigan 2000). Rita, the mother of a fourteen-year-old boy, was present when her partner self-inseminated with semen donated by Rita's nephew. Rita had picked the semen up in the morning and transported it back to the campground where she and her partner were staying for the weekend, all the while keeping the semen warm. She and her partner planned to parent together. Still, at first, she had a difficult time representing, and naming, her relationship to her son.

> At first, people would say to me, 'Oh, is he your grandson?' (because I was a bit older) or, 'Is he your son?' And I never knew how to react. I would either just kind of shrug or – you know? It took me a while to get into the groove of saying he's my son. Although, emotionally, I felt bonded with him before he was even born. I was the one who would get up at night and change his diapers and bring him in for feeding. So, over the long haul what actually happened – like, I have heard that mothers especially hear every sound the baby makes even if they're sleeping. That happened to me, whereas, for [my ex-partner], it didn't. Because I felt, well, she spent nine months carrying him, and this is something that I want to do and should do. This is my share. She actually stated after a while that she didn't hear him at night. And I always did. So there was kind of an interesting bonding that took place. But it took a while for me to sort of internalize all that. Now I call him my son, and I have to really stop and think at times that he's not my biological son. He's, like, my son. But it took a while for me before I – when somebody would say, 'Is he your son?' that I'd just automatically say, 'Yes, he is.' Now, I always say that, and so unless people ask further questions, that's as far as it goes.

Numerous ways of becoming a mother exist, and, as various researchers have identified, the concept of real motherhood is flexible and not reducible to biology (see Ragoné and Winddance Twine 2000; Layne 1999). Yet, a dominant normative discourse defines non-biological and non-legal mothers as non-mothers. Non-biological and non-legal mothers need to negotiate their 'mother' identity in relation to this discourse of exclusion. Rita's lived experience of bonding with her son, caring for him and meeting his needs, as mothers do, eventually enabled her to name her son as her son.[12]

Negotiating parenting relationships and one's identification as a parent is often most clear around the time of conception, pregnancy, and birth, or at the end of a relationship. When Rita and her partner began talking about separating, Rita assumed that her son would live with her partner.

> I always felt that I was second in [my son's] life, that [my ex-partner] was his number one, and that never bothered me. It was something I accepted. And so when the terrible time came and I was packing my suitcase and I was leaving, you know, kind of just after a major issue had come up, [my son] came and he just threw his arms around me – he was ten at the time – and, you know, just repeated this broken hearted 'Don't leave, don't leave, don't leave.' And I couldn't. I just couldn't tear him off of me and leave. So, after a couple more weeks when it became obvious that it wasn't going to work, Celine said, 'I will leave.' And she did.

Without an already legally recognized relationship to a child, a woman in a relationship with a woman who is already legally recognized as the mother encounters significant amounts of resistance to their claim for mother-parent status from friends, family, and the courts, if not from their own sense of distance. Rita assumed that she would be the one to leave, similar to the way in which Paula speculated that she could never take her partner to court to try to take away *her* child. Instead, Rita became the primary caregiver, and her son visits his other mom on weekends. Rita and her partner had encountered significant red tape when they attempted to find a way for Rita to adopt their son (prior to the 1996 Adoption Act). In contrast to the experiences of other women who found it difficult to maintain their status as parents – as non-biological parents – Rita's parental status was further solidified, and legalized via a custody agreement that was made when her relationship with her son's biological mother ended.

This chapter has addressed how the mediation of *knowing* within the context of parenting or planning to parent calls on women to explore their understandings of what biology, genetic relatedness, and everyday caring contribute to one's status as a parent and to claims to relationships with children. Women described how they had been confronted with an awareness of beliefs (their own and others') in the so-called biological truths when it comes to parenting, but also how experiences and time had challenged set categories. In the next chapter, experiences within a newer paradigm that emphasizes the possibility of 'contracting relationships' are explored.

9 Contracting Kinship

On the Cusp of Change

Many pivotal court cases took place throughout the 1980s and 1990s, in which lesbians and gay men challenged their denial of access to rights and benefits, due to the exclusionary definition of *spouse*.[1] However, without governmental action, amendments to policies or Acts only applied to the specific issues covered by such policies and Acts and only within a limited jurisdiction. Successful challenges set precedents, upon which future decisions could be made, but the cost of launching challenges to separate pieces of legislation was often prohibitive to individuals. In the light of legislative reform in a number of provinces and anticipation of the decision of *M. v. H.* in Ontario, Status of Women Canada[2] issued a call for proposals on 'The Intersection of Gender and Sexual Orientation: Implications of Policy Changes for Women in Lesbian Relationships.' The resulting reports by Lahey (2001) and Demczuk, Caron, et al. (2002) provide detailed accounts of the political history of lesbian women's status in Canada and the differential and stratified ways in which lesbians' lives and social and economic status are or may be affected by policy changes. The documents provide critical insight into the economic disadvantages and potential consequences of new legislation that recognizes same-sex or same-gender relationships. The report by Demczuk, Caron, et al. highlights the discrepancies among laws across Canada as well as within individual provinces. The authors draw specific attention to the ways in which recognition of spousal status is maintained as distinct from legislation governing adoption and filiation, writing:

Nevertheless, the current trend among lawmakers in Canada is to grant same-sex couples the same rights and obligations as are given to opposite-sex cohabiting couples, with the exception of certain provisions concerning adoption and filiation. The evidence for this comes notably from the enactment of Bill 32 in Quebec, specific statutes in some provinces such as British Columbia and recent judicial decisions. The inclusion of same-sex couples in the legal definition of 'spouse' is being achieved gradually and unevenly, as is shown by the provisions in Bill 5[3] in Ontario and more generally the differences in conjugal status granted to gay and lesbian couples in the provinces of Canada. These piecemeal reforms are producing a private family law regime that is asymmetrical and inconsistent because they are usually the result of legal challenges rather than the result of a declared political decision to put an end to discrimination based on sexual orientation. (Demczuk, Caron, et al. 2002, 51)

As mentioned by Talia in chapter 5, a key refrain in discussions regarding same-sex rights, as well as the justification for separate categorical status (such as same-sex partner, common-law partner, or domestic partner) and the exclusion of same-sex partners from the right to legal marriage, is the procreation argument. As the reaction of Erica's father highlights, a relationship between two adults is considered to be one thing, but sanctioning same-sex parenting is another. While one of the key shifts that took place in British Columbia was the amendment to the Family Relations Act, the amendment facilitated the recognition of parental status upon the dissolution of a relationship. Via the amendments, women who had been parenting children with a woman had rights and obligations to continue the parenting relationship with the child. The amendments, however, did not facilitate legal recognition of parental authority within the context of an ongoing relationship between partners. A number of women described commitment ceremonies as part of their process of establishing a family setting, by publicly declaring their relationship, for the child they hoped to have or were parenting. However, the Modernization of Benefits and Obligations Act (2000), the 2003 decision in British Columbia to allow same-sex marriage, and the federal 2005 decision to facilitate marriage between people of the same sex did not confer upon lesbian partners dual parental status from birth.

As discussed in the previous chapters, women had varying degrees of knowledge about their rights, donors' rights, and, if a partner (of either the inseminating woman or the sperm donor) was involved, that partner's rights. In British Columbia, legislative reform, especially the implementation of the Adoption Act in 1996 and amendments to the Family Relations Act in 1998 , worked to establish an environment for the legal recognition and status of lesbian parents and lesbian families. Women in my study described the province as 'progressive' and 'on the cusp of change.' The stories of women that are drawn upon in this chapter illustrate the ways in which women and potential donors navigated rapidly shifting terrain and legal uncertainties and ambiguities. Specifically, the focus here is on the social and cultural contexts of engaging with emerging (potential) legal technologies of recognition (and non-recognition) including known-donor contracts, adoption, and birth registration.

Legal Bridges:
Known-Donor Contracts and Second-Parent Adoptions

The experiential knowledge of friends or the information found in books or magazines about lesbian parenting shaped women's thoughts about having children and their interpretations of the various legal arrangements that might be possible. Known-donor contracts[4] have held a contested place within queer women's individual narratives of trying to become a parent as well as within publicly stated advice on the topic. They can be perceived as providing a potential form of legal protection but also a written acknowledgment of paternity. At a basic level, for men, donor contracts are a means by which to state in writing that they have no responsibilities toward any child or children conceived. For women, donor contracts represent a means by which to have the donor acknowledge that he will not be a parent to the child. On a general level, known-donor contracts aim to define the intentions of the parties involved. Sperm-donor contracts have progressed from statements by a donor consenting to the use of his sperm and 'signing away his [parental] rights,' to dense documents that outline in detail the parental roles of a donor and the recipient woman or couple. The viability of sperm-donor contracts is untested. However, their increasing use is, perhaps, indicative of the practices of contracting relationship obligations in various spheres.

Shortly after Jenna and her partner decided to go ahead with their plans to become parents, a friend volunteered to be the donor.

Although they were not clear about what would go into establishing a sperm-donor contract, they felt that it was an important thing to do. Jenna reflected: 'We were fearful that ... We had no idea what his reaction might be once the child had been born and, I think quite naively, believed that having this contract would offer some real protection. I'm still unclear as to whether it really did or not.' The donor contract which Jenna, her partner, and the donor established cost over $1,500 and, in its final version, was over eighteen pages long. Jenna explained what occurred after the initial draft was drawn up:

> We went through several more edits of this contract and got it to a place where we could all agree on it and then sign it off. And then, I guess, right around that time, once we had him identified and knew that he was willing to sign the contract, he said things like, 'I thought this was just something that we were doing, I was doing for you as a friend. I don't want the government to be part of this.' Well, at that time, and I think still now, until an adoption takes place, there is no really legal way within the law for the government not to have a hand in it. Maybe I can only say this because it worked out well for us, but it was really quite scary at the time to have that whopping document.

The process of creating a donor contract, especially between friends, formalizes the relationship between the donor and the recipient woman or women. Drawing up such a contract and involving lawyers, including a separate lawyer for the donor, challenges the concept of sperm donation as a gift, a concept that often defined women's and men's original ideas about the donor relationship. Jenna and her partner wanted a donor who would agree to be known to the child, and who might be involved in the child's life as a friend of theirs, but who would not be the father. As Jenna stated, 'There was no really legal way within the law for the government not to have a hand in it.' There was no legislation in place that would facilitate the abdication of a known donor's parental authority and rights and responsibilities to any child or children conceived.[5] Sperm donors' rights and responsibilities to children in Canada and many other jurisdictions are only severed through the use of sperm-bank programs and the clinical guidelines and norms of assisted-reproduction practice. Current websites for Canadian fertility clinics point to the ambiguous legal status associated with gamete donors.[6] By contracting their relationship with the donor, Jenna and her partner hoped to formalize his 'gift' in language that might be recognized by law if necessary. Although still unclear as to whether or not the document did afford them any protection, Jenna stated: 'I think it was really good because it brought all these issues out for us that we never would have had a way of kind of bringing to the surface ourselves. We were really confident by the time we went forward that we three all had a clear understanding of what his role was, and felt confident that we were all thinking about it in the same way.'

Although the process of working through the contract and agreeing on the various details was daunting and quite formal, Jenna's story took another type of twist that was familiar to many women who tried to conceive with semen from known donors and needed to coordinate the timing of ovulation with the donor's availability. As it happened, Jenna and the donor were living in different geographical locations and were both going to be in the same city on the weekend during which she was to ovulate – *before* they signed the contract.

> The timing was that we had just finished the last edits on this contract and verbally agreed that it was all okay. But because we were in different places, we didn't want to be couriering this thing back and forth. So we hadn't actually signed it, although it was close enough that we all agreed we were going to. Our lawyer delivered the final version of the contract to the desk at the hotel where I was staying. The donor came and met us in our room there. And he got there and we all read it over, and it said exactly what we expected it to say, and it had places for us all to sign ... and then it had this line that said 'witness.' So we ordered up room service and tipped the bellhop. So the witness on our contract is a bellhop from the hotel. And then we kind of made small talk and said, 'Okay, we're done, we're going to do this.'

At the time that Jenna and her partner were negotiating their relationship with the donor, 'talk' about the forthcoming Adoption Act was 'in the air.' Within the donor contract they included statements regarding the donor's consent to a second-parent[7] adoption by Jenna's partner if it became possible for same-sex partners to do so – which it did. The donor contract – the weight of which was uncertain – was to (hopefully) act as a legal bridge between the time of birth and the completion of the adoption. Although Jenna and her partner began looking into the process of completing a second-parent adoption just weeks after their daughter was born, complications related to obtaining their child's birth certificate delayed the process significantly. 'It was all very, very weird because she was more than a year old [by the time the adoption was processed], and by that time it was perfectly clear to us, and to her, who her parents were. It was us, right? So [when the adoption process was finalized], it was a really big relief for us, for [my partner], and I think for the donor, too, to know that under the eyes of the law now we are the parents.' Jenna articulates the differentiation between the parameters of clarity regarding relationships between her, her partner, the donor, and now a child in an interesting way. In the sense of everyday practices, the parenting relationships were clearly defined. The finalization of the adoption rendered the organization of their family clear within the law. However, by including the donor within the description of the relief they felt upon the finalization of the adoption process, Jenna highlights the shared experience of donors and women who together negotiate relationships that historically have not been recognized by law.

Amy and Liz had friends whose child was conceived using donor semen from one of the California sperm banks, and they had decided to follow suit. Amy said:

> That just sounded so easy. You get this [catalogue] in the mail and this list of guys, and then you just get the one you want. And so we sent away and we got our thing in the mail and we started going over the guys, and that night I couldn't even sleep because I realized it was just too weird to pick a potential father, the biological father, based on eye colour, height, this idea of what his personality is like. That's a bias, of course. If I were to describe myself, it would be completely different from the way you would describe me. It's just – it's unreal.

Amy, like a number of other women who thought about choosing a known donor, had been constantly on the lookout for a donor since the time her biological clock kicked in, when she turned thirty. A few years earlier she had made a mental note that a friend of a friend would be a good potential donor. Some women agonize over the appropriate way to ask a man to be a donor. Other women raise the topic in casual conversations to get a sense of the man's reaction to the idea. Amy simply called this potential donor (Zac) and asked him over the phone. 'I think we were both grateful that I'd done it over the phone because he was just floored. And he said, "It's really good that you can't see me now because my face is completely red. I can't believe that you asked me this."' After thinking and talking about it for three months, including over dinners with both couples who would be involved – Amy and Liz, and Zac and his partner, Benjamin – Zac decided that he did not wish to act as a donor. About a month later he called to say that he had changed his mind; he would be the donor but he wanted to remain anonymous to everybody.[8] Another condition – of his – was that they had to have a written agreement. Their donor agreement ended up being thirty-six pages long.[9]

The option of a second-parent adoption was also available to Amy and Liz, which they pursued after their daughter was born. Amy and Liz discovered that filling out the birth registration form was a bit tricky. Birth registration forms in British Columbia at the time included sections to fill out about the mother and the father of the child. If the father's signature would not be on the registration form, women were to identify the father as 'unknown' or 'unacknowledged.'[10] Amy filled in her information and stated that the father was unknown. She explained: 'Once the child [was] born, there was a lag time before Liz adopted her. On the certificate of live birth I put the father was unknown – which, of course, is me lying. It's weird, we got caught up in that because when we went to file for adoption, we needed consent from the biological father saying that it's okay that Liz is adopting her.' Jenna had also commented: 'I didn't want to lie on the form, but it was one of those things where the form did not fit with reality.' Children must live in the home of adoptive parents for six months before an adoption can be finalized. Although the Adoption Act made it possible for lesbian and gay individuals to adopt and, in these cases, adopt the child of their partner, the process did not permit adoption from the time of birth if the birth was to one of the partners. Thus, children born to lesbian couples could not be legally related to both their parents until six months following their birth.[11] As with Jenna and her partner, the adoption of Amy and Liz's child took place when their daughter was over a year old. Liz commented:

It's weird because there's a time period before the baby and then there's a time period after the baby. And after the baby is way different, it's way different from what you were thinking. So, before, I definitely wanted to adopt because, you know, I wanted to be a true family, and adoption did that for me, just made it legal. But after she was born – going through the birthing process and the pregnancy and everything – it wasn't such a big deal anymore because it was like I'd had her. She's not mine, really, but I think she is. So it wasn't that big of a deal, but it did make it feel complete.

The adoption proceeded without the consent of the biological father, and, according to Amy, Zac relaxed a bit once the adoption had gone through. Amy added that she felt that prior to the adoption Zac, perhaps, felt morally as well as legally responsible for their child. Liz's comment echoes Jenna's in that the processes of becoming a parent and parenting made her a parent. Yet, although the formalization of the legal relationship was not as big a deal as she had anticipated it would be, she notes that 'it did make it feel complete.' This sense of completion, then, perhaps also highlights the standing of a legal family within the context of Canadian law. The adoption was not what made her a parent, but it did solidify that status.

Claudia and her partner were the parents of a seven-month-old infant at the time of the interview. They had made arrangements with a man whom they knew through the local community to be the sperm donor. In contrast to other women who often defined a known donor's involvement in the child's life (if there was to be any) as that of an 'uncle,' Claudia stated: 'We made a conscious choice. We wanted there to be a dad. We wanted a known donor who would eventually at some point be involved in this child's life, should they both choose to have this happen.' Here, the relationship of 'dad' is associated with choice: Claudia and her partner chose to try to become parents with sperm from a known donor, and the child and the donor could then choose whether or not to have a relationship. This construction of the dad-child relationship as a choice infers that the relationship can potentially develop once the child is able to articulate such a choice. They did not want to have a written agreement. Claudia explained: 'Neither of us is necessarily that way inclined. He's a bit of an anarchist, so documentation was fairly meaningless. And an agreement is an agreement until it's broken.' They did plan, though, for Claudia to adopt the child. She continued:

> The thing with the sperm donor has changed. We had an expectation, perhaps naively so, that it wasn't going to be very involved, you know, that somehow magically at twelve they would get together and he would be a presence in her life. Partly because we picked somebody who we thought liked kids, he naturally has fallen in love with her. And he's

around, and he's quite a presence. He's over usually about two times a week, and we've met his extended family.

Although Liz had expected the adoption process to be a significant step in defining her relationship to her daughter, her story locates the adoption as a formality that only legally recognized what she had already experienced – herself as a parent to her daughter. In Liz and Amy's story, though, the donor (and an extended family on his side) was not present as a potential parent. In contrast, following the birth of Claudia's daughter, the man who was the sperm donor became a dad, and his daughter also became a part of his family:

It's gotten interesting. So, now there's a grandfather and a grandmother both. [My partner's] parents are both dead, my father is dead, my mother's the only other grandparent. So it's kind of nice to get this little bonus. And I wouldn't say that they've particularly embraced her as one of their own, but they do have a recognition of some kind of an attach-ment. His family was mixed in response. Well, his mom's having a bit of a fit. It's like all she wants to have is a normal child, and her kids keep doing odd things. This was just another – you know, the gay son saying, 'I have a daughter.'

Throughout the interview there is the assertion of the donor-dad's inclusion of the child in his life, and the inclusion of his family, as a bonus. There are also, though, the statements that 'the thing with the donor has changed' and 'it's gotten interesting.' The familial presence of the donor's relatives in both their and their daughter's life is much greater than that of Claudia's or her partner's own relatives. As she describes, even the roles of grandmother and grandfather (as a nor-mative couple unit) can only be fulfilled by the donor's parents. The finalization of the second-parent adoption, which could not take place before their daughter was six months old, was experienced as much more than paper work in this case.

I have legally adopted, which we did the minute we could. And what that means is the sperm donor consents – doesn't really give up anything, but kind of does – to my adopting this child. He has done that. It's all done legally at this point, which didn't change anything, you know. It doesn't change anything morally or emotionally, but it was something that we really wanted to do – especially because it changed for him as much as it did. That part's out of the way. That's great. I'm really happy about that. And now it's easier for us to be a little more gracious, I think, around him, knowing that our rights are secured. It's fine for him to be the dad, but we make it fairly clear that he's not a parent. He's the dad; we are the parents. We get to decide absolutely everything ... Anything they do in terms of their relationship is gravy for them both. And it's interesting because what's happened is we've ended up having him in our lives, and I don't know that it's somebody that we would choose, necessarily, but it's sort of like family. We don't get to choose.

Claudia describes herself as 'keenly aware that legally [the donor] had more rights' than she did for six months. Although she states that the donor does not really give up anything, the statement competes with the reality of family law. The donor can be seen not to have given up anything, because the agreement was that he would be the father and the two women would be the legal parents. Within the frame of the law, consenting to the adoption places him in the position of having the authority to do so (as a biological and legally recognized parent). That nothing has changed morally or emotionally stabilizes the potential tenacity of the relationship between Claudia and her child during the first six months by rendering the parenting constellation continuous and in accord with their originally conceived agreement. Also interesting is the way in which the relationship is no longer configured as one of choice but, rather, as one akin to family, where you have no choice. The donor is now their daughter's dad and not the man they chose as a sperm donor. Yet, in describing the events, she commented, 'The thing with the sperm donor has changed.' In contrast to a number of other women who discursively distanced the sperm donor from the child by describing the relationship as that of an 'uncle' rather than a 'dad,' Claudia distinguishes between an acknowledged status and role as dad and the status held by herself and her partner as everyday decision-making parents.[12]

Changing Visions:
Domestic and International Adoptions

Over the course of twelve years, Glynis and Virginia tried to get pregnant (each of them was inseminating), with donor semen from three different donors. The first donor was an anonymous live donor who lived in a small town down the highway. Glynis melodramatically recalled the 'crazy scheme' that characterized their first attempt at having a child:

> He was a friend of a friend. We didn't know who he was. He had volunteered to be a sperm donor, and he put his ejaculate in a jar and a paper bag and sent it [by taxi] to a hotel downtown, where one of our friends picked it up and brought it to the house where we were waiting upstairs with baited breath ... That was the craziest one. This guy was very sweet and he was very supportive. He wanted to know if he could build a piece of furniture for this baby when it arrived on the scene.

In this situation, the donor, although distanced from the act of conception and involvement in the parenting of the child, represented his imagined sense of connection to the child through his request to build a piece of furniture for the baby when it arrived.[13] Literature about donor insemination, and now more frequently egg donation, focuses on the distinctions individuals make between types of relatedness, revealing how varying practices are understood as producing kinship clarity (Ragoné 1999; Cussins 1998a). Women whose sperm donor is not completely anonymous (an intermediary knows the donor) and women whose donors are known found themselves negotiating kinship not only between themselves, their family, and the donor but also between themselves, their family, the donor, and the donor's relations. Glynis, Virginia, and the donor were comfortable not knowing each other's identities. However, it seemed that the donor's 'girlfriend actually was very, very curious about who we were, which was part of the problem.' Anonymous 'local' donors were often members of the same circles of friends, belonging to similar and sometimes the same community groups or involved in similar social or political activities. Thus, anonymity could be perceived as quite fragile: a girlfriend's curiosity would most likely result in a breach of anonymity in such small communities as those in which Glynis, Virginia, the donor, and his girlfriend were living. They only inseminated twice with his semen.

Women who are trying to find either anonymous donors or known donors look for ways of letting people know that they are looking for a donor. Like a number of other women, Glynis and Virginia employed the strategy of talking to everyone they and their friends knew in the hope of locating men who could be potential sperm donors. Glynis commented on the strangeness of searching for a donor: 'There were all these conversations, fascinating conversations, around people's kitchen tables. How do you approach the subject gradually? "So, um, you know, Virginia and I have been thinking about having children. How would you like to be a sperm donor?"' Virginia commented that another man who volunteered to be a donor 'didn't have any problem with the idea of being a sperm donor; he had a problem with the idea of jerking off into a paper cup. He wanted to actually have sex with Glynis.' Glynis grimaced, 'I think he was just a letch myself.' Passing on this opportunity, their second attempt involved anonymous donor semen from a sperm bank in California. Instead of having the semen transported via taxi from a town down the road, they now had the semen shipped on dry ice to a northern U.S. town just south of the Canadian border. For between six and eight months both Glynis and Virginia drove across the border, returning each time with a cooler of dry ice and a vial of semen. Both women inseminated over this period, but neither became pregnant. Leaning back on the couch during the interview, with her son Emmanuel curled up against her, Virginia sighed, 'It was about eight months we did it, and then we quit for a while and cried and cried a lot.' Looking up at her, Emmanuel whispered, 'But why did you cry?' 'Because nobody was getting pregnant. We wanted a baby.'

Glynis had both a hysterosalpingogram to check that her fallopian tubes were open and a laparoscopy to see if there was anything else that might be affecting her ability to get pregnant. She tried for another four months by inseminating with semen from the sperm bank. Next, a friend said that he would be willing to be a donor, and she tried to get pregnant by inseminating with his semen for a while. As the stories and the timeline became evident in her retelling of their experiences, Virginia exclaimed, 'God, we were persistent!' Glynis echoed her: 'We were very persistent. This was a big thing, and it just got to be too much, and we just quit. We gave up and were very sad. And then, in 1995, at work we were talking about who we wanted to be like. "If you could be anybody in the world, who would you want to be?" And [my colleague] said she wanted to be [someone famous], and I looked at [my other colleague], who has five kids, and I said, "I want to be you."' Glynis's colleague had adopted three of her five children. Although Glynis had been a member of the Adoptive

Parents Association for 'about a year around the turn of the decade,' she and Virginia had not actively pursued adoption. Following this conversation with her colleagues, Glynis decided, 'Okay. We'll run this one out until the end, and then I'll know for sure that there's no way to do anything.'

By 1995, the government of British Columbia had decided to implement the Adoption Act,[14] which would remove the restriction of adoption to married couples.[15] Early on in the process of applying to adopt, Glynis 'had a run in with the social worker at the Ministry office.' She stated:

> We were considering domestic adoption. We were considering all kinds of possibilities. But [the social worker] was quite adamant that the home study needed to say we were lesbians, sort of right up front. And it was clear to me – and she said as much – 'that'll pretty much preclude any domestic adoption ... Nobody will give you a baby.' I said, 'Well, thanks' ... And she said that anything that didn't say that right up front was going to be, you know, deceptive and unprincipled.[16]

Domestic adoption refers to the adoption of a child who has been placed for adoption within the same country. An international adoption is one in which a child is adopted from another country. Prior to the implementation of the Adoption Act, domestic adoptions were within the regulatory jurisdiction of the provincial government, whereas international adoptions were not. Social workers responsible for completing home studies for international adoptions were also outside of the purview of the provincial Ministry of Children and Family Development. The Adoption Act allows any woman to file a single or a joint (with a man or a woman) application for adoption and now also governs international adoptions. Based on my interviews with women throughout British Columbia, Ministry staff and social workers' reception of lesbians' requests for information and applications varied dramatically. Some women met social workers who supported their applications and actively pursued the possibility of a domestic adoption. Many queer women and men, before and after the implementation of the Adoption Act, adopted internationally through agencies that supported and advocated for placements of children with lesbians and gay men.[17]

Glynis continued:

There was an ad in the magazine that the BC Adoptive Parents Association publishes that said, 'If you're legally entitled to adopt in your
province, then wherever you live we can help you.' It was this agency in
Ontario that facilitates a lot of [international] adoptions. I thought, 'Well,
I'll just phone these people up' – because I'd already talked to the international adoption desk about China and about Haiti, and they said, 'No
way.' So I phoned the woman who ran this adoption agency and said –
I'd gotten to the stage where my opening line was, 'I'm a lesbian in a relationship and ...' You know, put the bad news on the table now. And she
said, 'Oh, well, what we do in that case is ...' They had facilitated several
adoptions, a number of adoptions for lesbian couples, and they knew
exactly what the [country] authorities needed to hear and didn't need to
hear, and basically talk the social worker through the home study.

The home study for Emmanuel reported that although Glynis would
be the legal adoptive parent, both women would parent the child. A
psychological study requested by the other government, and completed by a social worker affiliated with the Ontario adoption
agency, argued that this was an appropriate and supportive environment. Soon after they brought Emmanuel home to live with
them, Glynis and Virginia updated their home study, applied for a
second placement, and 'brought their daughter home' the following
year.[18]

   When Glynis and Virginia began the adoption application process, it
was legal for lesbians to adopt in British Columbia. The combination
of the legislative changes in the province, the negative run-in with the
Ministry social worker, and their noticing an advertisement for an
international adoption agency based in Ontario led to the adoption of
two children from another country. At the time of the interview Glynis
and Virginia planned to eventually do a second-parent adoption
(within the province) so that both women would be recognized as
legal parents of both children, but neither felt that it needed to be done
immediately. Glynis commented, 'We were greatly reassured by the
new Family [Relations] Act.'[19] The amendments to the Family Relations Act ensured that if she and Virginia separated, the law would recognize them as spouses and support each woman's claims for custody
and child support and the right to a continuing relationship with, and
continuing obligations toward, the children. Perhaps more relevant to
their sense of connectedness to each other and their children was their
seventeen-year history together, twelve of which were spent attempt-

ing to become parents. Virginia further explained: 'We're operating on trust to a large degree here, trust and good will. And, you know, some people feel uncomfortable about going through life shaking people's hands instead of signing on the dotted line, but I like it. The less that I have to formalize, the less that I have to involve lawyers and whoever else and that – but next time I have a couple of thousand dollars, instead of buying a new car ...'

In Virginia and Glynis' case, the use of anonymous donors was presented neither as a means of securing their relationship to the child via a socially and legally recognized (biological) connection nor as a means of establishing a biogenetic relationship between one woman and the child. Like many of the women I interviewed who had spent years planning and trying to have a child, Glynis and Virginia had pursued all the avenues they perceived to be possible routes to becoming parents. The experiences with the provincial social worker with whom Glynis had a run-in and the staff at the international adoption agency through which they adopted their two children were significantly different. The BC Ministry social worker believed that it would be 'deceptive and unprincipled' not to clearly identify Glynis and Virginia as lesbians, although in her view that information would 'preclude a domestic adoption – nobody will give you a baby.' In contrast, the staff at the international adoption agency framed Glynis and Virginia's application in such a way that their sexual identifications and relationship would not inhibit the adoption process.[20]

A number of the women I interviewed had positive experiences in gaining information about, and access to, assisted-reproductive services, sperm banks, and adoptions. Their desire to have children was supported by straight and queer service providers, social workers, and Ministry agents. However, many queer women who were trying to become parents, as well as the individuals who were supporting them, found themselves navigating a dominant discourse of homophobia, which purports that most people would not approve of providing insemination or other fertility services to lesbians and that few people would voluntarily place their child for adoption by a lesbian or a gay man. Women who were actively defining the foundations of the social world into which their child would be brought, by challenging friends, families, and co-workers to recognize them as *lesbian* parents and parents-to-be, were simultaneously responsible for representing a family image that conformed to the greatest degree to that of the normative heterosexual family. The most common normative identity that seemed accessible to the single and partnered queer women who were considering international adoption was that of a straight single woman. Hazel, another woman I interviewed who has adopted internationally, explained: 'Always adoption had been in the back of our minds if [donor insemination] didn't work. But we figured we'd probably have to do it in a covert manner. And, basically, that's how most lesbians do it; they represent themselves as single. So we were thinking that that's what we would do [once I decided to stop inseminating].' Hazel filed an individual application for adoption with the BC Ministry in 1996, the year that the Adoption Act was implemented. Then she and her partner met a lesbian couple who had been able to adopt internationally and who had been able to be out about their relationship. Hazel and her partner followed their path up until the final stage of the adoption when they were faced with a different judge than the one who had processed their acquaintances' adoption. At that point, in contrast to the women they knew, who had been successful in having both their names put on their child's birth certificate, Hazel individually adopted their son, Garret, becoming his only legal parent:

> I don't know that [the social worker] actually told us in as many words [to file for adoption as an individual rather than a couple], but at that point we were so close [to finalizing the adoption] that we didn't care. We were willing to do whatever we had to do. That was as close as we'd gone. It was almost a ten-year journey to do this, getting ready, then eliminating the AI, and then finding a child … We weren't going to say, 'Oh well, no, we won't do it your way.'

Whereas a number of the women whose partner gave birth to their child or children were planning to do second-parent adoptions, Hazel pointed out to me a concern that she and her partner had about the wording of the Adoption Act. She explained: 'The Adoption Act allows step-parent adoption of your partner's biological child; it doesn't necessarily allow adoption of your adopted children. So I have adopted a child. My partner may or may not be able to second-parent adopt.' Because of the similarity of their case, Virginia and Glynis may also face this issue. Hazel plans to adopt a second child, and then her partner will apply to do a second-parent adoption of both children. At that point their plan is to challenge the language of the legislation if necessary.

Legal from Birth: Recording Relatedness

The women I interviewed witnessed numerous shifts in the legal status of queer women and men in relation to children. Many women, like Virginia and Glynis, felt more secure in their family status given the amendments to the Family Relations Act and the recognition of same-sex partners within the definition of *spouse*. Looking at women's experiences within the context of these legislative changes, though, it becomes clear that an amendment to one piece of legislation does not immediately transfer legal status and recognition to a situation falling under the purview of another piece of legislation. Discussing second-parent adoption procedures, Susan Dalton states:

> One drawback for couples who use the second-parent adoption as a legal substitute for marriage is that the resulting legal structure is a family in which the two adults remain legal strangers to one another ... As the vast majority of legal benefits and protections afforded families in this society are funnelled through the spousal relationship (i.e. through legally married couples to their children), [a lesbian couple and their child] would [remain] unrecognizable as a family for the purpose of accessing these benefits. (2001, 212–13)

Applying Dalton's statement to the experiences of women I interviewed, it is clear that women seek legal recognition of their relationships to each other and their children through multiple means. It is often hoped that the recognition of parents and children as family in one context will equate to recognition in another context, but this is not always true. The amendments to the Family Relations Act meant that same-sex partners would be legally recognized as spouses with obligations and rights upon the dissolution of a relationship. Lesbian co-parents who separated would be responsible for supporting any children they were parenting and have a right to a continued relationship with those children. However, the Family Relations Act did not, and does not, confer rights or recognition to non-legal mothers throughout the duration of the relationship. The women I met who advocated second-parent adoption were often concerned with establishing these rights. They wanted to ensure that if something were to happen to the legal mother (if she were hospitalized or died), the non-biological or non-adoptive mother would be recognized as the child's parent. Many women also wanted the recognition afforded by the medical community, school systems, and customs officials so that a mother who did not give birth to their child or children or a mother who did not originally file for adoption would be authorized to make decisions and travel across national borders.

As mentioned earlier, filling out a birth registration form presented issues for various women in my study. A few women I interviewed who included the name of their partner on the birth certificate as the second parent were told by the Vital Statistics Agency that they had wrongly filled out the form. The evidence of the error, in the case of one couple I interviewed, was a name associated with a female gender which was written in the box designated for father's information. A decision in a case that came before the BC Human Rights Tribunal in 2001 once again shifted the landscape in which lesbian parents, donors, and donor-dads could define their family. Being named a child's parent from birth allows women to complete subsequent paperwork with the status of parent. Two lesbian couples who were denied the right to name the non-biological mother as a co-parent on their child's birth registration form filed separate human rights complaints in the late 1990s. In August 2001 the BC Human Rights Tribunal ruled that the BC Vital Statistics Agency had acted in a discriminatory fashion, and ordered the Agency to amend its forms to allow for the possibility of parents of the same gender (as that of the birth mother) to register as their child's parent at birth. The BC Human Rights Tribunal's decision was based on the evidence that 'in fact' the process of registering a birth does not equal the process of naming the biological parents. A manner of testing has never been implemented to determine the genetic paternal links between a man registered as a father and the named child. Furthermore, it is accepted practice for a father of a child conceived by donor insemination to be registered on the birth certificate. The ruling produced the category of a 'non-biological birth mother' and simultaneously challenged the established association between vital statistics data, genealogical information, and adoption records.

The case, however, was brought forward by four women, two of whom had become pregnant by clinical donor insemination with semen from a sperm bank. The analogy then, between male partners of women in the same situation being registered as the parent, worked. In most descriptions of this case, it is stated that lesbian women who conceive with anonymous-donor semen can register a same-sex partner as the parent of the child born. The government of British Columbia challenged the decision of the Human Rights Tribunal, upon which it was decided that the Tribunal had overstepped its jurisdictional boundaries in requiring the Vital Statistics Agency to alter its forms to facilitate the registration of a co-parent. The ruling in this situation found that the forms could only be required to be amended so that they were non-discriminatory. The original discrimination was based, as described above, on the practice of denying the registration of women co-parents and permitting the registration of male parents of children conceived by anonymous-donor insemination (at a clinic).[21] The forms have been amended and now distinguish between 'mother's information' and 'father or co-parent's information.' The separate category of 'co-parent' is defined in the form as 'a person who is in a spousal relationship with the mother of the child, is not the father of the child and the mother and co-parent have agreed to be the parents of the child.' In this construction, the mother category presumably remains stable. A presumably stable category of 'father' also remains, and an additional category of 'co-parent' is added. It could be assumed that this reconstruction of categories is meant to maintain the form (or reinvent the form) to be a reflection of biological parenting, with the men who are not biogenetically related to the child born acknowledging themselves as co-parent. Given the normative practices of secrecy surrounding donor insemination in heterosexual relationships, as well as perhaps a man's unwillingness to be named co-parent (and not father) of a child he parents as a father, I expect that this will not be the case. I also expect that a system of proving paternity will not be implemented. Thus, the forms will reflect an asymmetry of relationships between women parents, based on a normative narrative of biological and non-biological relationships. This construction continues to raise questions, given that there is no possibility for the co-existence of a father and a co-parent as registered parents, alongside the individual whose information is included under 'mother.' It is also unclear, based on this decision, which sets a precedent with respect to the use of clinical assisted-insemination services, what the ruling would be in the case of women who conceived with semen from a known donor.

More recently, other court cases have been decided that could also have an impact on future uses of registration documents as a means of recording, claiming, and determining parental status. In 2003 a case was decided at the Supreme Court of Canada (*Trociuk v. British Columbia [Attorney General]*) in which a British Columbia man challenged an ex-partner's declaration that 'the father is unacknowledged by the mother' on the Registration of Live Birth form. The case had been filed in 1996. In the written decision Justice Deschamps stated that the registration process is meant to reflect biological connections and that recording these connections affirms the importance of this link. This decision contrasted with those of the lower court and the Supreme Court of British Columbia, both of which had upheld a mother's right to state that the father is unacknowledged. This decision could have the effect of opening up the possibility for sperm donors who were not intending to be parents originally to apply for acknowledged status of their paternal relationship. It could also make the process of registering a co-parent on a Registration of Live Birth form more difficult.

Another decision was rendered in 2003, on the case of a couple who had entered into a surrogacy agreement with (as reported) another couple, in which a woman gave birth to a child following the transfer of an embryo created by the petitioning couple's egg and sperm. The intended parents were denied the possibility to register as the parents of the child. It was argued that the mother who is named on the Declaration of Live Birth form is the woman who gave birth to the child, which is affirmed by the submission of a Declaration of Birth form by a midwife or physician attending the birth and recording its details. Thus, it would not be possible for the commissioning parents to register as parents. The court decision found that denying the couple the possibility of registering as parents of the child was unjustified. Their parental status was also uncontested by the woman who had given birth.

The above three cases have been read as complementary,[22] but they also reveal the complexities of current legal decision making and the potential application of the scenarios in multiple ways. The role that the process of recording relatedness plays in Canada is highlighted, but each of the decisions places limitations on the potential for the scenarios in the other two cases, as well as many others, to be later recognized in support of a similar decision.[23] In June 2008 the relevant section of the BC Registration of Live Birth form read: 'If the father is not being registered below, for one of the following reasons, please check the following statement: I am the mother of this child and do solemnly declare that: the father is incapable or the father is unacknowledged by the mother or the father is unknown by the mother or the father refused to acknowledge the child.' For women who do not conceive with semen from an anonymous (unknown) donor, it might seem most logical to not acknowledge the father (because acknowledgment is seen as acknowledgment of a parental status and not a biological-genetic relationship). Given that the Supreme Court of Canada has deemed it unconstitutional to provide a means by which a mother can choose to not acknowledge a father, as it is seen to discriminate against fathers, this option may be unavailable in the future.[24] Time will tell whether or not this possibility changes women's ideas about the need to do second-parent adoptions, and how women who conceive with semen from known donors outside of clinical settings will interpret this ruling. Lawyers still recommend adoption as the legal route to parenthood.[25]

Unforeseeable and Uncontractable Relations

It is, of course, not always possible to imagine the relationship that one might have to a partner, a child, or a man who agrees to act as a sperm donor. Relationships are mediated and negotiated through experience. Paper tools may facilitate a documentation of relationships and a recording of intentions. Law, policies, and practices may critically restrict or promote various constructions or recognition of relationships. As Jenna noted earlier, one of the significant advantages of developing a comprehensive known-donor agreement was that it 'put everything on the table' and potentially provoked conversations about issues that might not otherwise have been discussed. However, not all relationships are foreseeable. A child's death, a partner's death, difficulties conceiving, miscarriages, the birth of a child with disabilities, and the termination of a pregnancy are situations in which changes take place to what seemed to be carefully thought-out, planned, and agreed-on relationships. In many cases, these changes do not occur within the same social frame as that of the original planning, in which, for example, there may have been time for a donor to discuss his potential role with family members or friends, or for a woman parenting a child to spend years negotiating her role as the mother of the child with her partner's family. In the previous sections of this chapter, I have emphasized the role that legislative changes played in conceptualizing parenthood, attempting to become a parent, and the practices of parenting. I provided examples in which women made use of the law and of numerous other strategies that were invoked. In the final paragraphs of this chapter I would like to look at a story in which the relationships with the donor, between the donor and a partner, and between the donor and a child, were not as planned and were also not (and perhaps could not be) re-encompassed within an altered frame.

Chandra was in her mid-twenties the first time that she gave birth to a child conceived by donor insemination. The donor was known, and the plan was that she and her then partner would parent the child. In her mid-thirties at the time of our interview, Chandra and her present partner were parents of a child conceived with donor semen from a sperm bank. Chandra related the decision to use an anonymous donor to a negative experience that she had had with the man who had been the sperm donor when she conceived her first child. Chandra's first child was born with a chromosomal disorder and died early in childhood. Commenting on the donor's breech of the initial arrangements, she stated that her child 'had medical problems, and even though [the donor] said he was going to be distant, the moment that we were dealing with the [healthcare] system he overrode my partner. He took all kinds of control in the intensive care unit, and it was just a nightmare.' Chandra's experiences with a known donor during her son's illness and death are part of her narrative of choosing an anonymous donor when trying to get pregnant with her second child many years later. She presents the donor's actions within the health care system and in the intensive care unit as stories of relatedness between the donor and her partner – 'he overrode my partner.' When I initially wrote about the experiences of the women I interviewed, I included a reference to Chandra's experience in a paragraph about the potential negative experiences of choosing known donors. This is no longer where I think it belongs. While not wanting to contest Chandra's narrative, I would like to look at this example for another reason and from another perspective. Many women discussed their thoughts about whom they wished to choose as a donor, or whom they eventually chose, with a view to various dimensions. However, at the same time that women spoke of creating larger networks of role models to whom their children could look, there was also a normative invocation of the *possibility* to construct and contain

relatedness. Women often spoke about the connections between decision making, responsibility, and parenting. In a normative sense,
parents are adults who have the *right* to make decisions regarding
their child, and spouses have the right to make decisions regarding
each other. Recall that at the same time Robyn stated that she 'would
take her rights,' she also remarked that she was not in hospital, with
her partner having to try to make decisions on her behalf.[26] A systemic problem within medical contexts is the emphasis that is placed
on particular definitions of *kin*, and the privileging of perceived biological relationships (see Luce 2005b) in the absence of any legal documents stating otherwise. While Chandra describes the donor as
having taken control in the intensive care unit, it is also possible that
he was, in contrast to Chandra's partner, at times recognized as
someone authorized to make decisions and to be *given* control. In a
system in which parents are authorized to make decisions regarding
the health care treatment of their child or children, the presence of a
father (donor) and mother (Chandra) would systemically close off the
options for Chandra's then partner (also the mother) to participate in
care or decision making.

At the same time that women contest the denial of recognition to a
certain related individual, a denial of someone else's assertion of relatedness is often enacted. The man who donated the semen by which
Chandra became pregnant was not an intended parent.[27] Perhaps if
the child had not had health difficulties, his storied location within this
assisted-conception narrative would have been different. Perhaps it
was also within the spatial and temporal limitations of the health care
setting and the child's anticipated lifespan that the donor asserted his
relatedness to a child who was dying, a relatedness that he would not
have the chance to perform differently over time. Although many
women spent a significant amount of time negotiating the intended
relationship between the donor and the child, as well as between the
adults involved, the act of having a child, as well as losing a child or a
partner, highlighted the very different ways and circumstances
through which relationships could change.

This chapter concludes part II by focusing on the emerging legal technologies that women employed to record their relatedness to a child or
children. It shows how practices of various kinds – and the now more
common understanding that relationships can be legally contracted –
have shaped women's anticipation of the formalization of relation-

ships. The stories also show, though, how some experiences contribute to an awareness of the limited scope of interactions to which legal technologies might apply. Part II has addressed the ways in which women negotiate relationships to a donor, a partner, and a child, as well as to friends and family, as part of the process of achieving parental certainty within shifting legal contexts. Part III will explore how the social and legal situations that women have discussed are interrelated with emerging developments in the field of reproductive health and science and the governance of assisted reproduction.

PART III

Reproductive 'Assistance'

Many people, including lesbian, bisexual, and queer women, straight friends and family, and health care providers, assume that lesbians do not sleep with men to get pregnant *because they are lesbians*. Therefore, using some form of donor insemination 'makes sense.' Some people, including lesbian and straight friends, family, and health care providers, assume that sleeping with a man would be an easy way to get pregnant. This assumption is often coupled with speculations that doing so will be inexpensive and, possibly, more efficient.

The women I interviewed sometimes spent years laying the social foundations for their family, navigating and evaluating various methods by which to establish a legal relationship to the child they hoped to have, and selecting a donor amidst new productions and interpretations of the medical knowledge related to HIV and STI transmission, genetics, and the science of fertilization, conception, and pregnancy. Throughout the process, women's choices about donors constrained their access to various methods of conception, and choosing to employ various methods of conception also constrained women's choice of donor. Women who attempted to conceive over the past two decades accessed assisted-reproduction programs or physician-assisted insemination during periods when there apparently was no access by lesbians to services. The women I interviewed also inseminated at home (as well as in campgrounds, parked cars, and the apartments of friends) throughout this same period. A number of women inseminated with semen couriered to a United States–Canada border town, which they then imported or 'smuggled' into Canada. Women who were trying to get pregnant, at a time when clinic doors were 'open' to single women and women with a woman partner, chose to inseminate on their own.

Although a number of the women I interviewed contemplated having sex with a man to get pregnant – sometimes as an initial speculation and sometimes as a last resort – most women in this study used various techniques of insemination that involved coordinating 'gamete traffic,' defined as the movement of donor gametes from bodies of origin to recipient bodies (Farquhar 1999). As one of the women I interviewed explained, once one decides that having sex with a man is not going to be a part of one's process of getting pregnant, the key issue becomes determining how to get the semen from A to B (that is, from a man's body to a woman's body). As many women discovered, this most often necessitates coordinating individual schedules so that women, donors (or semen), and sometimes health practitioners will be in close proximity to each other. Attempting to become a pregnant with donor semen, sometimes in combination with other forms of assisted-reproductive technologies, such as in vitro fertilization, egg donation, and ovulation monitoring, involves the transfer of gametes (sperm and sometimes eggs) from body to body *and* the movement of bodies (of women, donors and, sometimes, health practitioners) from place to place. It also necessitates women's engagement with a complex set of medical discourses (encompassing reproductive health and genetic knowledge) by which kinship and reproduction are governed.

The following chapters look closely at narratives of what one woman called the nitty-gritty (the details of actually trying to conceive) and the circumstances that influenced women's experiences. I examine the emergence of lesbian health literature and the framing of lesbian health issues, alongside dominant images of how lesbians should go about trying to get pregnant if they plan on doing so. Addressing the manners in which the women I interviewed tried to make sense of what could be hereditary or transmissible, what might influence the chance of getting pregnant, how they felt about being out or not being out to health care providers, and the experiences during health care encounters, this final section of the book brings the previous two sections into a conversation with understandings and experiences of health and the possible shape of questions that may emerge in the coming years.

10 Matters of Health

Technologies of assisted conception have been naturalized, and what were dominantly perceived to be natural conceptions via heterosexual intercourse have been denaturalized (Sullivan 2004; Franklin 1997; Strathern 1992). As scholars writing at the intersection of science, technology, health, and body studies demonstrate, new narratives of conception have defined technological reproductive assistance as merely 'giving nature a helping hand.' Emerging cultural understandings of *nature* and *natural* continuously incorporate technology (Davis-Floyd and Dumit 1998). Sarah Franklin states:

> As reproductive success is rendered tentative by increasing knowledge of how much can go wrong with the early stages of embryo-genesis, so too is reproductive failure rendered tentative by the increasing number of options available to assist the production of pregnancy. True to the pattern of Euro-American representations of the natural as both within and beyond human control, as so deftly described by Tsing (1995), both 'normal' and assisted conception are naturalized *at the same time both are described as miraculous* (1998, 106, italics in the original).

Along a similar train of thought, Pamela Moore argues that contemporary U.S. health care advertising practices counter representations of assisted-reproductive technologies as a 'high-tech miracle for the few' (1999, 83). Instead, 'fertility treatment seems more like a regular part of a healthy woman's pursuit of "wellness" than a remarkable feat of mythic proportion' (Moore 1999, 83). Accounts of assisted and unassisted conception work to normalize and naturalize reproductive assistance and the designation of pregnancy as an achievement (Moore

1999; Franklin 1998; Weschler 1995). Thus, it seems that infertility, in contrast to reproductive technology, is what disrupts so-called nature. Yet, it is argued, experiences of infertility can be managed – and avoided – by regular monitoring of a woman's fertility status and the use of reproductive assistance.

With the proliferation of public discourses on reproductive (and genetic) technologies, and both textual and visual depictions of scientific progress in the field of reproductive and genetic science, *infertility* acquires an understood and presumed static meaning (Franklin 1990). Its resolution is dependent on new advances in treatment, as well as the acquisition of necessary funding to develop new treatments.[1] However, 'having to try' to become pregnant with the assistance of technologies, such as IVF (Franklin 1997), has, by many scholars' accounts, become routine and, perhaps more importantly, expected (Franklin 1997; Modell 1999; Becker 2000). Gay Becker observes:

> The process of technological development in medicine culminates with the naturalization of a technology and its acceptance by the public. Today babies such as Louise Brown are seen as a normal part of life. *People have adjusted to the idea that conception may take place in the lab, not in the womb.* In twenty years new reproductive technologies have not only come full circle, they have come to be viewed around the world as simply another means of conception. (2000, 19, italics added)

Comparing the narratives of the women I interviewed to the findings of other scholars working in the field of assisted reproduction, it appears that the re-spatialization of conception is predominantly viewed as simply another means of conception when mediated by *visible* technology and clinical intervention. Clinical practice and the clinical management of the bodies of gamete (egg or sperm) origin and the recipient bodies (Kahn 2000) regulate 'gamete traffic' (Farquhar 1999) – the movement of sperm and eggs from bodies of origin to recipient bodies. Farquhar states: 'No longer does heterosex have a material or symbolic monopoly over procreation … Through reprotech's prenatal, indeed preconception, interventions, donor gametes radically displace the biogenetic family with myriad unintended effects and new ontologies – both social and corporeal' (1999, 30). However, although the potential of new reproductive technologies to engender new family formations has been at the centre of public and parliamentary debates due to the separation of sex from procreation, 'the postmodern collapsing, unhinging, and blurring of seemingly inevitable progressions and associations, relationships, and definitions of the body in general, and reproduction, sex and kinship in particular, cuts both ways. While gamete traffic threatens to remove reproduction from its heteronormative context (love marriage, sexual monogamy), it can also fuel its recuperation' (Farquhar 1999, 20).

Regulated by the individual practices of physicians, clinic policies, and fragmented legislation, the use of assisted-reproductive technologies does not overtly challenge dominant ideas about sexuality, parenthood, reproduction, and the family. The project of naturalizing reproductive assistance required the naturalization of exclusionary practices as well as the restriction of access to treatment to individuals whose use of the technologies would not challenge the concept of 'natural' family structures. Practices, policies, and legislation contained any potential 'threats' (following Farquhar's rendition) to a heteronormative image and construction of family, by restricting access to services and silencing the voices of 'unauthorized' users. Queer women and straight or queer donors may often have an ambiguous or uneasy relationship to the so-called naturalness conferred on a heterosexual couple's use of assisted-reproduction technologies. It is important to bear in mind the varied beginnings to the narratives of assisted conception that were related by women in this study and the ways in which experiences throughout one's life influence perceptions of what might be considered natural in one context or another.[2] Charis Cussins (1998b; Thompson 2005) uses the phrase *ontological choreography* to refer to performances of gender within the spaces of fertility treatment. The image of a choreographed performance emphasizes the notion of an accompanying script to which one should adhere. For the women interviewed in Sarah Franklin's ethnography *Embodied Progress*, 'having to try' was a key component of that script.[3] In my study, the fact that women who were trying to become a parent – on their own or within the context of a relationship with another woman or a man who would be a co-parent – were not part of the original planned cast, to follow this metaphor, simultaneously displaced their experiences from the normative clinical context, and often their individual experiences from normative attempts to include lesbians as clients.

Alternative Insemination and Women's Health

During the 1980s, as feminist scholars criticized the further medicalization of women's bodies and reproduction via new reproductive technologies (Arditti, Duelli Klein, and Minden 1984; Spallone and Steinberg 1987; Spallone 1989; Corea 1985), lesbians' and single straight women's use of donor sperm and practices of self-insemination were heralded as examples of women maintaining control over their body and reproductive experiences (Hornstein 1984; Wolf 1982). According to Haimes and Weiner, 'lesbian DI drew attention to the practice of DI itself: not as an unfortunate necessity to circumvent subfertility but as a positive opportunity' (2000, 478). Throughout the 1980s, debates ensued about who could access assisted-reproductive technologies. For the most part there was no support for lesbians' requests for access to services, and 'awareness grew that medical supervision was not a prerequisite for a procedure that is technically very simple' (Haimes and Weiner 2000). Practising donor insemination outside of clinical contexts contested the image of donor insemination as a medical practice.[4] Information about self-insemination, and recommendations about the 'technologies' – diaphragms, cervical caps, sperm cups, and needleless syringes – that could assist women in placing semen as close to their cervix as possible, countered the notion that in the absence of sexual intercourse with a man it would be necessary to have a health professional insert the semen into the vagina. Self-insemination and clinic-based donor insemination were quite similar in practice throughout the 1980s and, in many areas, the early 1990s. Like the women who inseminated at home – on their own or with the assistance of friends, partners, or lovers – most of the women I interviewed who were inseminated at a physician's office or a fertility clinic during the 1980s and early 1990s recounted a very low-tech experience of intracervical insemination (ICI). Semen was 'injected' into their vagina, sometimes using a cannula to deposit it as close to the cervix as possible.

Women interested in parenthood often formed discussion groups as described in chapter 2, and through these discussion groups, or sometimes workshops facilitated by lesbian parents, they learned about their bodies and insemination techniques. Knowledge about alternative insemination was shared with women through support groups, consciousness-raising groups, and workshops in much the same way that other knowledge about health was disseminated during the pivotal years of the women's health movement (Boston Women's Health Collective 1994). In an effort to de-medicalize reproduction and donor insemination, and to ensure the availability of donor insemination to lesbians and the heterosexual women without male partners who were being denied access to clinic-based donor insemination (Haimes and Weiner 2000; Hornstein 1984), feminist organizations and women's health clinics implemented both informal and formal donor-insemination programs. For example, The Sperm Bank of California and Pacific Reproductive Services – whose programs were accessed by women I interviewed – were established around this time. In 1984 Francie Hornstein wrote: 'It seemed particularly fitting that the same women who developed the practice of menstrual extraction, a procedure that could be used for early abortion, also were among the pioneers in the practice of self-help donor insemination. We figured if we could safely help a woman end her pregnancy without the help of physicians and patriarchal laws, we could certainly help women get pregnant' (374).

Many of these donor insemination programs provided women with semen that was acquired either through their own donor program or through a 'friendly' physician's access to a commercial sperm bank, and then they encouraged women to do the inseminations themselves. Writing from a UK standpoint and citing Duelli Klein (1984) and Wikler and Wikler (1991), Haimes and Weiner (2000) note that the first self-insemination group is thought to have been formed in 1978 (notably, the same year in which Louise Brown was born). In 1984, Francie Hornstein noted that self-insemination programs had begun in California, Vermont, and New York (1984, 376). In her account of self-insemination in Canada, Rona Achilles locates the development of self-insemination groups at an earlier date, stating: 'There is an increasing demand for DI by single women, and underground networks of women have developed since the early 1970s in Britain, the United States and Canada to facilitate SI [self-insemination]. This movement has grown in both numbers and sophistication' (1993, 539). Importantly, Achilles' statement renders self-insemination a contemporary rather than a historical practice. Furthermore, her comment regarding the growth of 'underground networks' of women sharing information with each other, and helping to match donors with recipients, points to the marginal location of self-insemination in relation to a dominant discourse of clinically managed assisted reproduction. Following Burfoot (1993), Haimes and Weiner state: 'There are many different types of [self-insemination] groups, but their defining characteristic is that they operate outside the professional structures of clinic-based DI' (2000, 479). Self-insemination networks are (and were) networks of knowledge exchange[5] – for the most part based in larger communities – that provide women with the information and confidence to inseminate at home.

Diagnosing Lesbian Bodies with Social Infertility

The experiences of queer women are concurrently both central and marginal to the debates and studies exploring the social, legal, and medical or health issues associated with the advent of new reproductive and genetic technologies. Lesbians' presence within the broader discourses of assisted reproduction historically took the shape of regulated absence from the practice of clinic-based assisted conception. Profiles of clinic clientele, and thus participants in research based on clinic populations, present an overwhelming image of middle-class, heterosexual clients.[6] The historical definition of lesbians as inappropriate consumers of fertility services served to also uphold the naturalness of heterosexual couples as appropriate users of the same services (cf. Haimes 1990; Cussins 1998b). As debates about reproductive technologies took hold in public and medical discourses, the issue of providing lesbians with access to fertility treatments was addressed as a 'moral' and 'ethical' dilemma. Lesbians' requests for access to assisted-reproductive services were designated 'special requests' (Englert 1994), and throughout the 1980s most of these requests were denied (Haimes and Weiner 2000). Significantly, the debates revolved for the most part around access to donor insemination. The debates seem to have been rejuvenated today as more queer women and donor-dads seek access to in vitro fertilization and donor-egg in vitro fertilization.[7] What seem to draw relatively few remarks are engagements in surrogacy practices, particularly by queer men wanting to become biological parents.[8]

Arguments for and against providing lesbians with access to fertility services and, more specifically, infertility treatments applied a discourse of social infertility to lesbian bodies (Daniels and Burn 1997; Englert 1994). Arguments against providing lesbians with access to assisted-reproductive technologies emphasized that lesbians' so-called infertility resulted from social rather than biological reasons, and, thus, assisted reproduction services were not justified. Arguments in

support of providing lesbians access to assisted-reproductive technologies – most often, donor insemination – emphasized lesbians'
infertility, irrespective of social or physical reasons. Addressing the
inclusion of lesbian couples within diagnoses of infertility, Julien
Murphy suggests the possibility that lesbians have 'relational infertility' (2001, 182). She writes:

> A few years ago, my partner and I began using assisted reproduction to
> conceive our first child, and it occurred to me as I wondered about les-
> bians' access to reproductive services, insurance coverage, and parenting
> rights for nonbirthing partners that there was little difference between us
> and the many infertile heterosexual couples for whom reproductive serv-
> ices were designed. While we lacked a medical reason for an infertility
> diagnosis, the similarities in the treatment plan and goal suggested that
> perhaps lesbian couples might be regarded as having a sort of 'relational
> infertility' that could be said to accompany lesbian relationships. (2001,
> 182)

Murphy argues that unlike most medical diagnoses, infertility is
defined relationally:

> Medical diagnostics allow for the possibility that the source of infertility,
> in some cases, may lie with the couple and not one of the individuals
> (Collins 1995; Daley et al. 1996; Siebel 1993). Given the relational aspect of
> fertility, two people may be fertile apart but infertile together. Infertility
> can be general or partner specific; it can be temporary or permanent.
> (2001, 190)

Throughout 'Should Lesbians Count as Infertile Couples? Antilesbian
Discrimination in Assisted Reproduction' (2001), Murphy considers
the possibilities of extending a definition of infertility to lesbian
couples. She argues that due to the lack of a diagnosis of infertility – a
recognized medical condition to be treated with infertility practices –
lesbians' requests for access to fertility clinics and sperm banks are recognized as 'optional' and thus, more easily denied. She wonders if
counting lesbian couples as infertile would challenge discriminatory
practices and provide lesbians with similar access to the benefits
obtained by heterosexual couples' infertility diagnosis, namely insurance coverage, recognition of the desire to parent, and parental rights
for the non-birthing partner.[9] Would a definition of infertility confer

reproductive status to lesbian couples, thus rendering it a positive act to assist lesbians to reproduce?[10]

Murphy proposes that self-insemination is still the most popular method of conception, yet she states, 'The trend in the 1990s is to seek out fertility experts when self-insemination fails to achieve a pregnancy' (2001, 184).[11] The strategy she employs in this particular piece of writing is to demonstrate the similarity between the lesbians and the heterosexual couples who use physician-assisted insemination (either intracervical or intrauterine), in order to argue in support of the possibility of a diagnosis of infertility for lesbian couples. She then problematizes the strategy of insisting on a medical diagnosis of infertility, arguing that (1) lesbians would then be required to fit their experiences into a heterosexual paradigm, (2) to do so might create social pressure on lesbians to become mothers, (3) it would medicalize an aspect of lesbianism, and (4) it would increase the medical regulation of lesbians' bodies. While Murphy takes on the discourses of social infertility and medical necessity that prevail in bioethics literature regarding lesbians' access to and use of fertility treatment, her analysis is limited to fertile lesbians.[12] Although she acknowledges that 'some lesbians and single women do have infertility problems and use assisted reproduction services to address diagnosed infertility conditions,' these women are peripheral to the debates which revolve around a notion of social or relational infertility and which continue to frame queer women's uses of assisted-reproductive technologies as a moral or an ethical issue. While broader discourses of medicine and bioethics debate whether or not lesbian couples should count as infertile, and continue to debate the issue of lesbians' access to fertility treatments, single and partnered queer women are using various methods of assisted conception and are experiencing difficulties conceiving, miscarriages and still births (see Luce 2004, 2005b). The women I interviewed negotiated the meanings of fertility and infertility within a broad context of their own experiential reproductive history, embodied histories of sexuality, and mediations of perceived risks and expenses. Some women sought medical assistance because they anticipated having difficulties conceiving, while others followed more of a chronologically ordered movement from low-tech to high-tech approaches. A number of the women in this study also took Clomid, an ovulation-inducing drug, for a number of cycles.[13] A move away from a concentration of analysis on access to clinics specializing in fertility assistance, often captured in the reference to an IVF clinic, highlights the proliferation of technology use – including ovulation predictor kits, pharmaceuticals, ultrasound monitoring, and cycle charting – that is often part of the process of trying to become pregnant and often includes encounters with health professionals.

Murphy states that to pursue a medical diagnosis of infertility for lesbians would mean having to fit their experiences into a heterosexual paradigm. The narratives of the women I interviewed suggest that queer women who are trying to conceive, regardless of a medical diagnosis of infertility, to various degrees relate their reproductive experiences to a heterosexual paradigm and measure their risks, failure, and success against heterosexual norms. With very little access to reproductive health literature directed at queer women (for recent exceptions see Pepper 1999; Toevs and Brill 2002), and even less to STI or HIV literature that addresses questions about negotiating safer inseminations, queer women are required to read their bodies, their histories, and their sense of sexuality into literature that assumes a heterosexual readership and promotes heterosexual coupling as natural to reproduction, reproductive health, and family.

More than Access

Women who are hoping to get pregnant assess their own knowledge about pregnancy and understandings about how women get pregnant. They are provided with the initial ideas about how to monitor and chart their cycle, by guidebooks such as *Considering Parenthood* (Pies 1988) and more recently *The Ultimate Guide to Pregnancy for Lesbians* (Pepper 1999) and *The Essential Guide to Lesbian Conception, Pregnancy, and Birth* (Toevs and Brill 2002; see also Brill 2006), as well as websites, such as that of the Lesbian Mothers Support Society; its website was accessible at www.lesbian.org and contained a significant number of links to Canadian-specific as well as international resources. The society ceased to exist in 2002. Books about 'natural' methods of birth control, including fertility-awareness methods, such as *Taking Charge of Your Fertility* (Weschler 2006 [1995]) provide useful and visual information about a woman's bodily changes during a menstrual cycle. Although lesbians are designated fertile consumers of infertility treatment or, in contrast, are designated as infertile, the queer women in my study who were considering parenthood became quite aware of their cycles and developed perspectives on their ability to conceive. The women I interviewed who tried to conceive outside of a clinical context during the early and mid-1980s often monitored their menstrual cycles by charting their temperature and noting changes in their cervical mucous. It was not uncommon for women to begin charting their cycle many years before their first insemination and to keep charting their cycle during breaks from inseminating. In comparison, many women who tried to get pregnant in earlier times in clinical contexts, and at home or in clinics during the 1990s, were more likely to seek a health professional's advice about preconception care (Franklin 1998; Moore 1999) and to perceive conception as the result of attention to details such as timing and technique. Women who inseminated in clinical contexts relied on the advice of fertility centre staff, and often on the use of ovulation predictor kits or on ultrasound monitoring of follicle development, to assess the right timing for an insemination. A number of women who were insemi-nating on their own – with a known donor or a sperm-bank donor from one of the California sperm banks – approached their family physician for detailed information about how and when to insemi-nate. The amount of support and information that they received, however, was significantly varied.

Heteronormativity and the assumed normalcy and naturalness of heterosexuality, especially in relation to reproduction and family, have a significant influence on queer women's health and well-being and queer women's experiences of reproductive health care. Queer women are habitually displaced from discourses of reproduction and repro-ductive health, sometimes by the very practices that physicians might believe validate women's sexual identities. For example, when Jenna, whose stories are told throughout this book, approached her physician for information about how to accurately time the insemination, the physician was surprised by the question. Perhaps following practice guidelines on providing appropriate lesbian health services, she had asked Jenna about her sexual practices and had charted the informa-tion that Jenna had identified herself as having a female sexual partner. Likely, charting the information had assisted the physician to not inap-propriately ask Jenna the typical questions about the birth control needs that most often characterize women's health care. However, this label carried assumptions, which lead to her surprise when Jenna declared that she was there for a visit because she wanted to get preg-nant. Jenna states, though, that her physician only 'missed maybe half a beat' before responding.

Other family physicians, of the women in my study, who were approached for information missed more than half a beat when women explained the reason for their visit. Fiona and Melanie, two other women whose narratives are included in earlier chapters, had a significantly different experience. Conversations with one potential donor concluded with a mutual agreement that they had different expectations regarding the role of the donor in the child's life. Next, they met a gay couple interested in acting as 'a donor.'[14] Melanie noted that HIV health issues were a concern 'because people right at that time started talking about a ten-year latency period.' Although Fiona and Melanie were comfortable asking the men about their relationship, including questions about sexual monogamy, and both men were willing to have HIV tests, they were uncertain about how to validate the results. Rhetorically, Melanie asked, 'Do we ask to see the results, the actual printed results of the test?'[15] While these 'negotiations' were taking place, they went to see Fiona's family physician to talk to her about how to inseminate. Fiona described:

> We went to this doctor that we had been going to, and she made some comment about how, if we were going to be using a gay man – and this was, you know, a nice woman physician; we'd been comfortable with her – and she made some comment like, 'Oh, a gay man as a donor? Oh, are you not worried about it being hereditary?' Homosexuality being hereditary. [Melanie laughed and said, 'I'd forgotten all about that.'] Oh? And that would be a problem? And she would love to help us when it came time to have the baby *but had no idea how she could help us get to that point.*

Fiona and Melanie had the good fortune to seek out and locate another doctor, a physician who 'just bent over backwards to help us in any way she could.' However, with a shortage of general practitioners taking new patients, and in many areas a paucity of health care providers, women were not always in a position to change physicians (see also Tiemann, Kennedy, and Haga 1998).[16]

The women I interviewed wanted to maximize the chances of getting pregnant within as few cycles as possible. In order to do so, they wanted to know: For how long does sperm survive outside of a man's body? How long can sperm live in a woman's body? How long does donor sperm, which has been frozen, remain viable after thawing? When is the best time to inseminate? What is the best way to inseminate? Queer women lack easy access to information that is specific to their experiences, identities, relationships, and ideas about sexuality and parenthood. Information must often be extrapolated from resources directed at heterosexual women and men. Thus, queer women's knowledge about their own fertility is often acquired by reading about the treatment or management of straight men's and women's experiences of infertility.

The Emergence of 'Lesbian Health' as a Framework for Health Services

In March 2000 the Society of Obstetricians and Gynaecologists of Canada (SOGC) issued the policy statement *Lesbian Health Guidelines* (Davis 2000). The first sentence under the heading 'Lesbian Women and Pregnancy' is 'Fewer lesbian women become pregnant than heterosexual women' (2000, 3). The paragraph outlines lesbians' theoretical increased risk for ovarian and endometrial cancer[17] and lesbians' theoretical reduced risk for cervical cancer.[18] There is no mention of how lesbians do get pregnant. The next heading is 'Lesbian Women as Parents.' Under this heading the first paragraph reiterates research findings, which conclude that, other than increased tolerance for diversity, there are no significant differences between children raised by straight parents and those raised by lesbian and gay parents. The second paragraph reads:

> Lesbians are no less likely to desire children than other women, and in one survey up to sixty percent of lesbians considered parenting. However, due to the lack of support from society and the medical community, these women are less likely to attempt to conceive. Adoption and fertility programmes can be difficult for lesbians to negotiate, so *they may subject themselves to health risks to conceive*, for example, intercourse with strangers or insemination with sperm from unscreened donors. No medical service should be restricted to an individual because of sexual orientation (artificial insemination with tested anonymous donor sperm or any other profertility technology). (2000, 3; italics added)

The first paragraph is arguably a means of reassuring practitioners who are advised to follow the recommendation in the second paragraph, that is, to not restrict a medical service on the basis of sexual orientation. These recommendations are in line with other Canadian health-service practice guidelines and statements. In 1993, *Proceed with Care*, the final report of the RCNRT, recommended that in compliance with the Canada Health Act lesbians should be ensured equitable access to fertility treatments (Canada 1993). In 1997 an advisory statement in the *Canadian Medical Association Journal* (CMAJ) cautioned physicians against discriminating on the basis of sexual orientation following a BC Human Rights Tribunal decision which found that a BC physician had discriminated against a lesbian couple by refusing them access to donor insemination services (Capen 1997). The Assisted Human Reproduction Act, proclaimed in 2004, explicitly states that 'persons who seek to undergo assisted reproduction procedures must not be discriminated against, including on the basis of their sexual orientation or marital status (Canada 2004).

In the practice guidelines described above, providing lesbians with access to 'artificial insemination with tested anonymous donor sperm or any other profertility technology' is presented not only as acting in a non-discriminatory manner (and thereby protecting physicians from involvement in law suits) but also as extending necessary protection to lesbians who might subject themselves to health risks due to the difficulty of accessing fertility and adoption programs. The possibility of inseminating outside of a clinical context and using semen from known donors who are not part of a sperm-bank program is not mentioned within these guidelines (see discussion below). Seldom are these possibilities identified as positive options in medical literature or practice guidelines pertaining to assisted conception or health care for lesbians (Moran 1996; for recent exceptions see Steele and Stratmann 2006; Ross, Steele, and Epstein 2006).

Practitioners have used the findings of research that assesses lesbians' use of clinic-based donor insemination in order to lobby in support of providing access to assisted-reproduction services (cf. Haimes and Weiner 2000). Yet, as Haimes and Weiner argue, within the medical literature the studies of lesbian families created by donor insemination, 'whilst encouraging a more open attitude, promote a narrow model of lesbian DI: of couples receiving anonymous DI in licensed clinics. That is, a model that mimics the "standard" model of heterosexual DI. Unlike the literature of the 1980s, where SI is hardly mentioned, the more recent literature acknowledges the practice but portrays it as a risky and dangerous last resort' (2000, 494).

How should physicians provide care to lesbians who have sex with a man whom they know in order to get pregnant, or lesbians

who inseminate with semen from donors whom they have
'screened'? Where are the women who choose to inseminate with
semen from known donors located within a health care framework
which normatively excludes that possibility? In 2006 two separate
articles appeared in key Canadian reproductive-health-profession
journals, which addressed the continuum of reproductive health
care with respect to lesbian women. As I have written in detail elsewhere (see Luce 2009 and part II herein), changes in legislation and
interpretations of legislation over the years have both facilitated and
restricted the use of assisted-reproductive technologies in general.
These changes – including the introduction of the Semen Regulations (1996), a Health Canada quarantine on semen stored in
Canada, and the prohibition of the importation of semen that does
not meet specific testing requirements (1999), the updated Semen
Regulations (2000), and the proclamation of the Assisted Human
Reproduction Act (2004) – have had particular consequences for the
women that I interviewed. For many women, one of the greatest
consequences resulted from the restrictions imposed on the importation of semen from two California sperm banks, which had a long
history of providing services to lesbian women and running donor-
identity-release programs (see Scheib et al. 2003; Agigian 2004). For
many Canadian women who wanted to use semen from a sperm
bank, these restrictions foreclosed the possibility of inseminating at
home. In both of the recently published articles, the authors clearly
identify the role that health professionals, significantly those who
are not working within fertility clinics, can play in relation to a
lesbian's experience of trying to become a parent. Steele and Stratmann, in 'Counseling Lesbian Patients About Getting Pregnant'
(2006), provide a detailed overview of the steps that a primary care
physician would take in counselling a lesbian woman and perhaps
her partner about reproductive health care with respect to pre-conception, pregnancy, and post-partum periods. This article both
addresses the specificity of lesbians' needs with respect to health
information and care *and* situates these specific needs within the
framework of 'counseling that family physicians provide regularly
to all women' (2006, 606). In doing so, false presumptions about the
exclusion of women who identify as lesbian from the categories
associated with infection risks due to fluid exchange are foregone, as
is the assumption that lesbians in general attend a fertility clinic and
attempt to become pregnant with semen from a sperm bank or, alter-

natively, engage in 'risky' home inseminations. The article places home insemination within the framework of a valid and safe choice in which a primary care physician can be included in the woman's health care as someone providing information on the recommended tests for the women attempting to conceive and the donors providing semen, or guidance on determining fertility patterns and monitoring ovulation cycles, or assistance with the insemination itself. The article states very clearly that within the new legislative framework governing assisted reproduction in Canada, it is possible for a family physician to participate in lesbians' reproductive health care and experiences. A number of women in my study assumed that their family physician would not be able to assist them in making various reproductive health care decisions, while others expected them to have information, which they were often unable to provide. This article is thus a critical contribution to the area of lesbian reproductive health care as it provides very different information in comparison to previous statements which, instead of providing active guidance material, concentrated more on warning physicians not to discriminate against lesbian patients.

The second article, 'Service Use and Gaps in Services for Lesbian and Bisexual Women During Donor Insemination, Pregnancy and the Postpartum Period' (Ross, Steele, and Epstein 2006), appeared in the *Journal of Obstetrics and Gynaecology Canada*. The article reports on analyses of focus group discussions conducted with women who were trying to become parents; biological parents of young children; and non-biological parents of young children or partners of pregnant women. In this article the authors highlight the dissatisfaction with health services as discussed by focus group participants in relation to (a) the high cost of semen and semen processing, (b) the limited donor selection, (c) the barriers related to sexual orientation, (d) the medicalization of conception, and (e) the legal barriers to conception (508-9). An additional theme discussed related to LGBTT-specific services,[19] especially regarding the possibility of analysis and screening for gay known donors and support services. With respect to pregnancy care, participants emphasized the role that educators and health care providers might play in rendering health services applicable, and thus experiences more comfortable, for women and couples who do not fit a heterosexual norm. The participants identified practices which reflect heteronormative assumptions of who is involved in pregnancy and birthing experiences

(509–510).[20] In terms of post-partum support, participants used very few services, with most of the discussion seemingly focused on legal issues and on the recognition of non-biological parents within the health care system (510). The article is a report of the focus group discussions and the themes arising out of them. The authors are very careful to state that the sample is small and has limitations but can identify steps that health care providers can take to improve services and reduce barriers to care. Reading the outcomes of the study, I was reminded of Rita's story of driving home after her partner had given birth to their son, because she had been told that only family could stay at the hospital, and of then driving back after deciding that the hospital was the place that she should be. I could also clearly recall the sign on the door of a delivery unit at a hospital in British Columbia which read 'Husbands and coaches only allowed.' Or Karyn's story of a physician entering her hospital room and then beginning to speak with the 'butchiest'-looking woman present in his attempt to identify the appropriate co-parent of the child to be born. Or Pam and Caroline's comments regarding a midwife who only addressed Pam, perhaps because Pam was the one who was pregnant or perhaps because she was uncomfortable with acknowledging Caroline as a prospective parent. Ross et al. make clear that there are discrepancies in care that are felt and have real consequences. What I find interesting, though, are the different framings of the discussions with respect to a chronology of attempted conception experiences, which I hope the stories and analyses in this book in some ways disrupt.

The authors concluding statement of recommendation to health care providers is: 'Finally, [care providers] can advocate for federal and provincial policies that establish the provision of assisted reproductive services that are accessible, equitable, flexible and cost-efficient' (510). While these are acceptable goals within a framework of equitable distribution of health care and resources, the ways in which these goals could potentially be met or even addressed are varied. The prevailing discussion within the section on pre-conception services concerns the cost of semen and of semen processing as a barrier. Yet, there is no evident contestation of the commodification of semen in the first place.[21] The frustration expressed in terms of the non-transparency of the costs associated with different procedures seems then to extend to a discussion of the non-availability (for purchase) of semen which would be of preference (from donors of colour,

identity-release donors, et cetera.). One of the difficulties is that regulations implemented by Health Canada prohibit medically assisted
donor insemination with non-cryopreserved (unfrozen) semen, and
clinical policies define men who are 'unrelated' (that is, not the
sexual partner of the inseminating woman) as 'donors.' Thus, in
cases in which women want to inseminate with semen from a known
donor with the assistance of a physician, or will undergo IVF, the
donor or semen must be tested, and the semen quarantined for six
months and then released upon subsequent testing of the man.[22] The
use of cryopreserved semen from a known donor thus becomes part
of the assisted-reproduction industry, with associated costs from the
beginning of this type of care or use of service. One could ask, for
example, what would be the cost of cryopreserving semen obtained
from a man if, on the day of egg collection from his female partner,
the treatment cycle needed to be abandoned? Presumably, due to
storage requirements, the man from whom the semen comes would
need to be tested. Would there be a way of extracting the costs for this
aspect of treatment and comparing them with the costs associated
with donor insemination in general or with designated donor programs specifically? On another line of thinking, how will the potential analysis of the costs of various dimensions associated with clinical donor insemination change with the implementation of the
Assisted Human Reproduction Act and the ban on the sale and purchase of sperm and eggs? Will narratives of the cost of donor insemination, currently articulated within the frames of both rights and
commercialization, change?

The past three decades have brought about considerable changes in
reproductive health care, including the advent of new reproductive
and genetic technologies, as well as in conceptualizations of appropriate lesbian health services. This chapter examines how queer women
have been situated in relation to developments in reproductive technologies, drawing attention to the sometimes problematic discourses
of reproductive autonomy, social versus physical infertility and risk, as
well as the common leap to identifying lesbian parenting as a health
concern, with little said about the plurality of possible routes to parenting. The final discussion of two papers which have recently
appeared in mainstream health profession journals highlights a potential shift in the framing of lesbian health issues. The articles offer guidance to physicians about providing continuity of care for queer women

considering pregnancy or trying to become pregnant, emphasizing the means of positive contributions rather than the avoidance of negative discrimination. The approaches that are taken – in which a physician's involvement is situated in accordance with recently implemented assisted-reproduction governance, and insemination with semen from a known donor is represented as a possibility – provide key entry points to the next chapter, which explores women's interactions with the reproductive and health knowledge emerging from various sources.

11 Screening Pasts

Only one couple I interviewed had attempted to conceive by an arrangement with an anonymous 'live' donor in the late 1980s, and one woman during the 1990s. Another couple in the process of thinking through their options at the time of our interview in 2000 mentioned the possibility of using an anonymous donor outside of a clinical context. However, most women I interviewed who inseminated with semen from a known donor emphasized *knowing* that individual. Knowing an individual meant knowing their sexual history, knowing their family and friends, and knowing their behavioural habits. This knowledge played an important role in women's narratives about choosing particular donors and particular methods of conception.

Pre-Aids to the Age of an Epidemic

The increased use of sperm banks and fertility clinics by lesbians since the early to mid-1980s is most often attributed to the perceived risk of contracting HIV/AIDS by donor insemination and the impact of HIV/AIDS on the donor pool available (Weston 1991). Kath Weston states:

> The onset of AIDS had a dramatic effect on the donor pool available to lesbians for alternative insemination. Before AIDS surfaced, the preferred means of facilitating lesbian motherhood had been to ask gay men to contribute sperm. The general feeling among lesbians was – and continues to be – that gay men represent that category of males most likely to recognize the lover of the biological mother as a full-fledged parent, and to

abide by any parenting and custody agreements reached in advance of a child's birth. For many, economics was also a factor in locating a donor, since informal arrangements are far less expensive than paying the high fees charged by sperm banks. But in light of the devastating losses AIDS has inflicted upon gay men in the Bay Area, and the risks for [the] child and mother-to-be of contracting the HIV virus through insemination, by the mid-1980s most lesbians and gay men had become hesitant to pursue this strategy (Pies and Hornstein 1988). (Weston 1991, 177)

The narratives of women in my study illustrate the connection between the impact of AIDS on queer women's reproductive experiences and the broader impact of AIDS on lesbians and gay men. In 1980 Rae and her partner travelled the better part of a day to attend a clinic in Vancouver where she remembers paying approximately fifty dollars a month for inseminations. Her partner conceived and then experienced a miscarriage. After some reflection, they decided to try inseminations at home, using semen from known donors. Rae recalled:

We started putting out the word that we wanted, um, sperm, and, basically, we started interviewing men, gay men. And this was also pre-HIV ... The two guys decided to actually – They mixed up their sperm. They made love and put both of their sperm in a jar. And they called it 'passion fruit.' And we had it ... It was all set right here [Rae gestures around us]. They made love up the street, and we were down the street. Because we knew at that time – according to our doctor's information, who was a lesbian – about the time frame, about if you do it with live [fresh semen], it's only half an hour. That's all. There's a time frame, and it needs to be done quickly because the little sperms are very fragile. And so they're up the street making love, and we're down the street waiting. And then at a particular time I went up the street, they gave me the jar, I went down and inseminated my partner.

Defining the period as pre-HIV, Rae located the practice of asking gay men to be donors in a historically particular context. Mixing semen served to blur the knowledge of paternity in a way that no longer makes sense, given widespread cultural understandings of definitive paternity by DNA testing. The practice of inseminating with semen from two donors simultaneously was also not perceived to introduce additional health risks. A few years later, AIDS became a visible presence in queer women's narratives of conception and insemination practices.[1] Small-scale, self-insemination networks that had provided access to live donors, like those described in Wilkes (1985), disbanded in the early to mid-1980s as knowledge about AIDS and HIV transmission spread.[2] Small networks of women and donors did not have access to laboratories to test and screen donors. Even in places where facilities for testing existed, men themselves were reluctant to get tested in light of the lack of treatment available (Weston 1991).

Queer women who were interested in having children witnessed increasing illness and death among their circles of friends and the effects of a homophobic backlash as AIDS was designated 'a gay disease.'[3] Fran, who started trying to conceive by using an anonymous donor in 1983, recounted: 'A very good friend of ours, who's a gay man, agreed to help us find a donor. There are a fair number of hippies where I used to live, and he lived in one of the co-ops and found a fellow. For the first three months that I tried to – that we inseminated, it was through this donor. And then [our friend] became very sick with AIDS, and he wasn't able to continue to be the courier back and forth.' As described earlier in chapter 7, the practice of using anonymous live donors often involved a sperm runner who couriered the semen from the donor to the recipient woman, thereby maintaining the anonymity of each party. When Fran's friend became ill and could no longer act as a go-between, Fran sought access to medically assisted insemination: 'I hunted around for an obstetrician/gynaecologist who would be willing to inseminate a single woman. I finally found one who was willing to do it. I went to interview him by myself, and he asked – he didn't ask me if I was a lesbian, but he made it pretty clear that he wasn't really willing [to participate in assisting] lesbian parenthood. But I figured something was better than nothing. So I asked [the physician] if I could bring a friend [to the appointments with me]. And this was in 1986 that we started to try to become pregnant.' According to Fran, locating a physician who was willing to inseminate a single woman was 'better than nothing.' This description identifies the clinical context as less than ideal. Fran went from trying to get pregnant at home with assistance from friends and community members to inseminating in a clinical context in which she could not talk openly about her life, her partner, her sexuality, or her sexual history. Her partner joined her at appointments as 'a friend.'[4]

Talking about an experience nearly a decade later than Fran's, Paula explained that 'gay men were pretty much out for us.' In contrast to locating the experience of HIV/AIDS as a devastating illness, Paula's comment is grounded in the ensuing context of discrimination associated with the dissemination of HIV test results, as well as the uncertainty regarding the management of this information.

> At the time – this was the early nineties – our reservations about asking gay men we knew [to be donors] were that we knew we would want them to have an HIV test. We also didn't think it was fair to ask a gay man to have an HIV test, considering what could happen to the information after the test results. We didn't know then – well, we still don't know, but we didn't know then what kind of privacy he would have. And so we thought if a gay man came forward and he already knew he was HIV negative, or he was interested in that information for himself and it wasn't linked to getting us pregnant, then we would use that as well. But we couldn't find any gay men who were willing or who were in that situation. And we just didn't think it was fair to ask anybody to go at that time and get tested.

The uncertainty about possible treatment options available for individuals who tested HIV positive, and the potential ramifications of a 'positive' result for those individuals' lives – for example, loss of job, housing, and health care – raised significant political and ethical questions regarding HIV testing during the 1980s and early 1990s. Emphasis was placed on the need for anonymous testing that would enable individuals to get tested and avoid potential breaches of confidentiality or discrimination.[5]

Self-insemination networks had emerged in the 1970s as a means to support those lesbians and single heterosexual women choosing to have children by donor insemination, by enabling women to attempt to conceive *outside of a medical framework*. HIV/AIDS and changing perceptions of risk influenced the choices that women in my study made and their reproductive experiences. The notion of risk, however, was not limited to the possibility of HIV transmission between the donor and the woman trying to conceive. Rather, concepts of risk extended to the social implications of HIV testing, privacy of information, and the receipt of results in a climate of inaccessible or unavailable treatment. The onset of HIV/AIDS does not *explain* queer women's use of spermbank donors, their use of physician-assisted or clinic-based donor insemination, or the perceived less frequent use of gay men as donors. The women I interviewed accessed medically assisted insemination prior to an awareness of AIDS. They had chosen known (and gay) donors and performed self-inseminations since the days of early awareness of AIDS and later knowledge of HIV. Awareness of AIDS, and later HIV and methods of HIV transmission, however, meant that some contact with the health care system would likely be necessary as women and men sought knowledge about the potential donor's HIV status.[6] Women wanted donors to have what was first referred to as an 'AIDS test,' and later, as an 'HIV test.'[7] The narratives of women in this study paint a complex relationship between HIV/AIDS, sperm donors, and various methods of conception.

Inseminations and Safe Sex

The AIDS epidemic holds a particular place in the development of agendas for lesbian health (Terry 1999; Winnow 1992). In *How to Have Theory in an Epidemic* (1999), Paula Treichler argues, 'The AIDS epidemic is simultaneously an epidemic of a transmissible lethal disease and an epidemic of meanings or signification' (11). She lists numerous characterizations of AIDS and then writes: 'Such diverse conceptualizations of AIDS are coupled with fragmentary interpretations of its specific elements ... Many believe that lesbians – a population relatively free of sexually transmitted diseases in general – are as likely to be infected as gay men' (13). On the other hand, 'researchers appeared to believe that sex between two women was so gentle and nonejaculatory it really wasn't sex at all, certainly it seemed much too wholesome to transmit so lethal a virus as HIV' (66). Women who have sex with women (WSW), whether or not they self-identified as lesbian or bisexual, did not constitute a 'surveillance category,' and 'little thought was given to the educational or social needs of women whose main sexual contacts were with other women' (66).[8] As Jennifer Terry writes, 'lesbian sisterhood had been powerful in the 1970s, but in many ways it was to be explicitly sexual in the 1980s and 1990s' (1999, 331). It became necessary to talk about the sexual and behavioural practices of women who have sex with women, in contrast to earlier lesbian health discourse premised on women's sexual identifications. Hence, safer-sex literature and health-promotion material were modified to address women who have sex with women, in order to work around (and in some ways to counter) the predominant notions of lesbian identity that had assumed, sometimes wrongly, that lesbians do not have sex with men, that they do not exchange bodily fluids, and that they do not engage in intravenous drug use. Making visible such assumptions that lesbians, by virtue of their identity, were not at risk from HIV was done in a fashion that could communicate with individuals who might be at risk from HIV infection but would not understand or primarily identify themselves as lesbians (Terry 1999, 332).

Although HIV/AIDS is viewed as a significant factor shaping the lesbian baby boom, health promotion and safer-sex campaigns targeted at women who have sex with women seldom mention donor insemination.[9] In general, the discussion of HIV transmission by donor insemination was restricted to the realm of policy and decision making with respect to clinical practices of donor insemination. These discussions centred for the most part on the implementation of screening practices and guidelines prohibiting men who were deemed as high risk from becoming donors (that is, those men who had had sex with a man).[10] According to the Institute of Medicine publication *Lesbian Health: Current Assessment and Directions for the Future*, 'HIV-related research on WSW, regardless of sexual orientation, has been scarce yet notable for its unexpected findings,' including 'risk for HIV infection of unknown magnitude owing to unprotected sex with women *and artificial insemination with unscreened semen*' (Solarz 1999, 76; italics added). Statements such as this, connecting lesbians, HIV, and insemination or reproduction are seldom made in broader discourses of lesbian health. The link that is consistently made between lesbians, HIV, and reproduction, however, is the need for access to *screened* semen, which is most often conflated with the need to provide lesbians with access to clinic-based donor insemination or sperm banks. Public health information about reproductive health assumes a heterosexual readership and does not identify nor address lesbian health issues. Within public health discourse, donor insemination is a medical practice that takes place under medical supervision. There were, however, a few notable exceptions that I encountered during the course of my research. For example, at the Dyke March in Toronto, June 1997, the AIDS Committee of Toronto launched a new brochure with information on lesbians and HIV. The pamphlet identifies a number of low and higher risk sexual practices. One of the centre panels contains a section on 'Getting Pregnant,' with the text: 'Many of us are choosing to have children. Whether you choose to self-inseminate with sperm from a donor or by having sex with a man, it's a good idea for you and your donor to be tested for HIV before inseminating.

Most babies of HIV-positive women are HIV-negative. If you are HIV positive it may be helpful to speak with a counsellor about pregnancy.' A year later, while leafing through files at AIDS Vancouver, I came across a safer-sex brochure from Australia that also identified insemination as a potential mode of HIV transmission. During the late 1990s, a number of workshops and outreach publications devoted to promoting discussions of LGBTI[11] health concerns emerged, rendering sexual-minority health experiences and needs more visible within a broader context.[12]

Which Knowledge Counts?

Before I met Meg, another woman I interviewed had described her as a woman who had conceived a child by 'AI [artificial or alternative insemination] years ago.' I never found out whether or not the woman who introduced us knew Meg's conception story; however, she framed it within the normalized discourse of alternative insemination. The phrase *AI* is often used as a shorthand for a number of the methods of conception used by women who become pregnant in the context of a relationship with a woman, regardless of the ·actual technique of insemination employed. Such usage differentiates these lesbian moms from queer women who had children while they identified, or were identified, as straight. Although most interviews lasted at least a couple of hours, Meg anticipated having only about twenty minutes available.[13] Hence, in response to my question, 'How did you go about trying to get pregnant?' Meg provided a condensed version of her experience: 'My partner and I were together for about two years, and we decided we wanted a family. And this sounds really funny – we had a list of five potential donors [she laughs]. Let's just put it that way. They had to qualify in health – no mental illness, no major illnesses like heart disease or TB or stuff like that. I just kind of out and out asked these guys these questions. And one qualified, and I just slept with him. Well, not just; it took a little while. But I slept with him and got pregnant.'

Meg laughed at her use of the word *donor* to refer to the man she and her then partner chose to be their child's 'father.' When *I* then used the term *donor* to refer to the man she had sex with in order to get pregnant, Meg interjected with, 'I can't say *donor*. I came out when I was eighteen and I had dated him a couple of times prior to that. So there was a window of opportunity there.' The first few minutes of the interview with Meg drew attention to the numerous ways in which queer women who inseminate at home and in clinics, as well as women who choose to sleep with men to get pregnant, use similar language to talk about screening donors and inseminating.[14] Both language and practice are adapted to match women's experiences with their perspectives on genetics and health and their beliefs about conception. Like other women who chose known or anonymous donors, Meg and her then partner developed a shortlist of candidates. Rather than asking them to fill out a questionnaire, like Nadine and Maureen did (see chapter 7), Meg simply casually inquired about the potential donor's family history. She explained: 'That was the way to do it. It's kind of easy to get pregnant, actually. But then, again, it's different nowadays. I didn't use any type of protection because I wanted to get pregnant. But again, *knowing* [italics added] that this person didn't have AIDS or venereal disease or stuff like that ... And that's really easy to talk to men about. Like, "I'm not going to sleep with you if you have something." It's easy enough to say that.' The man who qualified to be the donor was someone Meg had dated a few times before coming out, and, as she put it, 'there was a window of opportunity there.'

> I think it was just a bit of a head-trip for him, me wanting to sleep with him and me being in a relationship. It was like some kind of a fantasy or something. I'm not sure, I'm really not sure. I did ask him at one point, when I was going out with him when I was younger, if I happened to get pregnant what would he do? And he said, 'Well, I'd make sure you'd lose it.' But again, he had all the potential: good health, good mind, good body, strong person, strong personality. So I didn't care about that part because I knew that he wouldn't be let back in the door. And men are easy, anyways. I hate to say that, but they are, and not responsible either.

There was no question in Meg's mind about how she and her then partner would have a child.[15] They screened potential donors for histories of various physical and mental health attributes and, choosing a man who met their criteria, set about trying to get pregnant. There was never any decision to be made between sleeping with a man and using a 'turkey baster.' Meg never considered getting a sample. As she explained:

It was my own attitude. I didn't want to tell my child, 'Your father's a turkey baster.' I didn't even consider that. None whatsoever. [It was] all natural, 100 per cent natural. I have no bones about sleeping with guys, I really don't. I don't have any major hang-ups and that. It's just my preference is women. That's it, basically. So, in terms of – there was no pain; there was no pleasure either [she laughs]. Oh geez, I just remember relaxing and just saying, 'I have to relax, and if I want this to happen, to get pregnant, then I'm just going to learn to relax.' And he left immediately, which was fine with me. And I lay there for a little while and I tried really hard not to go to the bathroom and just little things like that, you know. Apparently the semen stays in your body for two to three hours or something, up to twenty-four hours, I've heard, but I was trying to get pregnant so I was doing things to enhance that.

Although I had explicitly included 'sex with a man' as a means of assisted conception in the poster used to advertise this study and to request participants, Meg was the only woman I interviewed who set out to have sex with a man in order to get pregnant, although other women considered it, and others conceived by having sex with a man.[16] Living in a small community, Meg had access to the donor's family health and sexual history *and* did not perceive there to be a risk with respect to potential custody issues.[17] Meg gave birth in the mid-1980s. The condensed version of her conception story foregrounds the issue of screening donors, yet, perhaps significantly, does not mention AIDS or HIV. Later in the interview Meg commented, 'It's different nowadays.' Meg's narrative of how she got pregnant draws attention to safe-sex discourses. What seemed to stand out in her mind was that she had unprotected sex with the donor. This was justified, though, *because* she was trying to get pregnant. She further explained her decision to have unprotected sex with him by emphasizing her knowledge of his history: 'But again, *knowing* that this person didn't have AIDS or venereal disease or stuff like that.' Meg's reflections reiterate her confidence in her ability to know the donor's health status and, thus, effectively screen him as a potential donor. Her story also points to the significance that other health considerations played in the choice of donor (see chapter 12).

Haimes and Weiner cite Macaulay et al. (1995) who 'suggest that scarcity of donors creates in SI [self-insemination] recipients a sense of indebtedness and an unwillingness to try to "set the terms" by demanding HIV tests' (2000). Haimes and Weiner note that in their study other health concerns were mentioned, but discussions about the health risks that lesbians considered 'tended to focus on HIV testing,' and women who used known donors had 'mixed experiences' (2000). In my study, HIV status and the risk of transmission were identified by women who chose to use sperm-bank donors, as some of the reasons for doing so. However, conversations and concerns about HIV testing expressed by the women I interviewed who had inseminated with semen from known donors were minimal. Most of the women who asked a man to be a donor, or were approached by men who wanted to be donors, relied on their knowledge of the donor's sexual behaviour and on their perceived accuracy of HIV tests and screening for other sexually transmitted infections. Women and donors, including those outside of the clinical context of donor insemination, accessed the health care system, sometimes separately and sometimes together. In a number of situations, potential donors had a complete physical, including HIV tests and STI screening, prior to agreeing to be a donor. Liz noted that although the man they had asked to be their donor took three months to respond (originally with a 'no'), he 'went to the doctor that very week and had all these tests.' The donor had also had an HIV test the previous year and since then had been in a monogamous relationship. Once he decided to become the donor, his partner was also tested for HIV and 'all this other stuff.' In contrast to stigma, concerns about confidentiality, and risks attached to HIV and STI testing, the STI screening and HIV testing prior to attempting conception was routine practice by the mid-1990s for many men (and women) in my study. The women interviewed did not feel they were taking risks but did note that they might have been more cautious if the donor had been someone else. Jenna speculated:

> The other thing about that was we knew that six months didn't elapse between the time that he got tested for HIV and when we actually used the sperm. So we had a conversation with him about that, because obviously you can't get an HIV test and know that you're negative and – like, you know how that whole thing works. And we just had a really frank conversation with him about it. Plus, he was married to a friend of mine, you know, who I know. She talks to me about her life and about their sex life and stuff like that. I knew that before they had gotten married, which was a year and a half before that or something, they had both been tested and were negative. There was enough trust between us that I was confi-

dent that when she told me, and also that when he told me separate from
her, that he hadn't had sex with anyone else, that a negative test at that
time meant that he was negative. I wouldn't do that with some other
potential donors though. I think I really would have had a test and then
a wait and then another test. But, you know, we just felt that it was okay
given the level of trust between us.

The current HIV assay tests for antibodies that indicate exposure to
HIV. Antibodies are believed to show up in the blood within twelve to
fourteen weeks of exposure in most cases, but public health brochures
state that it can take up to six months for antibodies to register. Jenna's
donor had an HIV test, but she states, 'Because obviously you can't get
an HIV test and know that you're negative,' she needed to talk to him
about his sexual practices. The concept of the window period is based
on the idea that one HIV test result can be negative, but the individual
may have been exposed to HIV within the six months prior to the test.
Thus, it is recommended that donors (men with whose semen women
inseminate or men with whom women sleep) have an HIV test, prac-
tise safe sex for six months, and then take a second test. Sperm banks
freeze and quarantine the semen provided at the time of the first test
and then release the semen six months later upon a second negative
test result.

Just as central to narratives about choosing donors and methods of
conception were examples of situations in which women did not know
the potential donor, or discovered new information about a man they
thought they knew. Bryn had a known-donor arrangement with her
neighbour. She stated: 'We were desperate for someone to donate, and
[the donor] actually had all the stuff I was looking for – I don't know,
I guess for phenotypic features. So, yeah, I did that weird thing. I
thought, it probably would work. My kid may have curly hair and
green eyes because he did. He was shorter than me, but I didn't mind
that too much because the tall genes are very strong in my family. But
I also wanted someone that I knew a little bit of their background.'
Unlike a number of women in this study, neither the donor and his
partner, nor Bryn and her partner, saw a physician or did STI or HIV
tests prior to beginning inseminations. Yet, they did discuss sexual
practices, substance use, and family history:

It was based truly on verbal – it was verbal. And because we had known
each other for a year, and they lived upstairs and we lived downstairs, we

figured that there was enough trust. And because we hung out almost every day, we figured there was enough trust that, you know … And for me, I wasn't sleeping around. My ex is my third partner, and so I figured for me, I know I was safe. And I knew that my ex was clean, too. And I had gotten tested in the past, for AIDS or, you know, hepatitis, or whatever. And I was completely clean … But I never asked [the donor] to get tested, or [his female partner]. But we did talk about it a lot, and they had said to us that they had gotten checked. But there was no papers to prove anything like that. So, it was really terrible.

After trying to get pregnant for nearly a year, Bryn noticed that she had a lot of vaginal discharge. At first she thought that perhaps her body was 'rejecting the sperm because we didn't make love to prepare my body for something entering it.' After a month of discharging so heavily that she needed to change her pads constantly, Bryn went to see a doctor and discovered that she had contracted an STI. Around the same time she found out that the donor was working as a 'male prostitute.' 'So I got treated for whatever it was, and I got a whole bunch of other tests to make sure that I didn't get any permanent diseases. But we didn't know about that side of his life; he kept it very private. And I also wanted someone that didn't drink, didn't do any drugs, no pot, no nothing. They had to be really clean. And [the donor and his partner] appeared to be like that. But then we found out that they lied.'

Bryn's story could potentially be used as evidence that self-insemination with untested anonymous-donor sperm is a risky and dangerous practice. Instead, I would point out the different ways in which women and donors can and do negotiate safer inseminations quite regularly and routinely. Known-donor semen is not always, and in my study seldom was, 'untested.' Most women I interviewed, and donors, accessed the health care system and used sexual and reproductive health services. Then they inseminated at home with tested *known donors*[18] rather than tested anonymous semen. However, in order for all women and donors to have access to information about the possibility of testing known donors, it is necessary to place self-insemination (including sexual intercourse), with semen from known donors, within the frame of reproductive health care and services. Denying lesbians access to fertility clinics does not force them to subject themselves to health risks; however, reducing lesbians' reproductive health care to a discourse of access to tested anonymous donors does.[19]

Clinical Inseminations and Risk Reduction

The increasing number of lesbians seeking access to medically assisted insemination is, as noted above, often linked to HIV and the ability of clinics to provide women with access to clean sperm. Clinic-based donor insemination is often conflated with safety, yet clinical practices over the decades have varied considerably. AIDS was first recognized as a disease that afflicted gay men and seemed to be sexually transmitted. AIDS was not connected to the clinical practice of donor insemination for quite some time.[20]

In 1982 Dawn decided to travel across the border to a women's clinic in Seattle, Washington State, which she knew was doing inseminations for 'women without husbands.' She told me that the health practitioners in Seattle were already using frozen semen, in contrast to the local Vancouver doctor who was inseminating women with fresh semen.[21] Dawn explained that this meant she 'didn't have to worry about the whole AIDS virus and a lot of viruses. And they screened [the donors], and most of the people were medical students – but that doesn't mean that they wouldn't have some kind of disease. They had a screening … And, as far as I know, they never had any problems because of the frozen sperm. It tends to knock out a number of the viruses.' Interestingly, Dawn identified the process of freezing the semen – not the testing of donors nor the quarantining of semen – as being related to the reduced risk of viral infection from insemination. Her narrative also pointed to the associations that are presumed between health and an individual's status; Dawn herself noted the mental association that she had made between a donor's socio-economic or educational background and his 'risk' status. Historically, many sperm donors who were associated with local physicians' clinics and sperm banks were medical students. Socio-economic status, education, and professional occupation were typically part of the 'screening process,' although, as Dawn pointed out, 'that doesn't mean that they wouldn't have some kind of disease.' This aspect of the screening practice, however, does appeal to many peoples' images of a healthy donor because indicators of health are often taken to be correlated with other lifestyle factors. When I asked Dawn about her experience at the clinic, she recalled:

> The only kind of weird comment was, 'Why didn't I go out –' and that was amazing to me, that the doctor asked me. The doctor asked me why

I didn't go out and pick up somebody in a bar. And I looked at her like she was out of her mind. I said, 'First of all, you never know who you're going to meet … I'm not looking for Mister Goodbar, thank you very much. And then, two, you never know what disease you might get.' I mean, in this day and age a doctor saying that was a little bit off to me.

Note here that there is a temporal blurring taking place concerning the onset of concerns regarding STI (including HIV) transmission as well as the prominence of any one form of infection. Rae's partner and Dawn would have been trying to conceive around the same time, with Rae situating the period as pre-HIV and Dawn being shocked that the doctor would not have considered the risks that would be undertaken by having sexual intercourse with a stranger.

In 1999, Erin, who was in the process of thinking through the possibilities of pregnancy, told me that she had had a few disagreements with friends about how she should try to get pregnant. 'My straight friends are like, "Oh geez, it's not like you've never slept with guys."… Because before I realized where I wanted to be, I was supposed to be married. I had slept with men, and what would it mean for one more time?'

The suggestion of 'picking a guy up at a bar' or sleeping with a man 'one more time' held different meaning for women in this study. Erin felt that sleeping with a man to get pregnant would introduce into her life a set of risks that she was not prepared to deal with:

Nowadays you've got to think about more than that. It's not that healthy out there. I'd be worried about what I'd be conceiving and the fact that you have this male figure that would be coming back ten months down the road saying, 'That's my kid, too, and I want rights.' So, yeah, that would be the easiest way to go, definitely the least expensive way to go about it. So, yeah, I have thought about that, but just no. There are too many things to consider. You have to go through all this testing, and even then some of the results, or symptoms, don't show up for five years. I don't have five years to wait. So that's probably not the way I would go.

Contrary to the speculative narrative that lesbians could have a one-night stand with a man, preferably a stranger, get pregnant, and live happily ever after, many women do not conceive following the first insemination, whether with fresh or frozen semen, or with intracervical or intrauterine insemination, and few are willing to take chances on strangers. Furthermore, in the context of these proposals, talk about the risk of HIV transmission and other STIs is non-existent[22] or rests on the 'just once isn't risky' rule, a rule that has resulted in many unplanned pregnancies and, for many, the contraction of an STI. Most of the time, people who suggest that women just pick up a stranger seem to forget that the timing of the sex would need to coincide with ovulation and that often one such encounter is not enough. Most of the women I interviewed who thought about having sex with a man to conceive did not consider that picking up a stranger was a viable option, noting the potential lifelong repercussions for women and their children in terms of both health and custody issues.

A discourse of HIV/AIDS risk governs and normalizes the practices of clinically managed donor insemination, and constructs donor insemination outside of this context as risky and dangerous (see Haimes and Weiner 2000). The women who sleep with men and the women who use fresh semen from known or anonymous donors (at home or in a clinic) undertake the same risks in terms of HIV and other STI transmission, and consciously assess these risks. As well, so-called risks are not non-existent in relation to semen accessed via sperm banks (see Luce 2009). However, women who sleep with men view themselves as taking on the additional risk of the man's involvement in the child's life, and it is this risk that many women perceive to be alleviated with the use of medically assisted reproductive services.

This chapter has addressed the ways in which screening donors in terms of the health risks associated with the transmission of infectious diseases often reflects an orientation toward the past, which is then incorporated as knowledge of the present. While reflecting on their experiences, women often noted the period in which they conceived, the duration for which they had known a donor, and the level of trust between the donor and themselves, which often had been established over time. In the next chapter, I focus on another dimension of screening donors which has become increasingly prevalent and is captured in Erin's comment, 'I'd be worried about what I'd be conceiving.' Significantly, the 'era of AIDS' (Weston 1991) is also the same era in which a growing 'fathers' rights' movement sought equal recognition of paternal claims to children (most often grounded in a genetic definition of fatherhood), and an emergent emphasis was placed on genes as the blueprint of life. Screening donors was not only articulated in terms of assessing the risk of contracting HIV or sexually transmitted infections. Women in this study negotiated the risks of HIV transmission alongside a host of other perceived risks such as family histories of mental health issues, alcohol and drug use, heart disease, tuberculosis, and a host of potentially hereditary physical and behavioural traits. In this sense, screening donors was also based on an orientation toward the future.

12 Screening Futures

Preconceptions

Observing the proliferation and appeal of guidebooks on pregnancy, Lisa Mitchell writes: 'The guides are aimed at heterosexual, married, middle-class, ideal-weight, able-bodied women, and the authors presume that their readers have both the time and money to eat right, reduce stress and learn how to be pregnant "properly." The "Every Woman" of these books is actively and effectively engaged in lessening the demands of work, supervised prenatal care, and otherwise arranging her life to ensure the right conditions for her pregnancy' (2001, 88-9). Mitchell notes that women who fall outside of the normative parameters represented in these books 'require special treatment: a separate chapter, or a special group (e.g., AA), or more medical care' (2001, 89). The guidebooks Mitchell refers to are marketed to already pregnant women who, reading the books, 'learn that many of the dangers in pregnancy are located in the bodies, histories and activities of pregnant women ... Choices made long before pregnancy, activities engaged in before pregnancy was suspected, and behaviours during pregnancy may all pose a risk to the foetus. Yet, promise the books, women can reduce these risks' (2001, 91).

Women who are *intending* to get pregnant are expected to be aware of these preconception risks and to begin monitoring their body for months, and even years, prior to attempting to conceive (Luce 1997; Mitchell 1993, 2001).[1] In *The Ultimate Guide to Pregnancy for Lesbians*, one of the current available pregnancy guides for women who do not fit the heterosexual norm, Rachel Pepper states:

Women of all different body types, weights, and physical abilities can conceive, give birth, and become good mothers. But because pregnancy is often physically and emotionally draining, it pays to be in the best shape you can be before you begin to inseminate. Eating well, drinking lots of water, quitting smoking, cutting back on caffeine and alcohol, and exercising regularly are all good preparation for pregnancy. You should talk to your doctor about any prescription medicines you are taking and decide whether you might be able to go off them for the duration of your pregnancy. Self-care is very important during both the conception process and pregnancy. The better you take care of yourself, the better your odds of enjoying your pregnancy and delivering a healthy baby. (1999, 6–7)

Again, although it is possible for 'women of all different body types, weights, and physical abilities [to] conceive, give birth, and become good mothers,' it is also possible to better the odds of having an enjoyable pregnancy and a healthy baby.[2] Following Pepper, conception, an enjoyable pregnancy, and a healthy baby are all results of a woman's ability to control and manage the 'maternal environment' (cf. Mitchell 2001) pre- and post-conception. Surveillance and self-monitoring of women's bodies does not begin at conception but, rather, is extended to women who might be or become pregnant. In Anne Balsamo's words, 'as a *potentially* "maternal body" even when not pregnant, the female body is also evaluated in terms of its physiological and moral status as a potential container for the embryo or fetus' (1996, italics in original).

Most of the women I interviewed who were planning to get pregnant began paying attention to their body, monitoring their menstrual cycle, and assessing their fertility odds long before they tried to conceive. The medicalization of pre-conception practices, as well as pregnancy, and the geneticization of health (Finkler 2000) led ever more frequently to an emphasis on the risks already present prior to pregnancy. However, as Margaret Lock and Patricia Kaufert suggest, 'attitudes towards medicalization can be positive, negative, or ambivalent, and in any case are not stable. The response of women to medicalization is often mixed. They rarely react to the specific technology, or simply to the manipulation of their bodies, but rather on the basis of their perceptions as to how medical surveillance and interventions might enhance or worsen their daily lives' (1998, 17).

In contrast to other studies in which women discounted the impact of the genetic father on fetal health status (Daniels 1997; Mitchell 2001), women I interviewed asserted that choosing a donor or genetic father offered an opportunity to assert some control over the health of the fetus and of the child to be.[3] Women assessed the risks to the fetus that they presumed to be contained within their own genetic history and that would potentially be passed on. Then a number of women sought donors whose genetic background was perceived to either complement or counter their own. Thus, women examined their own genetic health histories (if they were available),[4] and all donors, whether ordered by number from a sperm-bank catalogue, contacted anonymously through an intermediary, or known to the woman or couple, were screened. This practice of screening, articulated very clearly by the women I interviewed, challenges the frequent assertion in medical journals that women engaging in donor insemination with semen from known donors are at risk due to their use of 'unscreened' semen. It is the meaning attributed to the technologies of screening used (social and/or technical, informal or structured) that differ, as well as the interpretations of the information acquired, but not the concept of screening itself.

Scholars have highlighted the growing list of supposedly genetically determined (or influenced) diseases and behaviours (Hartouni 1997; van Dijck 1995).[5] José van Dijck states:

Part of genetics' appeal is its promise to cure congenital disease, or even eliminate disease from the roots of human reproduction. Since the 1950s, we can notice a clear shift in the public perception of genetics, from an obscure scientific paradigm (genetic engineering) into a preferred solution to a pressing medical problem (genetic therapy). The cause of ever more diseases is purportedly fixed in the genes. This attribution of genetic causes is not restricted to so-called single-gene disorders, such as cystic fibrosis and Tay Sachs disease, but seems to have been extended to a number of multi-factor diseases, and even to behaviour deviances. Naturally, the idea of genetics as a remedy for congenital diseases raises different concerns from the prospect of genetics as a remedy for behavioural deviance. Yet through media and other public channels, we are confronted, in one and the same breath, with genes for single-gene diseases, breast cancer, alcoholism, violence or manic depression. (1995, 7)

On the one hand, the women I interviewed often contested the determination of parental status by genetic relatedness. Women in a relationship with a woman often conferred parental status on a non-genetic mother, and 'uncle' status on a genetic father. Some women were comfortable with relationship constellations in which a woman's brother was both uncle and genetic father, or a woman's nephew was her child's genetic father and social dad. On the other hand, women choosing donors are immersed in a discourse of genetics that suggests the possibilities of tracing and mapping (or at least influencing) an individual's life and health potential prior to conception. One woman, whose potential donor took a long time deciding not to be a donor, joked that that was okay because she couldn't imagine having a child who was a procrastinator. In a more serious tone she explained that she wanted to be sure to choose a smart donor whose genes would counter the potential for a learning disability that she herself might transmit. Another woman with poor vision stated that she wanted a donor with good eyesight. What women 'knew' to be genetic and what women perceived to be related to genetics were seldom differentiated when they were talking about choosing sperm donors. Similar to the discussion above about screening for HIV and other STIs, 'knowing' the donor often supported women's decisions. Again, for women who chose to use sperm-bank donors, the information produced by clinic staff – even if produced in a fashion similar to that outside of a clinical context – was often perceived to be more reliable.

Genetic and Health Knowledge

Whereas women's narratives about choosing known or anonymous donors in accordance with the relationship that women envisioned for the donor and child are explored in part II of this book, known donors also represented an opportunity to access a tangible sense of the history of an individual. Women who chose known donors often (but not always) knew the men in various aspects of their lives. They knew their partners, their reactions to particular life events, and their family backgrounds. Having a first-hand sense of who the donor was figured largely in the narratives of women who chose not to use a sperm-bank donor. Rachel explained: 'I also wanted to know, like, health history and have more of a sense of who the person was, not just sperm I was using. That would be a huge impact potentially. Their genetic material has a huge impact on the child, and it was more important for me to know who that person would be than to not know. Because I know you can go through clinics and you can get information about who the donor was, but you never know who that person is.' Rachel uses a grammatical framing of the past and present in an interesting way here. In the present, she refers to her wanting to know the health history of the donor and to have a sense of who the person *was*. She again repeats her location of the donor to the past (who the donor *was*), making reference to the separation of information from the present *person* that the donor *is*. This tension between a donor rendered static, the sperm that could be used, and a person about whom one can develop an ongoing sense is one that is negotiated by women when they are making decisions about donors in relation to a number of factors. Recall that Hilary discussed the decision that she and her partner made against a donor who would have a photograph available, given that the photograph (representing his embodiment) might lesson the degree of his anonymity. She thought that choosing not to purchase a photograph that exists might make them feel that they had withheld potential information from their future child. In Rachel's case, it seems that the process of knowing a person or donor is ongoing, in contrast to information which can only be associated with, or represent, the donor at a particular point in time.

The distinction that Rachel made – between having *information* about a donor and *knowing* the person – was one that other women I interviewed made as well. For many, both interpreting information and knowing an individual involved an element of trust. Like Fiona and Melanie who chose to use a sperm-bank donor after meeting with a man or men who were interested in being known donors, some women placed more trust in the information and screening procedures provided by the sperm bank than in their ability to know a couple whom they had just met. Amy and Liz, whose friends had conceived using a sperm-bank donor, ordered a donor catalogue (donor profiles were not yet available online) and 'started going over the guys' as soon as it arrived. Liz commented: 'We had it down to a pick, too, and then the more we thought about it the more we thought, "This is just too weird." Because we had decided to pick a donor that looked like me, right? So, blonde hair, blue eyes, and athletic.' Instead, Amy and Liz asked a man who was an acquaintance through mutual friends to be the donor. They explained to him that he was their first choice because of 'his sense of humour.' Although neither of the women were close friends of his, they had known him and 'knew he was a good guy' through their relationships with mutual friends.

Clean Semen

Although the risks of STI and HIV transmission through the use of fresh semen are commonly raised by health practitioners as a reason not to use known donors, women who chose sperm-bank donors were also interested in reducing the risk to the general and genetic health of their future child. I interviewed a number of women for whom an experience of learning new information about a donor or a potential donor had provided the backdrop to their decision to pursue the use of a sperm-bank donor. In the story shared earlier about Bryn's experience of contracting a sexually transmitted infection (via insemination), the discovery about the donor's substance use figured just as significantly into her narrative as did the fact that he was a sex-trade worker. When she referred to wanting to inseminate with semen from someone who was 'clean,' HIV and STI status was inseparable from issues related to alcohol and drug use. Similarly, when Erin countered her friends' suggestion that she sleep with a man to get pregnant with the declaration, 'It's not that healthy out there. I'd be worried about what I'd be conceiving,' she was not only referring to sexually transmitted infections; she had recently found out through a friend that the man she had considered approaching about being a donor had been 'quite into hard drugs' a few years back. Erin declared:

> I'm very anti-drugs. He was into the heroin and cocaine and what have you. And so that really turned me right around. Okay, no, he's not who I want to approach. Because [my friend] says, 'That's still in his system, and there's been some damage there from the use of the drugs previously, even though he's not doing them anymore.' I said, 'Thank you. I didn't realize.' Because I think he probably would have agreed to it, and maybe without telling me what his past history was. I really appreciate that she let me know. I don't think any less of him; it's just not who I want to have in my child.

Here, Erin's conceptualization of the man whom she might have asked to be a sperm donor in no way renders him disembodied but rather frames his past in an embodied orientation toward the future. She states, 'It's just not who I want to *have in my child*,' leaving open the question of whether she believes that the 'damage' supposedly caused by the drug use or her aversion to drugs is behind her response, but vocalizing her belief on the potential impact of the substance use on a future child. The formation of this expression provides a vivid image of the role that any donor might play in the shaping of a future child: not only does the donor's sperm help to create the child, but also the donor is configured as literally present within the child. Both Rachel's and Erin's ways of discussing these ideas, while drawing on notions about heredity and genetics, establish a distance from a discourse that could be reduced to talk about cells or genes. It is the wholeness of the individual that would be contributed to the anticipated child. Further to her statement above, Erin explained: 'I'm not saying that anyone is perfect, and I don't expect a perfect child, but someone with a little bit more of a chance right from the start would be nice.' For most women, getting pregnant was not going to happen by chance but, rather, by choice. Since women were choosing, they wanted to choose wisely.

Women were not the only ones to engage in screening practices. Donors provided women with various reasons as to why they did not want to be donors, ranging from questions about their sense of responsibility for children who might be born, to respecting the concerns of their partner, to being HIV positive, to not wanting to contribute to the passing on of their genes. If you recall from chapter 7, Pam and Caroline asked a number of men to be donors. The last man whom Pam and Caroline approached immediately said yes. Yet, a few months later he 'screened' himself out of the donor pool. Caroline explained:

> He said that he had changed his mind, not for any reason other than the fact that he realized that, looking at his family, there were lots of drug and alcohol issues in his family – not for him personally but for his extended family – which, of course, we could never have known because his family is back east. And he just sort of said he thought that there was a possible genetic concern and, 'I don't feel that in good conscience I would feel very good about doing this type of thing' – which we actually really respected and we appreciated as well because we do think that there is something to that. Fortunately for Pam and I, that's not really at all a part of our lives or our families' lives. It's like an unknown for us. So that's something that we really wanted to know.

New Ways of Knowing

Women who inseminated with sperm-bank donors did not have access to much information until fairly recently. In some cases, physicians simply matched the inseminating woman's (or sometimes her partner's) physical characteristics with those of a donor. In other cases, women compiled an autobiographical profile, including interests and hobbies, and were given a shortlist of donors from which to choose. Most of the women I interviewed who used sperm-bank donors in the mid- to late 1990s had long detailed descriptions of their donor, complete with donor profile, essay, genetic and family history, and most recently, photographs and videotapes. Hilary stated that their donor's essay is what sold them on him: 'We just really lucked out. And this guy, fortunately, on top of [writing an essay], was very much fifty percent my personality and fifty percent Bridget's. He's an eternal optimist like me and is very grounded like Bridget. He's an academic like me and a jock like Bridget. [Professionally,] he has a very similar background to mine, and he's a coach, so he's very much an athlete like Bridget. And his values! He's a couple of years younger than me and has tremendous values.' Hilary explained that some of the donors did not include essays, which she took as a sign that they were in it 'just for the money.' She added:

> And then on top of [the similarities], the health statistics are phenomenal. Because you get the health statistics on everyone, right? – their parents, their sisters, their brothers, and their grandparents. Their education, their colouring, their health. You get to know not quite as much as you do on the donor but everything you want on the family. His grandparents were all living other than one. They were all in their mid-nineties – and one had died at eighty-nine and that one was a smoker. The other ones were all living in their mid-nineties. None of his family had any health problems. He had virtually perfect health. There was no issue with respect to – we don't have to concern ourselves with AIDS fortunately, because that screening is done for us.

Donors usually have a limited number of vials available at any given time. Having found the 'perfect' donor, Hilary and Bridget bought the nineteen vials of his semen that were in stock. It is interesting that Hilary described the donor as a blend of herself and her partner. In some ways, Hilary's description enables the possibility of the donor producing a child on his own that could appear to be the genetic outcome of the combination of herself and her partner. Perhaps by seeing both Bridget and herself in the donor, Hilary moved away from the more common narrative of reproducing herself through the donor's genes. Instead, Bridget is the one to get pregnant, but little is mentioned about her contribution to the social and genetic make-up of the child, other than via the commonalities between her and the donor, which are complemented by commonalities between Hilary and the donor. The donor is a reflection of them both, which, it is hoped, will be reproduced in the child.

Hilary commented on the impeccable health of the donor and the incredible health of his family. 'Phenomenal' health, or at least representations of it, seemed to be expected by some women not only of the donor but of his family as well. Denise, who first chose a known donor (someone she did not know well) and then chose a donor from a sperm bank, was incredulous about the discrepancy in the information about the donor as provided to her by the fertility clinic and the information which was included in his detailed and updated profile from the sperm bank.[6] She exclaimed, '[The] guy's no longer teaching, he's like working as something else, and he's gained thirty pounds. Plus, there was [a mention of] cancer that wasn't on the profile that [I saw] … It turned out [that his brother has] testicular cancer.' Denise was told that she could change to her second choice of donor for her next cycle, but would have to go ahead with her first choice if she chose to inseminate during the current cycle. When the time came for the following cycle, the semen from the donor of her second choice, a man with a 'stellar history,' was still in the required six-month quarantine. Her first choice, the one with the evident discrepancy in information, was still available. Telling her story, Denise was uncertain about the decision she would make. Her comments about the first donor's new job and the shift in his weight offer insight into the characteristics which had influenced her initial decision regarding this donor. However, while she was surprised at the difference in the information acquired via the fertility centre where she would be inseminated and that acquired via the sperm bank with which the donor was affiliated, the irritation can also be viewed in relation to aspects of temporality associated with semen donations and inseminations. Going back to Rachel's comments discussed earlier, in which reflections on a donor are framed in terms of not knowing who the donor was, it is possible to look further at how Denise addresses her discovery of other information about the donor, which leads her to want to change donors. She had chosen the donor on the basis of particular characteristics. Given that vials of semen can be cryopreserved, somewhat indefinitely, the semen with which she would have inseminated may have been donated at a time when the representation of the donor that she received (perhaps even the absence of information about his brother having testicular cancer) was true. However, it is also possible that she may have been inseminated with semen that was donated at a time when the updated details better reflected the donor's reality. The combination of factors about which Denise seemed astonished illustrates the difficulties embedded in reducing semen to biological substance.

Lesbian conception guidebooks stress that screening is never 100 per cent, regardless of whether or not it takes place in a clinical context. The authors of a new lesbian conception and pregnancy guidebook raise an interesting question by noting that many sperm-bank donors are in their early twenties and may not have encountered various health issues by that time (Toevs and Brill 2002). The image of a donor that emerges from the information included in his profile is somewhat static. It does not take into account his life history, nor life change, but rather inscribes his values, current athletic ability (and able-bodied state), entrepreneurial skills, educational status, mental health, and genetic health in his genes as if they will always be so. One of the questions I am left with in terms of Denise's story is whether it was perhaps the evidence of change, rather than the actual new state of being, that had a greater influence on her wish to inseminate with semen from another donor. An indication of change can work to contest the embodied figuration of 'the donor' by the recipient woman, rendering him also perhaps a person whose everyday life may contain occupational stress, illness, and fluctuations in physical characteristics.

No Longer Strangers

Medically assisted insemination is dominantly constructed as a safe method of assisted conception. Today, *representations* of clinical donor-screening practices suggest that they are more thorough and more accurate than what women and men could do on their own. Historically, women and fertility specialists engaged in similar practices of screening. The women I interviewed who chose to use semen from sperm banks (or from local physicians who had access to a donor pool), like the women discussed above, spoke about knowing or not knowing donors. Women clearly stated that inseminating with semen from strangers introduced a set of risks with which they were not prepared to deal. Contemporary practices of requesting donors to write essays on why they have chosen to be donors or of providing women with photographs and videotapes of donors further embody the donor. This enables recipient women to produce an image of an individual, even if that image is from a particular point in time. For many women, clinically generated information about donors minimized their status as strangers and seemingly reduced the perceived risks that inseminating with semen from strangers presented. Someone *knows* these donors.

The supposed cultural and medical significance of donor offspring's ability to access their genetic identity (that is, their genetic health history as opposed to the identity of an individual donor) was written into the legislation on assisted reproductive technologies which was put forward as I was completing the fieldwork for this book. When the Assisted Human Reproduction Act was proclaimed in March 2004, in spite of significant lobbying by children conceived with donor gametes, a donor registry was implemented which could only facilitate full release of the identity of the donor upon the *donor's* approval. However, genetic health information would be regularly maintained. Much greater emphasis had been placed by adult children of donors on their wish to know who the donor *was* and *is* (Skelton 2006). This next-generation discussion points to the complex imbrications of notions of genetics, contemporary ideas of health, and concepts of relatedness. The first children born as part of the donor identity-release programs from The Sperm Bank of California and Pacific Reproductive Services have now turned eighteen and may request the contact details of the donor (see Scheib et al. 2003). A donor sibling registry, initiated by Wendy Kramer and her son Ryan in 2000, manifests another route to relations, by which the mother and the son attempted to link the latter to genetic relatives, namely by matching individuals conceived using the same donor. The registry enables individuals to enter the information that they know about the donor, the sperm bank or the clinic with which the donor was affiliated, and their own birth details, in the hope that a sibling match or a donor match might be made.[7] Some of the individuals who have been active in the Canadian public media, namely Shelly Kreutz and Olivia Pratten, have also established a separate site for individuals born by anonymous-donor insemination in British Columbia as a result of treatment at the practice of Dr Gerald Korn and a few other physicians who had small donor pools (Skelton 2006).[8] In 2007 a man who had been a sperm donor and read about two young women who had found themselves to be genetically related through California Cryobank donor number

150 (his code) decided to enter the relationship (Harmon 2007). In Britain a teenage boy used genealogical software to trace 'his' donor (Von Radowitz 2005). An industry has emerged by which information about and images of donors are made available for purchase. This industry capitalizes on the meanings that information holds within current societies and the ways in which particular types of information and their communication have a certain currency.

This chapter explores the numerous and competing concepts of genetics which informed women's reflections about the heritability of disease, genetic predispositions, and the traits they perceived to be negative or positive. Women in this study weighed their assessment of their knowledge of their own family history (if it was available) against that of potential donors, sometimes becoming or being already self-consciously aware of their engagement in this process. Most of the discussions around genetics did not have to do with providing the child with genetic information but rather, as Erin commented, with the best chance in life that is possible. Information was associated with knowledge and knowing, but as illustrated by Denise's comments, knowing could be presumed to be of a static state, which in Rachel's perspective just was not enough. As new studies emerge, which address the meanings attributed to genetic relatedness, genetic information, and notions of knowing by children born following gamete donation, we can begin to look at the complexity of intergenerational perceptions and discussions of such concepts.

In the final chapter of this book I will examine the location of queer women in relation to assisted reproduction and developments in the area of reproductive science and medicine, now more than thirty years after the announcement of the world's first baby born following in vitro fertilization, an announcement that brought all forms of assisted-conception technologies into public view.

13 Reflections

> If they are going to engage in this pursuit of reproduction at any cost anyway, it might as well be with my eggs. (Pollock 1998)[1]

Since 2002 I have lived in two European countries – first England and now Germany – conducting research on projects which have addressed the use and development of more 'high-tech' technologies than those used by the majority of the women I had interviewed during the fieldwork for this project in Canada. When I returned to the stories that form *Beyond Expectation*, I did so with new knowledge and a growing interest in the constellations of governance that are very much part of the sense-making processes invoked within narratives of assisted-reproduction technologies and assisted conception. Over the course of my work on issues related to reproductive health and politics I have kept track of news bulletins about emerging research, novel techniques, and especially the representations of the 'queer' reproductive possibilities that they could enable. The quote above, for example, comes from a journal article written by a self-identifying lesbian egg donor which I came across in a bookstore in Australia. Although critical of the ways in which these representations are disseminated and taken up in public discourse, I had not extended my analysis to the politics of such *research* as it interrelates with new (or amended) assisted-reproduction legislation and queer women's involvement. The following pages address how queer women are situated in the whole of assisted reproduction with respect to clinical practice and research and the ever more explicit governance of both.

Parameters of Governance: Family Law and Medicine

To conclude an ethnography of assisted reproduction with a remark about the birth of Louise Brown, known as the world's first test-tube baby, who was born in 1978, may be clichéd. In fact, reference to her birth and the story of in vitro fertilization (not donor insemination) may still seem out of place. It is 'in place' for a few specific reasons. There was a significant history of research in embryology and repro-ductive science prior to 1978, which informed the in vitro fertilization experiments undergone by Leslie Brown in her attempts to conceive a child (Clarke 1998). However, it was the widely publicized *announce-ment* of Louise Brown's birth, and the quick pace of subsequent devel-opments, which compelled feminists, public representatives, and par-liamentarians in many countries to address the so-called challenges that new methods of conception presented to normative images of family and the presumed naturalness of procreation (see Franklin 1997; Haimes 1990; Cannell 1990; Stanworth 1987a). The description of a test-tube baby connotes the potential laboratory development of embryos, fetuses, and babies, akin to the image used on the cover of Susan Squier's book *Babies in Bottles* (1994). In vitro fertilization involves the extraction of an egg (or, more often, eggs) from a woman's uterus, fertilization outside of the body (either by sperm added to eggs in solution in a Petri dish or by micromanipulation and injection), incubation of the hopefully cleaving fertilized egg, and transfer of an embryo or embryos to the same or a different woman's uterus. The potential for fertilization to occur outside of the body (and with donor gametes – egg or sperm cells), and the hormonal stimulation of a woman's ovaries, often resulting in the retrieval of more than one egg and the establishment of more than one embryo per IVF cycle (which could then be donated), raised numerous concerns about the ways in which new reproductive technologies disrupted 'nature' and, within feminist circles, instrumentalized women, technologized reproduc-tion, and potentially reinforced imperatives to become a mother (see Corea 1985; Spallone 1989). The debates surrounding the introduction of IVF into medical practice extended to other assisted-reproduction practices, such as donor insemination and gamete intrafallopian-tube transfer (GIFT).[2] In 1987 Michelle Stanworth speculated that repro-ductive technologies received such widespread attention 'because they crystallize issues at the heart of contemporary controversies over sex-uality, parenthood, reproduction and the family' (1987a, 18). At a time when single motherhood was becoming not necessarily 'normal' but visible, and lesbian women were also visible mothers, the possibility for women to have children without having sexual intercourse with a man sparked further debate (Shore 1992; Cannell 1990).[3] In the United Kingdom, where in vitro fertilization was first practised, assisted-reproduction technologies both supported and contested the Thatcher-era political perspectives on family values (see Franklin 1997).

It was in the United Kingdom that the first English-language publications of studies and critiques of the new reproductive technologies emerged and that legislation regulating assisted reproduction and embryo research was implemented.[4] Franklin and Roberts state: 'Since 1990, the Act has been copied by countries all over the world and is widely seen as a unique, exemplary, and distinctively "British" achievement that continues to set the global "gold standard" for governance of the post-IVF reproductive "revolution," while reinforcing Britain's self-proclaimed role as the home of "the Mother of all Parliaments"' (2006, 40). The legislation implemented in the United Kingdom established a system of governance which facilitated the use of assisted-reproduction technologies but contained the degree to which their use would destabilize the normative status quo conceptualizations of both procreation and who should procreate. Not only does the HFE Act stipulate the permitted practices of assisted reproduction, but it is also the legislative authority which determines the status of relationships produced through the use of reproductive technologies. Thus, for example, the HFE Act put into place a system by which male partners, of women who gave birth to a child conceived with donor sperm, were named as 'father' on the birth certificate, a practice which on the basis of its premise, when subject to review, extended the right of dual female parentage in cases where donor insemination was used (Porter 2008). The Act also included from the outset section 13(5), which stated that in determining access to assisted-reproduction services, practitioners must consider the welfare of the child, 'including the need of that child for a father.' This clause supported the denial of fertility services to women in various situations and/or their coverage by the National Health Service.[5] The clause was only amended by guidance on its interpretation in 2006 and reworded by removing the word *father* in 2008.

As discussed throughout this book, the legal status of women and donors in relation to children was a question and/or concern for women at various stages of their experiences. I recall that during my fieldwork, text on the website of one fertility centre changed from a statement that a child conceived by assisted reproduction would be the legal child of the intending parents to read that the child would be the legal child of the mother. Now, ten years later, most resources concerning legal parental status following assisted conception in Canada still cite ambiguity with respect to the recognition of a sperm (or egg) donor as parent. For example, the Victoria Fertility Centre states: 'The federal law is that the only exchange of monies between the intended parents and egg donor can be for the expenses incurred during the process. Although there is no specific B.C. statute regarding ovum donation, *the understanding is* that the intended parents of the child will be recognized as the child's legal parents rather than the egg donor. The same applies for sperm donation.' In Ontario the Hamilton Health Sciences Centre for Reproductive Care[6] included a section on 'legal considerations of donor insemination,' which I reproduce here as a means of illustrating the complexity of the situation:

> At present, there are no laws in Ontario governing the status of the donors, parents and children. For legal issues, you may want to consult with your lawyer. *It is usual* for couples who conceive a child with DI to put both their names on the child's birth certificate. Custody cases in Ontario involving donor conceived children have resulted in the father who has raised the child being given the same consideration, as would a biological father. However, at present, there is no legislation to guarantee that the non-biological parent is the legal parent. There are no laws to clarify the rights or responsibilities of donors towards the children conceived with their anonymously donated sperm.

An additional two points under the heading 'Legal Considerations of Donor Insemination for Single or Same Sex Couples' are:

> A single woman, as the only guardian for her child, may wish to ensure that she has made provision for additional legal guardianship. The non-conceiving partner in a same-sex relationship may wish to consult a lawyer to determine her legal rights. She may wish to consider a private adoption of her partner's biological child or have her lawyer develop a parenting agreement.

The current emphasis, thus, continues to be on the norms which have shaped the use of medically assisted reproduction services by heterosexual couples. The recognition of lesbian parents in Canada, although supported by analogies drawn with opposite-sex couples using donor insemination, has not been facilitated through assisted-reproduction legislation but rather through developments and changes in the area of family law. The legal status of LGBT parents changed incrementally across Canada, with more broadly applicable (and visible) changes occurring in 2000 and then in 2005. Across Canada, while certainly not all aspects of legislation have been changed to facilitate the recognition of LGBT parents, the changes have been significant enough that provincial governments are perhaps clearer that it would be futile to challenge deficiencies that are pointed out.

A number of other areas deserving of attention relate specifically to the implications of assisted-reproduction practices and reproductive experiences under the new governing framework of the Assisted Human Reproduction Act. Until 29 March 2004, when 'an Act respecting assisted human reproduction and related research' (the AHR Act) received royal assent, the structure of assisted-reproduction governance in Canada had differed significantly, for example, from that which had been implemented in 1990 in the UK as described above. Assisted reproduction had been governed by individual practice, professional best-practice guidelines, a voluntary moratorium since 1995, and subsequent Health Canada regulations and directives aimed particularly at practices of so-called therapeutic donor insemination (see Luce 2009). The women I interviewed very clearly made reference to anticipated regulations and changes in assisted-reproduction policy. In most cases, reference was made to the possible ban on the payment of egg and sperm donors[7] and, by those who were trying to get pregnant in 1999 and 2000, to the prohibition of the release or importation of semen that did not comply with the conditions of a Health Canada quarantine and the updated Semen Regulations (2000).[8] Between 1993, when the Royal Commission on New Reproductive Technologies was completed, and 2004 when the AHR Act was proclaimed, a number of bills had been introduced in Parliament, accompanied or followed by papers outlining the desired scope of legislation. Each of these, however, had been shelved.[9] The final bill, C-6, banned a number of activities and put into place a means of regulating a number of others.

The social, health, and scientific contexts in which the AHR Act passed in Canada were significantly different to those in which the Royal Commission activities were carried out, as well as those in the mid-nineties when the guidelines for the voluntary moratorium were circulated. In 1993, recommendations were made to restrict in vitro fertilization services to situations in which a woman's fallopian tubes were blocked. Following the publication of the report, insurance coverage of in vitro fertilization in Ontario, for example, was limited to women experiencing this condition. Unlike as suggested by Murphy (see chapter 10), infertility treatment was not normatively based on a relational diagnosis. Even then, fifteen years following the birth of the first child born by IVF, there was a sense that its use should be restricted to particular indications. By placing an emphasis on what now may seem to be a very mechanical understanding of the function of in vitro fertilization – that is, to bypass the need for the egg to travel through the fallopian tube – the use of IVF in situations of male-factor infertility or suboptimum fertility was excluded from coverage. By 2004, IVF had become entrenched as a Canadian health service, available (at a cost) for a number of indications, including the 'treatment' of male infertility and suboptimal fertility by intracytoplasmic sperm injection (ICSI), and as a component of egg donation and surrogacy practices. Embryo-screening technologies had also become available in Canada. The first instance of preimplantation genetic diagnosis (PGD) – the screening of an embryo prior to its transfer to a woman's uterus and following in vitro fertilization (with or without ICSI) – took place in the early 1990s. A clinic in Montreal, Quebec, states on its website that it has been offering PGD services since 1998. A Health Canada information website notes that prior to the AHR Act PGD was not regulated in Canada and it is estimated that fewer than twenty children have been born following PGD.[10] This statement, however, does not provide an indication of the number of IVF cycles involving PGD that have been started.

The introduction on the Health Canada website dedicated to the Assisted Human Reproduction Act states that the goals of the act are three-fold: 'it prohibits human cloning and other unacceptable activities; it seeks to protect the health and safety of Canadians who use AHR procedures; and it ensures that AHR related research, which may help find treatments for infertility and diseases such as Parkinson's and Alzheimer's, takes place in a controlled environment.'[11] Working in the UK when the AHR Act was passed, I was surprised to hear the legislation being referred to as Canada's 'cloning bill.'[12] Yet, it seemed that the technological possibilities arising from the combination of somatic cell nuclear transfer and techniques for isolating, characterizing, and differentiating embryonic stem cells had rendered the possibility of human cloning plausible enough for its prohibition to be perceived as a central purpose of legislation.[13] In *Bodies in Glass*, Deborah Lynn Steinberg articulates clearly the relationship between assisted-reproduction practices and embryology research (1997a). Mariana Valverde and Lorna Weir (1997) also underlined the need to pay attention to the implications of embryological research for women, pointing to the gap in governance discourses at the time. That the prohibition of 'human cloning' is listed first in the itemization of the purposes of the AHR Act, alongside other 'unacceptable activities,' obscures the distinction that is subsequently made between *reproductive* and *research* cloning – the prohibition of the latter being subject to reconsideration in a few years' time. A key area of research taking place within the scope of the third listed purpose is human embryonic stem cell research. The AHR Act was passed in the spring of 2004, just a few months prior to the announcement of a license granted by the HFEA to the Newcastle Fertility Centre in the United Kingdom to carry out research involving somatic cell nuclear transfer (research cloning). Stem cell research involving somatic cell nuclear transfer or other 'cloning' techniques relates to the third area of activity mentioned within the purpose of the AHR Act, namely, the conduct of AHR-related research with respect to diseases such as Parkinson's and Alzheimer's. The AHR Act, so it has been reported, was meant to restrict embryonic stem cell research to that involving 'spare embryos,' which were unused in IVF treatment, and to prohibit the creation of new embryos for research purposes (Nisker and White 2005). Reports of the first derivation of a stem cell line by researchers at Mount Sinai hospital in Toronto demonstrated that so-called fresh embryos, those donated at the time of an IVF cycle, were used (Nisker and White 2005). As Nisker and White note, the assumption that spare embryos are those which are cryopreserved and then later 'donated' was only implicit in the legislation. These seemingly discursive distinctions may factor significantly in the health and reproductive experiences of women and men (Luce 2008). The embedding of research issues (and possibilities for research directions) within legislation governing what many might understand as a medical practice or set of health services highlights the entwinement of embryological research and fertility treatment.

The principles of the AHR Act clearly state that the denial of services on the basis of sexual orientation is not allowed. Legislated access – that is, visible statements of who can access assisted-reproduction services – may or may not influence the number of women who choose to try to become a parent within clinical settings. Legal recognition of parental status through non-biology-based routes may also shape the decisions of women. It is important to recall that queer women attempt to become pregnant or parents through a broad variety of methods and for different reasons, and they may also attribute different meanings to these assisted-conception experiences. While the contribution of an egg or eggs by one partner and gestation of a fetus by another may initially be due to the inability of one woman to carry a fetus to term or that of the other to conceive, this practice may turn out to facilitate parental recognition outside of the jurisdiction in which the child is born. Women who are undergoing in vitro fertilization may combine it with intracytoplasmic sperm injection, not because of male subfertility but in order to maximize the potential for an embryo in the face of limited semen available (perhaps there is only one vial left, and the women are hoping for a sibling). Women may conceive and then have embryos in storage, which they are asked to donate for research purposes. Women may undergo an egg-collection procedure, or a follicle reduction if too many follicles develop while they are taking ovulation medication, and be asked to donate the eggs for research or for the treatment of another woman. Women may have had previous experiences of losing a child or terminating a pregnancy due to a chromosomal anomaly and opt to pursue preimplantation genetic diagnosis. Just as women identifying as lesbian or queer cannot live outside of the law, the broader discourses and material practices associated with assisted-reproduction and genetic technologies have the potential to be a part of our lives regardless of how we might try to become parents or relate to children. This is not to say that science or medicine is the agent within these processes; rather, it is to call attention to the increasing linkages between the commercialization of reproductive tissue, embryo research, egg donation and surrogacy and thoughts about genes and heritability. Queer women may not end up in the imagined scenarios that are depicted with the announcement of novel technologies or extrapolations from new basic research. Yet, women may face any number of emerging questions associated with contemporary assisted reproduction.

Conclusion

Throughout this book, as a means of producing a larger narrative of women's experiences of assisted conception, I have disentangled the women's narratives to some degree in order to facilitate the retelling of queer women's stories through the particular lenses of social, legal, and medical discourses, expectations, and contestations. This exercise also, through the obvious overlaps in narratives and disruptions to experiences, reiterates the inseparability of the social, legal, and medical contexts in which the women I interviewed thought about becoming, or attempted to become, a parent. Throughout the initial research for this book I was fairly consistently in the position of having to justify my focus on the experiences of queer women and to challenge the statements commonly made about the non-issue of lesbian uses of assisted-reproduction (most often reduced to assisted-insemination) services. Through their narratives the women I interviewed both reproduced and challenged conceptualizations of a lesbian ontology: this notion of being lesbian, bisexual, transgender, or queer did not *define* their experiences. However, women who do not meet the (albeit shifting) normative image of a woman trying to become pregnant – women who are not partnered with a man, women who are partnered with a woman, and individuals who do not identify as either woman or man – are differently located with respect to children, health services, heterosexism, homophobia, transphobia, legal risks, and expectations. Significantly, in line with recommendations made in the *Final Report of the Royal Commission on New Reproductive Technologies*, the Canada Health Act, and the Canadian Charter of Rights and Freedoms, and with the status of same-sex rights legislation in Canada, written into the principles of the Assisted Human Reproduction Act is the statement that treatment is to be provided. Access to assisted-reproduction technologies by women identifying as lesbian (and hopefully bisexual, transgender, or queer) is a matter of legislation. Perhaps it is now time to re-emphasize the importance of analysing the politics of reproduction and queer reproductive politics beyond clinic access, beyond donor insemination, and beyond the narratives of becoming a mother.

Appendix A:
Timeline of Significant Events

Throughout *Beyond Expectation* there is mention of earlier and later periods within which women attempted to become or thought about becoming a parent. These correspond to shifts in the social, legal, and medical contexts, some of which are related to the developments below.

1980–5   Pacific Reproductive Services, The Sperm Bank of California, and California Cryobank are established

1985   The Warnock Report is published in the UK

1986   Dr Gerald Korn appears in a custody case between two women

1989   Royal Commission on New Reproductive Technologies is launched

1990   Human Fertilisation and Embryology Act (1990) comes into force

1991   Human Fertilisation and Embryology Authority is implemented

1993   *Final Report of the Royal Commission on New Reproductive Technologies* is published, recommending equal access to fertility services

1995   BC Human Rights Tribunal decision in the case *Potter v. Korn* [1995] 23 C.H.R.R. D/319. Lesbians cannot be denied access to fertility services

          Creative Beginnings Fertility Centre opens in Vancouver, British Columbia

          Voluntary moratorium on certain reproductive-technology practices (including the buying and selling of gametes) is announced

1996   Health Canada introduces Semen Regulations

          BC introduces the Adoption Act, making it possible that 'any person or any two persons may adopt'

1998   Bills 31 and 32 come into force, amending the Family Relations Act and conferring legal recognition on same-sex partners in the definition of *spouse*, thereby allocating to same-sex parents the rights and obligations of child support, custody, and access in the event of the dissolution of a relationship

1999   Health Canada implements quarantine on semen stored at facilities in Canada and prohibits the import of donor semen
The court finds the definition of *spouse* to the exclusion of same-sex partners unconstitutional in the decision of *M. v. H.* in Ontario, and orders the legislation to be revised

2000   Semen Regulations are revised and updated to include mandatory nucleic acid amplification (NAT) testing of donors (and stored semen) for Chlamydia. Health Canada's quarantine ends, and semen meeting the new guidelines can be released for use
The Modernization of Benefits and Obligations Act is proclaimed by the federal government, giving same-sex common-law partners in Canada the same rights and obligations as those of heterosexual common-law couples in the areas of legislation that confer rights or obligations through the category of 'spouse'

2001   BC Human Rights Tribunal determines that the BC Vital Statistics Agency had discriminated against same-gender partners by refusing the inclusion of two women's names together. BC same-sex couples win the right to have two women's names on the Registration of Live Birth form and on the birth certificate of a child

2003   Same-sex marriage becomes legal in British Columbia

2004   Assisted Human Reproduction Act is proclaimed, establishing the Assisted Human Reproduction Agency of Canada (or Assisted Human Reproduction Canada)

2005   Same-sex marriage is legalized across Canada after the introduction of Bill C-38, which becomes the Civil Marriage Act

2007   Ontario court awards legal status to three parents

Appendix B:
Biographies of Women Interviewed

The biographies below are ordered according to the approximate time at which the assisted-conception experiences of the woman began. They are also divided along the temporal lines which relate most closely to the significant social, medical, and legal changes which may have influenced their experiences. Not all women are mentioned by name in this book.

Pre-1985

Rae became a parent with her former partner in the early 1980s. They employed both physician-assisted insemination with anonymous-donor semen, and donor semen from two friends (a male couple) during their attempts to become pregnant.

Glynis and **Virginia** became the parents of two children adopted in the mid- to late 1990s, following twelve years of trying to become parents together.

Dawn has two children who were conceived during the early and mid-1980s after she accessed donor insemination services at a U.S. women's health clinic.

Fran tried to become pregnant during the mid-1980s with anonymous donor semen couriered by an intermediary and then physician-assisted insemination, at which she disclosed neither her sexual identity nor her relationship. She has been in a parenting relationship to children of different partners over the years.

Meg co-parents her teenage daughter with her ex-partner and both of their current partners.

Rita's partner, Celine, became pregnant in the early 1980s.

June is the mother of a fifteen-year-old who was conceived following known-donor insemination.

1985–95

Estelle has a child conceived by insemination with semen from a known donor and whom she continues to parent with a former partner. Estelle also has ongoing family relationships to children of other partners, who are now in their twenties.

Nadine (and her former partner, Maureen) co-parent two children. They had approached a physician about donor insemination services. Each gave birth to a child following insemination with semen from the same known donor.

Yvonne experienced a miscarriage after becoming pregnant following sex with a man in 1988. She then founded a support group for lesbians trying to become parents and tried to become pregnant in the early 1990s over the course of five physician- assisted inseminations with donor semen.

Hannah's former partner tried to become pregnant, employing various methods. They experienced a stillbirth late in pregnancy.

Talia tried to become pregnant during two separate phases – a year and a half with physician-assisted anonymous-donor insemination and one year of self-insemination with a known donor. She is a parent to her late partner's children, now in their twenties.

Paula and her partner initially sought a known donor, and then Paula tried to become pregnant with physician-assisted insemination. She and her partner at the time were founding members of a support group for lesbians trying to become parents.

Bryn tried to become pregnant with donor semen from a friend in the early 1990s. She is still considering becoming a mother.

Rachel tried to become pregnant by insemination with semen from a known donor over an eighteen-month period.

Cynthia is the mother of a child conceived with semen from a known donor.

Hazel is the co-parent of a toddler who was adopted after many years of Hazel's trying to become a parent. She and her partner also parent a child to whom her partner gave birth in a previous relationship.

Georgina has a child who was conceived during a relationship with a former female partner.

Astrid has two children, one conceived in a relationship with a previous male ex-partner and one conceived by clinical donor insemination while she was in a relationship with a woman. She and her former female partner have joint custody of their youngest daughter.

Marcia is the mother of a nine-year-old. She thought about becoming a parent through pregnancy for a long time before trying, made arrangements with a known donor, and then tried to become pregnant with semen from a different known donor for approximately one year. She became pregnant with donor semen shipped to Vancouver from a U.S. sperm bank.

Carol adopted a baby through a private arrangement, whom she has parented together with **Mona** since the child was an infant. Mona also has two other children in their early twenties.

1996–2000

Fern and **Mareika** adopted two children. The first adoption took place just prior to the implementation of the BC Adoption Act, and the second after the changes were in effect.

Jenna is the parent of a young child who was conceived following insemination with known-donor semen. Her partner has adopted their child.

Sonja has tried at different times in her life to become pregnant. She experienced a miscarriage after becoming pregnant, following self-insemination while she and a friend were trying to become parents. After not becoming pregnant again for over a year, she was inseminated with anonymous semen at a clinic.

Ena and **Laura** have two children, one who is adopted and one who was conceived following insemination with semen from a known donor.

Janine is the self-identified single mother of two children under two years old. She became pregnant with her first child following self-insemination, and with her second following physician-assisted insemination, both times with semen from a willing-to-be-known donor from a U.S. sperm bank.

Ellen and **Pia** have adopted two children.

Amy and **Liz** are the parents of a young child who was conceived following home insemination with semen from a known donor. Liz has adopted their child.

Chandra and **Marlene** have a young child together. Chandra experienced the death of a child conceived in another relationship.

Karyn and **Theo** have one child and recently experienced a late-trimester termination of pregnancy. They have both tried to become pregnant by combining willing-to-be-known donor semen with physician-assisted insemination and are planning a third pregnancy.

Hilary is the mother of a toddler to whom her partner, **Bridget**, gave birth. She had originally planned to co-parent with a close male friend who would have also been the donor, but after relocating to the west coast, she and Bridget decided to use the anonymous-donor services of a local fertility centre.

Nora and **Terry** parent a twelve-year-old. After receiving fertility treatment, Nora is in the process of letting go of the idea of trying to become pregnant. They also provide respite care for a young child.

Fiona and **Melanie** are the parents of a toddler. They had initially made arrangements with a known donor, then Fiona inseminated at home with semen from a U.S. sperm bank. After many cycles, Melanie tried to become pregnant, and they combined home inseminations with physician-assisted inseminations each cycle. Fiona later tried to become pregnant by in vitro fertilization.

Heather co-parents her young child with her friend Brian, who is also the donor. Her partner has teenage children, and she has a stepdaughter who is now in her twenties.

Kara is the mother of an infant whose father (Kara's ex-partner) is present as a parent in their child's life.

Jeanette and **Katharine** are the parents of a toddler.

Grace has been trying to become pregnant after making arrangements with a known donor and has recently decided to take a break. She is in a relationship with Morgan, who has one child.

Claudia is the parent of an infant conceived by her partner with a known donor. She has adopted her child.

Rose and **Kirsten** are the parents of a new baby.

Tracy and **Monique** have been foster parents to four children for two and a half years and are the new parents of a child conceived by donor insemination.

Caroline and **Pam** are expecting their first child. They first sought a known donor, then decided to combine a willing-to-be-known donor from a sperm bank and home insemination, and finally conceived, following an intra-uterine insemination with anonymous-donor semen at a fertility centre.

Theresa and **Nadia** are expecting their first child. After a very long process of trying to make arrangements with a known donor, Nadia conceived following insemination with semen from a friend. They have established a known-donor contract.

Eva and **Imogen** have two adopted children whom they parent together, and Eva is currently pregnant. The sperm donor is known and also is already a parent.

Alice is trying to become pregnant and shares in parenting her partner's young children. She has tried inseminations at a U.S. clinic and self-insemination with a known donor and is now seeking further fertility assessment.

Denise is currently trying to become pregnant by combining sperm-donor access from a fertility centre with physician-assisted insemination.

Olivia and **Roxy** are trying to become parents by known-donor insemination. Olivia recently experienced an ectopic pregnancy.
Paige is in the process of adopting a child.

2001–

Lilly and **Rowena** are presently looking into the possibility of combining the choice of a known donor with physician-assisted insemination. Lilly is adopted and believes that she would prefer a known donor.
Sara and **Kim** are actively planning to have children and have identified a potential known donor.
Beth and **Faye** are making plans to start trying to become pregnant.
Adele and **Vivian** are in parenting relationships to Vivian's children. Adele has thought about trying to become pregnant and has tried to gather some information.
Sybil and her partner, **Ann**, are considering various options with respect to becoming parents.
Erin is considering having children.
Erica plans to become a parent in the future.
Bess has recently begun a relationship with a woman who has children. She has never planned to have children.
Sam has considered having children in the context of different relationships, was previously married to a woman who had children, and is most recently considering fostering and adoption.
Jessica is considering becoming a parent in the future.
Wynne is considering becoming a parent in the future.
Robyn is considering becoming a parent in the future.

Overview

59 interviews were conducted with 82 women. At the time of the interview:
- 15 women were living in a northern region of British Columbia
- 17 women were living on Vancouver Island or affiliated west coast islands
- 17 women were living in the interior of British Columbia
- 33 women were living in Vancouver and the Lower Mainland

- 5 women were parents of or in parenting relationships to a grown child or children in their twenties
- 8 women were parenting a child or children between the ages of thirteen and eighteen

- 11 women were parenting a child or children between the ages of six and twelve
- 19 women were parenting a child or children between the ages of two and five
- 10 women were parenting a child or children under the age of two
- 6 women were experiencing pregnancy (3 women were pregnant)
- 10 women had stopped trying to become parents
- 5 women were trying to become parents (4 by pregnancy, 1 by adoption)
- 8 women were planning to become parents in the near future (within five years)
- 5 women were thinking about parenthood
- 3 women had considered the possibility of parenting
- 1 woman had never considered becoming a parent, and has most recently entered into a relationship with a woman who has children
- 11 women had had experiences with either domestic or international adoption (excluding second-parent adoptions).

Notes

Preface

1 *New reproductive technologies* was first most commonly used to distinguish the questions raised by new technologies facilitating reproduction from the technologies of birth control or abortion. It expanded to *new reproductive and genetic technologies*, as genetic screening and testing was integrated into prenatal, pre-conception, and preimplantation health care. *Assisted reproduction technologies* then came to be used separately from *genetic technologies*. In this book, I do not make sharp distinctions between the terminology but rather draw attention to how images created by the usage of various terms (even if contradictory to uses in other spaces) support acts and technologies of governance.

2 Each participant in this study was self-selected, having seen a poster about the project or heard about it from someone. Each woman was provided with a project information sheet, and before each interview I verbally explained my project and invited questions about the research. Each participant then signed a project consent form and stipulated whether or not she gave permission for someone other than me to transcribe the interview. Many women invited me to their homes; other women came to my apartment or met me in public settings such as restaurants or parks. Children's questions and interruptions were a familiar backdrop to conversations. The interviews were transcribed verbatim, but I have made minimal changes to the narratives included in this book in order to obscure any identifying phrases or statements. To ensure full confidentiality, each participant was assigned a code, which was used to identify interview tapes and transcripts. The names used throughout the book are pseudonyms.

3 The political meanings and lived experiences of what constitutes *coming out* and *being out* are varied. Throughout this book I have employed the language because of its currency within particular discussions and also to draw attention to the complex experiences that women articulate about being out, being out to others, and being or feeling 'visible' as lesbian, bisexual, or transgender in different spheres of their life (work, home) and to different people (friends, family, strangers, co-workers).

Chapter One

1 This discourse has been extended more recently to egg donor availability (see Luce 2005a, 2008; Roberts and Throsby 2008).
2 In the period 1995–1996, I conducted an ethnographic study of women's embodied experiences of pregnancy with an emphasis on how frameworks of low-risk maternity care inform women's narratives of reproductive health and normalcy, and vice versa (Luce 1997). As well, concurrent with the fieldwork for this book, I participated in a collaborative study of the integration of Ontario and BC midwives into the respective health care systems (Bourgeault, Luce, MacDonald, and Winkup 2006, forthcoming).
3 Stanworth (1987a), for example, orders reproductive technologies according to the categories of fertility control, labour and birth management, antenatal and visualising technologies, and conceptive technologies. Employing a similarly broad scope, Beckman and Harvey (2005, 1) define reproductive technologies as 'the drugs, medical and surgical procedures and devices that facilitate conception, prevent or terminate pregnancy, and prevent the acquisition and transmission of sexually transmitted infections.' The 'new' which was employed in various frames often drew attention to the advent of technologies associated with the development of in vitro fertilization but extended the scope of analysis to already present technologies as well as those which could be imagined to belong to the future. This representation of novelty was perhaps also avoided in various contexts in which the seemingly rapid 'routinization' of so-called new technologies was analysed. The current, in Beckman and Harvey's collection, points to the shifting status of reproductive technologies, reflecting both their enduring and future presence and also their transformations.
4 While there is some overlap, by the end of the 1990s a clear distinction seemed to exist between research on reproductive technologies that was associated with new kinship studies and research that remained tied to

earlier work in the anthropology of reproduction. The contestation of categories of gender and nature within anthropology very much informed both. See Yanagisako and Collier 1987; Franklin and McKinnon 2001; Carsten 2000; Ginsburg and Rapp 1995.

5   As well, in 2007, a research team lead by Craig Venter applied for a patent for what they proposed would be a new artificial organism. Such emerging research in the field of synthetic biology provides examples of new formations of life and the value that may be attributed to them.

6   In response to a query made on my behalf by a colleague working at a British hospital that provided fertility treatment covered by the National Health Service (NHS), I was provided with a set of data detailing the number of enquiries and participants in the donor insemination (DI) program who identified themselves as lesbian. The numbers (and the record keeping itself) are indicative of interest in clinic-based medically assisted reproduction and the provision of services to lesbian women.

7   See 'Concern Over Three-Parent Embryo' at http://news.bbc.co.uk/1/hi/health/4228712.stm.

8   See Hennessy and Marsh (2006).

9   For details of changes to the Act, see http://www.dh.gov.uk/en/Publicationsandstatistics/Legislation/Actsandbills/DH_080211 (accessed 29 March 2009).

10   See the Health Canada website for an overview of the legislative activity which culminated in the Assisted Human Reproduction Act, http://www.hc-sc.gc.ca/hl-vs/reprod/index-eng.php (accessed 29 March 2009).

11   For a description of the agency's mandate, as well as reports on activities, see http://www.ahrc-pac.gc.ca/index.php?lang=.

12   Thus, I interviewed 'out' lesbians who accessed donor insemination services in British Columbia but who were not 'out' to the fertility specialist.

13   See Luce (2009) for an examination of the politics of cross-border donor inseminations and the stratified implications of assisted reproduction governance.

14   The temporal order of these two events, the reporting of the infection and the inspection of the facilities, varied in discussions of the events leading to the quarantine of semen in Canada.

15   Commercial U.S. fertility and tissue banks, fertility clinics, and surrogacy programs play a large role in the development of the assisted reproduction industry worldwide. Women living in countries where assisted reproductive technologies are not available regularly seek the services made available by institutions in the United States. The commercializa-

tion of donor insemination in the United States, and the availability online of information about sperm banks, has enabled many women to access what participants in this study referred to as 'clean sperm' from facilities equipped to run screening tests.

16 The Adoption Act is available at http://www.qp.gov.bc.ca/statreg/stat/ A/96005_01.htm (accessed 16 June 2008). As well, extensive information on current adoption policy is available at http://www.mcf.gov.bc.ca/adoption/index.htm (accessed 16 June 2008).

17 See Lahey (1999).

18 This legislation seems to facilitate the combination of a known donor (whose paternal rights would then be abdicated) and self-insemination, given very loose interpretations of the physician's role in these instances.

19 See 'Eggs Fertilised Without Sperm' at http://news.bbc.co.uk/2/hi/ health/1431489.stm (accessed 22 June 2008).

20 See 'Concern Over Three-Parent Embryo' at http://news.bbc.co.uk/1/hi/health/4228712.stm.

21 In 1999 the Institute of Medicine published *Lesbian Health: Current Assessment and Directions for the Future*, a report that made steps to outline a research and service priority agenda in the area of lesbian health (Solarz 1999). At the turn of the new millennium LGBT health issues were addressed in a number of funded research projects, coalition-building initiatives, conferences, and workshops (see Fisher 1995; Mathieson 1998; Ponticelli 1998; Anderson, Healy et al. 2001). See also bibliographies identifying lesbian and bisexual women's health research, such as Luce et al. 2000 and Hudspith with Rabinovitch (2002). References to lesbians and reproductive health care are often limited to statements regarding the number of lesbians who are parents and the need for physicians to recognize the heterosexism in questions such as 'What type of birth control do you use?' Lesbian health literature cites nulliparity – not giving birth to children – as placing lesbians at a higher risk of breast cancer, and lesbians' absence of a need for birth control (and thus yearly contraception prescriptions) as contributing to lesbians' decisions to forego regular access to primary care (White and Dull 1997). The findings of these studies were echoed during the interviews for my study as women told me about, for example, the 'health benefits' of pregnancy and breast feeding. Clarifying, Kim, who was planning to become pregnant, added that the health benefits were not *the* reason she was going to have a child, biologically, but that she did think about it 'as a plus.'

Chapter Two

1 Ellen DeGeneres starred as Ellen Morgan on the television sitcom *Ellen*. In 1997 both DeGeneres and Morgan came out. The television character Ellen started dating a woman who had a daughter conceived by alternative insemination. In real life DeGeneres and Anne Heche became partners. After they separated, Heche began a relationship with a man, became pregnant, and now has a son. In many ways Heche's relationship with DeGeneres challenged normative understandings of *lesbian* (she expressed that she had never felt gay; she simply fell in love with a woman), and her subsequent status as a married mom engendered commentary on her 'never lesbian' status. Such 'truth' narratives about sexuality continue to dominate public discourse, even in the age of so-called queer challenges to heteronormativity.

2 The article is titled 'Two Moms, Better Than One?' and repeats a common narrative of decision making, addressing questions regarding who will bear the child, the use of fresh or frozen semen, choosing a donor, and inseminating. Another common story told within the frame of lesbian parenting is about the validation that children and parents receive by other children who claim that children with two moms are luckier. The emphasis on two-parent families, queer or straight, in the act of 'staking claim to Mother's Day' (the caption next to the headline) continues to marginalize straight and queer single parents and those family configurations comprising more than two parents.

3 Statements like the following are commonly cited as an indication of the number of lesbian and gay parents in North America: 'Widely cited figures suggest that ten percent of women are lesbians and that between twenty and thirty percent of lesbians are mothers. A recent study estimated that there are "between 3 and 8 million gay and lesbian parents in the United States, raising between 6 and 14 million children"' (Arnup 1995, vii). Only recently has sexual orientation been included as part of the Canadian census. Longstanding uncertainty about the discriminatory effects that declaring one's sexual orientation or status as being in a same-sex relationship may have an impact on the (lack of) demographic data.

4 See Katherine Arnup (1994) for a historical analysis of the role of advice literature in women's experiences of motherhood. As pre-conception care has become an increasingly salient focus within women's reproductive health care and experiences as a mother-to-be (a category often extended to all women regardless of their intention to get pregnant or not), a host

of fertility management books have appeared, integrating the sometimes separate discourses of contraceptive and conceptive education. *Taking Charge of Your Fertility: The Definitive Guide to Natural Birth Control, Pregnancy Achievement, and Reproductive Health* by Toni Weshler (1995) appears to be one of the most often cited and was most commonly referred to by women in my study.

5 One woman who decided to try to get pregnant in the early 1980s described it as an era in which it was 'illegal to adopt if you were queer.' Prohibitive adoption legislation and practices (and the cost of international adoptions) were cited by a number of women who chose to try to conceive on their own or in a relationship with a partner or future co-parent. In Canada, adoption is primarily governed by provincial law. In the case of inter-country adoption, citizenship and immigration policies, which are within the federal jurisdiction, also play a significant role. In British Columbia the introduction of the Adoption Act in November 1996 made it possible for self-identified lesbians and gay men to adopt. The shift in adoption legislation in most other provinces followed the 1999 ruling in the Ontario case, *M. v H*, which determined that the exclusionary definition of *spouse* was unconstitutional (see Lahey [1999] for a pre-decision analysis of the case). Interestingly, it was in Ontario in 1995 that a court decided in favour of second-parent adoption by women of a child born to their partner.

6 The sexual and reproductive histories of queer women (explicitly meant to include lesbian, bisexual, and transgender individuals identifying with the category woman and women who have sex with women [WSW]) are often obscured by a dominant and normative discourse which constitutes lesbian sex and lesbian sexual identity as 'non-procreative.' This assumes that lesbians do not have sex with men and renders invisible women's histories of consensual and non-consensual sexual relations with women and men. These histories are a significant part of a queer woman's embodied sexuality and were both literally and figuratively inscribed in and on the 'lesbian' bodies of women I interviewed as memories, stress, and scar tissue.

7 Yvonne's friend had placed an ad for a sperm donor in a local newspaper but then decided to try to conceive by having sex with her ex-husband. Although most women I interviewed connected with donors through someone they knew, a few women placed ads in local newspapers in their attempt to meet potential donors. Advertisements (placed also by men wanting to act as donors and/or co-parents) seemed quite common in the queer newspapers and magazines that I encountered

during a trip to the UK in 1998, although they were less common across Canada. The Internet has become a site for donor-recipient-co-parent matching.

8   At the time Yvonne was trying to get pregnant, employment insurance was known as unemployment insurance.

9   See chapter 11 for a discussion about Paula's hesitation to ask gay men to be donors during the first decade or so of the AIDS epidemic.

10   *Considering Parenthood* is the title of Cheri Pies' influential workbook (1988) for lesbians thinking about becoming parents.

11   The Lesbian Mothers Support Society page (1996–2002) at www.lesbian.org/lesbian-moms/ provided comprehensive information and links to other organizations.

12   Email lists and chat rooms were often initiated by community centres or programs. A number of women mentioned the Lesbian Mothers Support Society (see footnote 11 above). The website of the Toronto Women's Bookstore maintains a list of other support and information organizations that may be relevant to queer moms. However, the links to some organizations are no longer valid. See http://www.womensbookstore.com/links-queer.html (accessed 16 June 2008). The Family Services Association website provides an online platform for the LGBTQ Parenting Network. The website notes that the network is now fully funded by the Ontario Ministry of Health and Long-Term Care, and it is expected that the URL may change. Information is currently available at http://www.fsatoronto.com/programs/lgbtparenting.html (accessed 16 June 2008)

13   Mothers have historically been identified as the cause of homosexuality and lesbianism (see Terry 1999, 317–28). Single mothers, raising children in the absence of men, presented even more of a perceived threat to the development of their children's 'proper' gender or sex role.

14   'That Alberta one' referred to the Lesbian Mothers Support Society page (see above).

15   This history of inaccessibility is complicated by the nuances of identification. While most women I interviewed maintained that the one physician who operated a sperm bank did not inseminate lesbians, I interviewed lesbians who had accessed services in Vancouver during the 1980s and early 1990s. These women had not disclosed their sexual identity to the physician, and one woman felt that the questions asked by the physician purposely enabled her to avoid disclosure. Another woman wondered if he knew her sexual identity when he started a conversation about whether she liked K.D. Lang's music (an out lesbian Canadian singer).

16 See chapter 10 for details about some of the California sperm banks with roots in feminist health centres. Details about clinics that emerged in the San Francisco Bay area, which were also accessed by Canadian women in this study, are included in Agigian (2004) and Mamo (2007).

17 The clinic offers access to services including therapeutic donor insemination, in vitro fertilization, and donor egg in vitro fertilization services.

18 See chapter 7 for narratives regarding the meaning of *live donor*.

19 Creative Beginnings is a pseudonym which I have used in other publications. Reading Almeling (2007), I was surprised to see that she had chosen the same pseudonym for the clinic where she conducted research. I have retained the name, partly because this incident reinforced its fictional status.

20 Few provincial and territorial jurisdictions in Canada have implemented legislation to define a donor's relationship to offspring. The normative practice of anonymous donor insemination, coupled with the commercialization of gametes (donors are compensated for their time), acted to regulate anonymous donors' conceptualizations of donor offspring as kin to whom they have a paternal-genetic relation. At the time of birth opposite-sex couples would, according to normative practice, register the 'social' father as father, thus establishing the legal rights of that child to support from that particular individual.

21 One of the men I met during my fieldwork had planned to be the donor for two lesbian friends. The woman who was planning to conceive pursued fertility assistance and was told that her chosen donor could not be included in the infertility treatment process. Given that in 1995 the BC Human Rights Council had awarded $3,400 to a lesbian couple who had been denied access to insemination services by a BC obstetrician-gynaecologist, finding that the doctor had discriminated against the women on the 'basis of sexual orientation and/or family status' (Capen 1997), I anticipated a suit of a similar kind to take place regarding the restrictions placed on gay men's reproductive rights. In 2003 a lesbian woman in Ontario was denied the possibility of undergoing clinical donor insemination with semen from a known donor which had not undergone testing and cryopreservation. She had tried to conceive at home with semen from a known donor, but did not become pregnant and was told that she could not access the fertility services of a clinic using the same donor, as he was not her spouse nor her sexual partner (see http://www.egale.ca/index.asp?lang=E&menu=1&item=922). The woman argued that to have the donor undergo the testing procedures associated with the Special Access Programme constituted discrimination

(this would also mean that the semen would have to be cryopreserved, which many associate with a lower success rate) (see Agigian 2004, 95). It was found that the refusal of health services did not contradict her rights but was in line with regulations. The case was framed as one concerning *her* rights, not the rights of the man acting as a donor. It would perhaps be interesting to think of this case in terms of discrimination against the women who are permitted to be inseminated with men who they state are their spouse or sexual partner. The asymmetrical practice is a reflection of the significant normative expectations about the monogamy and risk status of a heterosexual couple undergoing fertility treatment. In another case in Ontario, a gay man who became a father via an egg donor and a gestational surrogate arrangement was granted the right to be the sole parent named on the birth registration form (see Boyd 2007).

22 Note that deciding to try to conceive with semen from a donor with whom one does not have a personal relationship does not result in a disinterest in or non-relatedness to the donor. What is discussed is a pragmatic assessment of the potential legal complications, the necessity of medical assistance, and the preservation of important relations, which may be strained by a recipient-donor relationship. Jeanette and Katharine's son was born with a disorder that medical professionals associated with the donor's genetic history. The ties which had been established to the sperm bank donor were evident in Jeanette's astonishment as she told me that they had been advised to choose a different donor if they decided to have more children.

Chapter Three

1 See John Fisher (2000) for a response to one Canadian Alliance member's apologies for making an anti-gay remark. An article published online by PlanetOut News staff, on the day following the 27 November 2000 election, highlights the political climate that had preceded the election, noting that 'many politically-oriented Canadian gays and lesbians [who] felt the imperative to defeat the Alliance made this the most important election of their lives' (Tuesday, November 28, 2000 / 12:53 AM). In 2003 the Canadian Alliance and the Progressive Conservative Party of Canada merged to form the Conservative Party of Canada, which, with Stephen Harper as prime minister, became the governing party in Canada in 2006.

2 The books were banned by the Surrey school district in 1997 from use as part of the regular curriculum. The case was heard in 2002 at the Supreme Court, which countered the decision of the school board and

advised that the books be reconsidered according to 'the broad principles of tolerance and non-sectarianism underlying the School Act' (cited in Egale 2002). The press release also cites paragraph 69 of the judgment by Supreme Court Chief Justice McLaughlin, who writes: 'It is suggested that, while the message of the books may be unobjectionable, the books will lead children to ask questions of their parents that may be inappropriate for the K-1 level and difficult for parents to answer. Yet on the record before us, it is hard to see how the materials will raise questions which would not in any event be raised by the acknowledged existence of same-sex parented families in the K-1 parent population, or in the broader world in which these children live. The only additional message of the materials appears to be the message of tolerance. Tolerance is always age-appropriate.'

The judgment of the Supreme Court of Canada for the case *Chamberlain v. Surrey School District No. 36*, [2002] 4 S.C.R. 710, 2002 SCC 86, is available at http://scc.lexum.umontreal.ca/en/2002/2002scc86/2002scc86 .html. Articles pertaining to the five-year challenge are available to download on the Egale Canada website. Following the 2002 Supreme Court decision, the Surrey school board has continued to refuse the use of books with so-called same-sex-parent content.

3 Heterosexual Pride days have been held in a few cities across Canada. In Regina the mayor proclaimed 18 June 2001 to be Family Pride Day after the organizers had threatened to sue in light of the fact that Gay and Lesbian Pride Day is proclaimed in that city. However, the mayor refused to proclaim a Family Pride Day in the following year (however, it did take place on 29 June), stating that 'the group is promoting a message of hate' (Peters 2002).

4 This research characteristically presumed that lesbian and gay parents would negatively impact on children, or the research was begun to contest this assumption in order to provide data to be used in custody cases involving lesbian and gay parents.

5 See http://www.colage.org.

6 These were common units of comparison, most likely based on the assumption that it allowed for the variation of sexuality to be the influencing factor on children's development. The politics and benefits of and access to the identity of *single parent* would be interesting to address. *Single* is often considered to mean 'un-married,' excluding partnerships and co-parenting relationships configured outside of marriage.

7 An important longitudinal study, conducted by Nanette Gartrell and colleagues, has been following a cohort of lesbian families for over fifteen

years. See Gartrell, Hamilton, et al. 1996; Gartrell, Banks, et al. 2000; and the website of the National Longitudinal Lesbian Family Study at http://www.nllfs.org/ (accessed 22 June 2008).

8 For films see *Camp Lavender Hill* (Tom Shepard), *That's a Family* (Debra Chasnoff and Helen S. Cohen), *It's Elementary* (Debra Chasnoff and Helen S. Cohen), and *Sticks and Stones* (Jan Padgett). For representations of children with queer parents in books see *Best Best Colors / Los Mejores Colores* (Hoffman 1999), *A Name on the Quilt* (Atkins 1999), and *Holly's Secret* (Garden 2000). Also see *Love Makes a Family* (Kaeser and Gillespie 1999).

9 Courts ruled on cases regarding the right of 'same-sex marriage' across Canada, and between 10 June 2003 and 23 June 2005 nine jurisdictions extended marriage to same-sex couples. On 10 July 2005 the federal government implemented the Civil Marriage Act, making same-sex marriage legal across Canada. See the website of Canadians for Equal Marriage (http://www.equal-marriage.ca) for details of the history of the campaign for same-sex marriage and for links to specific case decisions.

10 The Defense of Marriage Act (DOMA) was passed in the United States in 1996 in order to restrict the possibility of same-sex marriage, by defining marriage as the union between a man and a woman. The Act, implemented at the federal level, meant that marriages legalized in one state would not be recognized in other states. Sullivan (2004, 28–30) discusses these events within a framework of resistance-assimilation. Lahey (1999) notes that in the United States significant energy was directed at challenging the DOMA by those who would and would not have focused on the issue of same-sex marriage previously. See Smith (2007) for a case-focused comparative analysis (United States and Canada) of the discursive framing of same-sex marriage lobbying, cases, and decisions.

11 The 20 May 1999 Supreme Court ruling in the case of *M. v. H.* declared unconstitutional the restriction of the category *spouse* to opposite-sex partners. The strong wording of the decision provoked other provinces and territories to implement legislation amendments in order to include same-sex partners within the definition of *spouse*. British Columbia had already done this on a certain level with the proclamation of Bills 31 and 32 in 1997. The federal government then passed Bill C-23, changing the meaning of *spouse* in sixty-eight pieces of legislation but maintaining the definition of *marriage* as applicable only to opposite-sex couples.

12 See Layne (1999), Ragoné and Winddance Twine (2000) and the *Journal of the Association for Research on Mothering* for contemporary analyses of motherhood and mothering.

13 Note that Erica used the phrase *artificial insemination* as a referent for clinical insemination or higher-tech insemination, in contrast to *self-insemination*, which many would argue is not artificial.

14 See Sullivan (2001) for an account of co-mothers' experiences of claiming their relationship to children and engaging in public outings and education.

Chapter Four

1 The wording describing Adele's parenting role was produced in part during the interview. Both Adele and Vivian moved in and out of language that clarified and obscured their different relationships to the children. Much of the discussion highlighted the differences between *parenting* as activities and *parent* as a normative term to define a particular (and supposedly understood) relationship between a child and an adult.

2 Vivian and her children were part of the Pride Day festivities that I attended later in my fieldwork period.

3 During my fieldwork I encountered a few support and discussion groups in smaller cities and towns, which were perhaps continuing an approach to creating community in places without a larger LGBT community service infrastructure in place.

4 The Centre is a community centre 'serving and supporting lesbian, gay, transgendered, and bisexual people and their allies.' I was a member of the community advisory committee from 1999 to 2001 and a member of the Queer Women's and Trans Health Series Planning Committee from 2000 to 2001.

5 This exhibit is included in the documentary *It's Elementary* (Deborah Chasnoff and Helen Cohen) and is available in book format.

6 Now see http://www.ProudParenting.com, which acts as a news and networking portal for information about issues related to queer parenting.

7 Queer magazines and queer parenting magazines were also not widely available.

Chapter Five

1 The women I interviewed who adopted children (as a joint adoption or a second-parent adoption) were able to apply for a second birth certificate on which both of their names would be listed as parents. The original birth certificate would then remain sealed until the child reached the age

of majority. Women who gave birth to children while in a relationship with a woman and who listed both women as parents on the birth registration form were told that they 'had filled the forms out wrong, having listed a "female" name in the space provided for the "father."'

2 See chapter 3 of Lahey (2001) for a thorough analysis of the implications of these distinctions and their relationship to previous decisions.

3 Reports note that following a human rights complaint made by two women married to each other (one of whom had just given birth) who were told that they could not both be registered as parents, the Government of Nova Scotia responded within days to change the birth registration form (Smith 2007; http://rightsforhumans.blogspot.com/2007/12/changing-laws-for-same-sex-couples-in.html (accessed 16 June 2008).

Chapter Six

1 See *Vriend v. Alberta*, [1998] 1 S.C.R. 493, Supreme Court of Canada decision available at http://scc.lexum.umontreal.ca/en/1998/1998rcs1-493/1998rcs1-493.html (accessed 16 June 2008).

2 The claims made by grandparents of children for custody add a critical dimension to pre-conception negotiations of relationships, as discussed in chapter 9, where women explored the implications of parental recognition by their parents and those of a partner and donor if involved.

3 See Robson (1995) for a discussion of the norms defining the appropriate behaviour for lesbian mothers, the court distinctions between *good* and *bad* lesbians, and the emphasis on the non-visibility of lesbian relationships.

4 For example, in *Lesbian Mothers* (Lewin 1993), the partners of the women interviewed are not included in the definition of *lesbian mother* – even if they are living with the women interviewed and co-parenting the children. In *Lesbian Motherhood* (Nelson 1996), women who are parenting children are included within the frame of *lesbian mother*, but women's sense of entitlement to this identity raises questions. These tensions and the distancing of oneself from claiming motherhood are also present in some of the narratives in *The Family of Woman* (Sullivan 2004).

5 Along similar lines, Jennifer Terry states: 'Lesbians have been prompted – and often compelled – to try to understand themselves to a very great degree in relation to a discourse, medicine, that construes their difference as primarily pathological' (1999, 324).

6 In traditional kinship theory, the term *affinity* would refer to relatives by marriage. See Mamo (2005) for an analysis of what she refers to as *affinity-ties*.

Chapter Seven

1 See chapter 1 for an explanation of the amendments.

2 For example, the Rainbow Flag Sperm Bank has a policy that sperm donors cannot be anonymous. Their identifying and contact information is provided to women at three months following the birth of a child, and women are under the obligation to contact the donor within one year. See http://www.gayspermbank.com and Agigian (2004).

3 At this time, *live* referred to someone who was around and not to the disembodied sperm that was frozen in liquid nitrogen tanks at the sperm banks. The language invokes a different image today, as it is possible to obtain sperm for insemination from deceased donors and dying men. See Andrews 1999 and also the UK case in which Diane Blood petitioned for the right to be inseminated with semen that had been procured (and then cryopreserved) from her husband while he was dying.

4 One of the women I interviewed had both a donor contract and a written agreement between herself and her partner in which they agreed to share custody in the event that they ever broke up. Many women inseminating during the same era, the early 1980s, believed that anything in writing could work against them in the court system.

5 Local donors were often men who lived in the same geographic community, whereas sperm-bank donors were sometimes from Washington State, California, and, more recently, Georgia.

6 Women and men who became parents by employing donor insemination, men who have acted as sperm donors, and children conceived by clinical donor insemination have been involved in lobbying for the removal of donor anonymity in Canada. See, for example, Gravenor (2004), Kinross (1992), and Mick (2007).

7 See Johnston (2002) and Bissessar (2005) for contrasting discussions of donor anonymity in Canadian legislation.

8 Women noted that potential donors' partners (women or men) also voiced objections to them being donors based on cultural notions about the intimacy that such substance-sharing entailed. Women and men did not want their partner's semen to be inside the body of another individual.

9 According to Linda Villarosa, 'Sweden, Austria and the State of Victoria in Australia have mandatory donor identification release' (2002). In April 2005, amendments to the Human Fertilisation and Embryology Act (United Kingdom) came into place, removing donor anonymity.

10 Interestingly, Becker states, 'In contrast to donor insemination, in which the identity of the donor is usually strictly concealed, the use of a donated egg is often characterized by considerable openness' (2000, 133).

11 This means that women must often take hormones, have their eggs aspirated, and attempt an in vitro fertilization cycle, which is often not successful. Intracytoplasmic sperm injection cycles in 1998 accounted for 9,361 pregnancies and 7,712 births in the United States (Villarosa 2002). Although the use of ICSI has been linked to genetic anomalies, it is regularly cited as a treatment for male infertility.

12 Cussins also notes, 'For women, accepting donor gametes is reportedly easier than for men, which correlates well with the lay belief that women find the idea of adoption easier to accept than their male partners' (1998a, 44). Caroline Gallop's (2007) recent book, *Making Babies the Hard Way*, offers a narrative of her experience which strongly counters this statement.

13 The Adoption Act and amendments to the Family Relations Act were made under the NDP provincial government. The liberal government was not expressing commitment to LGBT rights and benefits.

14 Becker (2000) notes that the guidelines do not require confidentiality or anonymity; it is just practice.

15 See http://www.thespermbankofca.org/.

16 See https://www.pacrepro.com/index.htm.

17 See http://www.cryobank.com.

18 In Canada, concurrent with discussions of the proposed 2004 legislation, there was significant attention given to the lack of access to even minimal information about sperm donors, and much media coverage of personal experiences of sperm donors and donor offspring. In discussions surrounding an earlier version of assisted-reproduction legislation, a conference on the subject of donor-conceived people organized in 2000, raised a number of issues, including calls for the implementation of a gamete-donor registry (McKeague 2000). Especially visibly active have been two women (Olivia Pratten and Shelley Kreutz), whose mothers conceived with donor semen in the 1980s (McClelland 2002). Shirley Pratten (Olivia Pratten's mother) was a founder of the New Reproductive Alternatives Society in British Columbia (see Kinross 1992; Skelton 2006).

19 Women also used the services of California sperm banks because they provided the option of inseminating at home and, in contrast to discriminating against lesbians, were established to meet the needs of lesbians and other women who were being denied access to other clinics and

sperm banks. For an in-depth analysis of narratives of conception across the U.S.-Canada border, and the stratified implications of newly implemented guidelines and legislation, see Luce 2009.

20 Vials of semen are typically sold in quantities of 0.5 cc (washed semen) and 0.8 cc (unwashed).

21 Between March and June 1999, Health Canada conducted inspections at Canadian sperm banks and storage facilities, finding that many programs did not meet the screening guidelines implemented in 1996. Donor semen stored in Canadian facilities was quarantined. In July 2000, Health Canada released new guidelines. Donor semen which does not meet these testing requirements cannot be distributed in Canada, nor can it be imported into Canada. PRS and TSBC are two sperm banks, notably the two facilities with willing-to-be-known donors, which did not follow the guidelines for testing Chlamydia as outlined by Health Canada. See http://www.hc-sc.gc.ca/dhp-mps/compli-conform/info-prod/don/gui_41-eng.php.

22 Xytex is based in Augusta, Georgia. Following the Health Canada quarantine, which reduced the availability of donor semen across Canada until it could be tested according to the new regulations, Xytex opened a satellite office in Toronto, Ontario. They recruited Toronto donors, whose semen was then shipped to Georgia for testing. Their website provides a list of current Canadian-compliant donors.

23 See http://www.xytex.com.

24 Xytex introduced 'open identity donors' around the year 2000. These donors, like the donors from TSBC, agree to have their identity released to the offspring at the age of eighteen. A quick glance at the online catalogue reveals that the number of open-identity donors is extremely small.

Chapter Eight

1 Note that this is not indicative of the number of women choosing known donors versus anonymous donors, but it is a statement made on the basis of Sullivan's sample. Intriguingly, a distinction in Sullivan's study is maintained between the categories of known donors and anonymous donors, which in my study became a contested distinction.

2 In a U.S. case in 2005, a man who had acted as a sperm donor to a friend on the basis of a verbal agreement was found liable for child support (on the bases of an action implemented by the woman, who had given birth to twins) (McElroy 2005). In a subsequent 2008 ruling in this case, the decision of the lower court was overturned, and the verbal agreement

was upheld as valid. Shapiro (2008) provides an overview of the frameworks governing the legal status of donors in various U.S. states. In another case in the United Kingdom – alternatively depicted as instigated by the lesbian parents (whose relationship had recently ended and who sought child support from the donor, also a friend) or by one of the woman parents of the two children – an emphasis was placed on the risk implied by becoming parents outside of the regulated medical system of assisted reproduction. See Williams (2007) and Byers and Malvern (2007). When this case was first heard, it was expected that new legislation would be coming into effect which would render women couples (but only those who had registered a civil partnership) the legal parents of children born within the legal union. This would then apparently resolve such distinctions between donors from licensed clinics and agreements made outside of that context. In May 2008, in discussions about the Human Fertilisation and Embryology Bill it was decided that the clause requiring clinicians to consider a child's need for a father would be removed from the HFE Act (Watt 2008). Porter (2008) reports, 'The Bill says that where there is reference to the father of a child such as on birth certificates this is to be read [as] a reference to the female parent who did not give birth,' and that this will apply to women both within and outside of a civil partnership. This change came into force effective April 2009.

3 Schneider's work has inspired generations of kinship theory within the discipline of anthropology and beyond.

4 Cussins suggests that these women are possibly enacting a kinship of shared motherhood: 'From the heart of biomedicine they are changing and extending the reference of the word mother' (1998b, 46).

5 Surrogacy arrangements have been at the forefront of key cases concerning the determination of parental status (see Hartouni 1997; Grayson 2000). The Assisted Human Reproduction Act prohibits commercial surrogacy arrangements but permits 'altruistic' surrogacy. The issue of registering parental status was raised with respect to a surrogacy arrangement, whereby the woman giving birth was viewed as the 'mother' to be identified on the registration form.

6 Invoking biogenetic continuity through the use of an already recognized family member as a donor seemingly naturalizes the use of a donor in a way that differs from the practice of choosing a friend, an acquaintance, or an anonymous donor. The background of a non-inseminating partner is reproduced through the genetic history she shares, for example, with her brother. Interestingly, though, it is most often assumed in these scenarios that brothers *are* biological or genetic siblings.

7 Many queer women whom I interviewed perceived donor-egg IVF as
   facilitating an equal biological relationship to the child, in contrast to the
   distinction made between the gestational and genetic relationship that is
   increasingly significant in heterosexual donor-egg and surrogacy practices. At a conference, a woman shared with me that she and her female
   partner had been among the first cases in Canada in which the donor egg
   with which a woman conceived by IVF was the egg of her female
   partner. This scenario is an interesting contribution to discussions I heard
   concerning the ethics of egg donation and the contested status of egg
   donation by relatives (most often conceptualized as mothers and sisters).
   In some cases, the possibility that a woman would be under pressure (of
   familial obligation) to donate an egg (or, in other cases, act as a surrogate)
   was considered to render the practice unethical. The case of egg donation
   and gestational surrogacy between women in a relationship is interesting
   in that, if both were planning to become parents, this plan would be fulfilled. However, this does not render inapplicable the potential to feel
   obligated to undergo fertility treatment.
      In a feature story that appeared in the news during my fieldwork, two
   U.S. women who had become parents in this way then used the Uniform
   Parentage Act to petition for (and achieve) recognition for both as
   parents. It was also reported that in South Africa the same situation was
   to result in the recognition of two women as the biological parents of the
   twins to which one woman had given birth, the embryos having been
   created with the other woman's eggs and with donor sperm (de Bruin
   2003). This practice, which I had originally heard described in an academic setting as egg 'swapping' (is an egg swapped for a womb?), is
   referred to by Crews (2005), and in the case she analyses, as *ovum sharing*.
   This is again problematic terminology, given the privileging of the ovum
   and the embedded altruistic connotations. Notably, Crews' discussion is
   with respect not to the petitioning for recognition of two-mother status at
   the time of the birth of a child (based on an equivalency of normatively
   ordered concepts of gestational and genetic motherhood), but to a case in
   which a judge ordered such recognition of two-mother status upon the
   end of a relationship and an application for parental rights by the woman
   whose eggs had been 'donated/provided/shared' (to employ the competing descriptive language) in the conception process. In Crews' view,
   the decision in this case jeopardizes the autonomous reproductive decision-making capacities of various individuals, including women who
   may act as surrogates and women who donate eggs.

A number of the women that I interviewed about their experiences of considering parenthood in the early 1980s mentioned in vitro fertilization, perhaps due to its newness in the media.

8 Note the parallels in thinking between the plans of Sara and Kim and those of Nadine and Maureen.

9 Some women were also familiar with scenarios in which a donor's family members, especially children's biological grandparents, have been awarded custody or visitation rights to children of lesbian parents (Gavigan 2000).

10 A number of women whom I interviewed chose willing-to-be-known donors, otherwise known as 'yes' donors (see also Mamo 2007; Agigian 2004). The identity of the donor will be released at the age of eighteen to the child. Women expressed these future relationships as being between the donor and their child, rather than between the donor and the family. It is more accurate these days to state that this relationship is *not expected* to be an issue. However, there have been a number of instances in the past few years in which teenage children have identified the donor, or the donor has come to identify himself to the children (see Luce 2009; Von Radowitz 2005; Harmon 2007).

11 This 'logic' is still formalized on the Registration of Live Birth forms in British Columbia, where although two women can be named as parents, the categories provided are 'mother' and 'father or co-parent.' Given that the attending physician or midwife provides a separate form on which the details of the woman who gave birth are listed, there is still a sense of recorded certainty and privilege concerning the body from which the child came.

12 See Wozniak (2001) for an account of foster mothers' claims to unmodified kinship status as mothers in relation to children.

Chapter Nine

1 See Lahey (2001) and Demczuk, Caron, et al. (2002).

2 Status of Women Canada is described as 'the federal government agency which promotes gender equality, and the full participation of women in the economic, social, cultural and political life of the country.' See http://www.swc-cfc.gc.ca/index_e.html.

3 Bill 5 was the omnibus bill introduced by the Ontario government in March 2000 in response to the decision in *M. v. H.* in 1999.

4 Sample donor contracts are available on various lesbian mom websites,

and other women in my study pointed out the sample contracts at the back of books such as *Considering Parenthood* (Pies 1988) or *The Ultimate Guide to Pregnancy for Lesbians* (Pepper 1999).

5 The contract was drawn up prior to the introduction of the Adoption Act in British Columbia. However, as discussed in this chapter, prior to the finalization of an adoption, the donor could assert parental rights. In California, if women inseminate with semen from known donors under the supervision of a physician, the donor has no paternal rights or obligations to any child conceived (Mamo 2007). Physicians in British Columbia will not inseminate women with fresh semen from an 'unrelated' donor, thus requiring the use of a designated (or directed) donor program, which also involves freezing and quarantining the semen. Potential donors must qualify under screening guidelines, the first of which prohibits semen donation from men who have had sex with another man, even once, since 1977. There is now a special access program through which it is possible for men who do not qualify according to the guidelines to participate in a 'directed-donor' program.

6 Internet sites of Canadian fertility clinics have amended the information provided regarding legal parentage after clinical donor insemination, during the years in which I have been involved with this area of research (1996–2008). See chapter 13 for further discussion.

7 There is a discursive and material-legal distinction between step-parent and second-parent adoption in legislation implemented in various jurisdictions. See Dalton (2001).

8 During the time between saying no and agreeing, Zac broached the subject of being a donor with his mother. She reportedly defined her kin status with the following reflection: 'I would be a grandmother by sperm donor. That would be all right.'

9 Although I do not delve into the structural commonalities between a number of the stories I heard and those available in other ethnographies of assisted reproduction, the reference to the length of the document was an interesting point. There is often an emphasis placed on the detailed planning and prenatal arrangements in which queer women engage prior to attempting to become a parent. Being able to recount this planning process sometimes serves as a useful tool in discussions concerning the potentially negative impact on children of having lesbian parents, but it can or could also obscure the experiences of women who do not have the resources to engage in such plans, who become pregnant accidentally, or who do not choose to organize their life in such a manner.

10 On the current form there is a section with the heading 'Statement.' The form reads: 'If the father is not being registered below, for one of the following reasons, please check the following statement: I am the mother of this child and do solemnly declare that: [blank box to check] The father is incapable or the father is unacknowledged by the mother or the father is unknown by the mother or the father refused to acknowledge the child.' It is thus possible to see why, even with the form now including the possibility to list a father or a co-parent (but not both on the Registration of Live Birth), women may not know how to proceed. Forms for the registration processes related to Vital Statistics concerns for many provinces are available online.

11 This time lag is also one of the reasons that BC lawyers advised that a known donor agreement be in place prior to conception, as it could potentially act as a document attesting to the reproductive and parenting intentions of those involved if questions were to arise during the six-month period.

12 In 2007 an Ontario court ruled in favour of a three-parent family, again demonstrating the emphasis on legal decision making as part of relatedness, but also providing a legal opening for other approaches to processes of enactment and displacement.

13 Notably, many women's narratives convey the variability of the men's reasons behind their decision to act as a sperm donor or not, but the arrival of a child was not questioned. One couple I interviewed experienced a late-term termination of pregnancy following the receipt of the results of an amniocentesis. The analysis had shown a fetal chromosomal translocation, which could not be attributed to the pregnant woman (whose egg had also been the one to be fertilized). The sperm bank with which the donor was affiliated contacted the donor to conduct tests on him as well, but still no reason for the translocation could be determined. This particular trisomy was not associated with living individuals, and faced with significant uncertainty about the life potential of the fetus and, if the pregnancy continued to term, of a child, the women decided to have an abortion. It is unknown how much information about the situation was shared with the donor or is shared with other donors in similar cases. In other situations known donors accompany women through the experiences of conception difficulties, miscarriages, and abortions and must also negotiate the meanings of infertility and a potentially new awareness of genetic carrier status. How men who act as sperm donors experience 'infertility,' miscarriage, stillbirth, or the death of a child is a

field which is still very much in need of exploration. This holds true both
for men who know the woman who is (or the women who are) trying to
become a parent and for men who participate in sperm-bank programs.
Additionally, the increasing availability – due in part to novel technologies and cost reduction – of genetic tests may also shape a sperm donor's
understanding of himself and his future reproductive possibilities.

14 In British Columbia it was the Adoption Act which facilitated both
second-parent adoptions and adoption on its own. In other provinces, for
example Ontario, court decisions made it possible for lesbians to complete step-parent adoptions, but continued to prohibit joint domestic
adoptions by same-sex couples.

15 In 1995 in Canada, marriage was only legally available to heterosexual
couples or a two-person composition of opposite-sex individuals.

16 In relation to the experiences described earlier, whereby Jenna and others
stated that they got caught up in situations of having to fill out birth registration forms that did not fit their reality, the experiences of women
confronted with emphases on being upfront about their lesbian identification – even though it was understood that this would preclude the possibility of adoption on the basis of prejudicial assumptions – raises the
question of what constitutes either deception or ethical behaviour.

17 Following the implementation of the Adoption Act in British Columbia,
inter-country adoptions are also provincially governed. There are six
licensed adoption agencies in BC. Inter-country adoptions in Canada
proceed in accordance with the Hague Convention on Protection of Children and Co-operation in Respect of Intercountry Adoption, which
requires authorities in both countries to authorize the adoption. Inter-
country adoptions between Canada and a country which has not ratified
the Hague Convention require a Letter of No Objection from the BC
Director of Adoption, to be presented to Citizenship and Immigration
Canada. Inter-country adoptions can be expensive, with costs of around
$15,000 to $30,000.

18 The language of *bringing a child home* resonates with stories of returning
home following a hospital birth. In these cases, international adoptions
involved travelling to the country where the child was living.

19 The Family Relations Act was amended in 1998, extending the definition
of *spouse*, and thereby rights and obligations to children, to include non-
married opposite and same-sex partners.

20 It is important to note that the commercial dimension to international
adoption could have also been seen as a motivation to support the policies that facilitated adoption by single individuals and people in same-

sex relationships. However, this was not articulated by any of the women I interviewed about their adoption experiences.

21 See the BC Family Law blog of the MacLean Family Law Group, http://www.bcfamilylawblog.com/bc_family_law_blog/2005/12/bc_fa mily_law_k.html (accessed 1 September 2007).

22 See the BC Family Law blog at http://www.bcfamilylawblog.com/ bc_family_law_blog/2005/12/bc_family_law_k.html#more (accessed 16 June 2008).

23 See Boyd (2007) and Crews (2005) for analyses of recent decisions, which have implications for court determinations of parenthood.

24 The case was decided in June 2003. In 2004 the man who had petitioned for recognition as 'father' launched a case against the British Columbia government, stating that there were unnecessary delays to the processing of the order from the Supreme Court of Canada.

25 It is necessary to note that there are provincial differences between the processes of birth registration. In 2007 an article posted on the Egale Canada website highlighted the case of a woman married to a woman in Nova Scotia, who was told that she and her partner would not be allowed to both register as parents on the birth registration form. Unable and unwilling to pay for the costs of adoption, the woman planned to give birth in Quebec, where registration of both parents would be possible. The case highlighted the fact that the legal relation- ship between parents and children in the case of same-sex partnerships is not conferred through the recognition of marriage. Also in 2007, a few months following the above report, the government of Nova Scotia received a complaint regarding the discriminatory registration process and agreed to amend the forms without contestation (Smith 2007). As names are not disclosed, there is a possibility that the cases refer to the same individuals.

26 Although Robyn was not making reference to a particular case, examples of situations in which this had happened were present within queer media, legal discourse, and general conversation. For examples of narratives illustrating such situations, see Luce (2005b) and Rockhill (1996).

27 My reading here is done within a particular frame in order to address the possibility of predetermining relationships. Chandra's experiences, however, also speak to other means of defining or not defining relation- ships, as the known donor was the brother of her partner. Chandra and her partner counted on some of the nurses who would intervene, in attempts to defer his actions.

Chapter Ten

1　The cyclical nature of infertility and its relationship to research is
addressed in Deborah Lynn Steinberg's analysis (1997a) of the development of the Human Fertilisation and Embryology Act in the United
Kingdom. The absence of attention to the relationship between assisted-
reproductive-technologies treatment and the broader fields of biomedical
research was also noted by Mariana Valverde and Lorna Weir in their
analysis of the recommendations made in the *Final Report of the Royal
Commission on New Reproductive Technologies* and proposed legislation
(1997). These relationships have become a greater focus of attention in
recent times due to developments in stem cell biology research, which ·
does not have the betterment of fertility treatments or the resolution of
infertility as its central aim (see Franklin 2006; Haimes and Luce 2006),
but at present requires donated embryos or eggs to proceed (Luce 2008).

2　For example, Erin, like many of the other women I interviewed,
responded to suggestions that she sleep with a man to get pregnant, by
asserting her present attractions as key to her sexuality and identifying
the potential health and legal risks involved in sleeping with a man to
get pregnant. Whereas Erin's friends seemed to think that it would be
natural for her to sleep with a man to get pregnant since she had done it
before, Erin's response suggests that, in fact, that would have been an
unnatural method since it would go against her assessment of the health
of the population of men from which she would be procuring semen and,
ultimately, a key contribution to her child's make-up. Meg, on the other
hand, never considered self-insemination (or, in her words, 'getting a
sample'), although the selection criteria by which she and her partner
narrowed their choice of donor closely resembled the criteria and process
of selection used by women choosing known or anonymous live donors
or frozen sperm.

3　One can also look back to Glynis's comment that she and Virginia
decided to 'run this one out to the end' as though there would be an end
that could be reached. One of the enduring difficulties with respect to
decisions about parenting is that the understanding and experience of
that end point in time can very often shift with the introduction (and
absence) of social, legal, and medical technologies that present new possibilities and foreclose others.

4　Amy Agigian (2004, 24) captures the politics of early parliamentary discussions of AI in the UK, citing Naomi Pfeffer's assessment of the 'threat'
that AI presented. Mary Anne Coffey notes that the Ontario Law Reform

Commission report on new reproductive technologies recommended 'the criminalization of AI when it is practiced without medical supervision' (Coffey 1989).

5 Although not a self-insemination network, a now long-running program in Toronto (Canada), Dykes Planning Tykes, can be viewed as reminiscent of earlier spaces devoted to knowledge exchange and empowerment. The LGBTQ Parenting Centre in Toronto runs programs for people in a variety of family and would-be-parenting constellations and maintains a resourceful website.

6 As well, recent qualitative studies of lesbian families, often based on samples from lesbian support groups or fertility clinics, are frequently comprised of middle-class couples. See discussions in Mamo (2007) and Sullivan (2004).

7 In 2000 a lesbian woman and a gay man were taken to court for having misrepresented their relationship status and undergone IVF treatment in Melbourne, Australia: the Infertility Treatment Act in Victoria prohibits a single woman's access to IVF. It was found that there was insufficient evidence that the man and woman had knowingly given false information to the IVF clinic, and the charges were dismissed. See Kissane (2000) and Burstin (2000). In 2007 the HFEA decided to remove the condition from the HFE Act that clinicians had to consider the need of a child for a father. The assumption represented, however, was that this would open up the possibility for single women and lesbian couples to access donor insemination services. It is seldom mentioned that the use of a donor might be combined with IVF, IVF-ICSI, or preimplantation genetic diagnosis (PGD) (which includes IVF).

8 Growing Generations, an organization specializing in surrogacy and egg donation, with offices in Los Angeles, New York, Boston, and the Ohio Valley, was founded in 1996. Its origination includes the story of two gay men who made private arrangements with a woman for her to be the surrogate mother of their child (that is, become pregnant, carry the fetus to term, and give birth). The woman self-inseminated with the semen of one of the men. She then left the United States while pregnant, breaking the arrangement. The normative practice at Growing Generations (according to the website) seems to be for men to choose an egg donor and a surrogate. One woman's eggs will then be fertilized in vitro with semen from an intending male parent, with the resulting embryo(s) being transferred to another woman's uterus. The presumption perhaps is that this relinquishes the attachment of the pregnant woman to the fetus (see Ragoné 1994).

An advertisement for an annual seminar hosted on 17 September 2007 by the LGBT centre in New York, called Men Having Babies, was sponsored by two commercial surrogacy organizations and was described as being a seminar about biological parenting for gay men.

There seems, in the U.S. discourse at least, to presently be a framing of the use of surrogacy by gay men as a route to biological parenthood, a framing that is also used in the context of a male couple who are trying to become parents. One article on surrogacy reported that the egg donor's eggs were fertilized *with the couple's sperm*, somewhat reminiscent of the story that Rae told in reference to her experiences in the early 1980s. The article goes on to explain that four of the donor's eggs were fertilized with sperm from one man, and four with sperm from the other, giving both men a chance at biological fatherhood. The article does not report whether or not the men then sought clarification of who was the biological father upon birth. The biological contribution of the surrogate mother is noted in references to the previously unknown 'toll' that pregnancy takes on a woman's body, but neither the potentially symmetrical biological contribution of the egg donor (that is, the effect of hormonal stimulation drugs on her body, as well as egg collection surgery) nor the genetic contribution is mentioned.

9 In the UK in 2006, reconsideration of the HFE Act and, specifically, the clause concerning the welfare of the child resulted in amendments which solidified the rights of lesbians to licensed fertility services. The most recent parliamentary debate of the Human Fertilisation and Embryology Bill resulted in recommendations that existing legislation, which recognizes the partner of a woman undergoing treatment as the father, be employed to recognize the lesbian partner of a woman who gives birth to a child or children conceived by assisted reproduction as the parent of the child or children. In 2008 a decision in Australia also found that it was discriminatory not to allow lesbian couples who had conceived using assisted-reproduction technologies the same parental recognition as provided to heterosexual couples becoming parents in the same manner (Blackburn-Starza 2008). My concern, here, is that the emphasis within these decisions is on the use of assisted-reproductive technologies within medical settings and the potential preclusion of other routes of access to legally recognized parental status.

10 Maureen Sullivan puts forward another image with respect to the relationship between lesbians and reproductive technologies, focusing not on the need for a definition of infertility to secure a lesbian's right to access fertility services but on the right of any individual to support for procreation. She writes: 'Families of the two-mother kind where at least one

mother is biologically related to the child due to mothers' access to certain procreative technologies represent, for some, an unambiguously beneficial application of the new technologies. In fact, some would argue that gay and lesbian couples present the most socially and politically defensible case for the need for procreative technologies because without them no gay person would be able to exercise biological kinship or reproduction rights, which are increasingly defined legally and culturally as human rights' (2004, 10–11).

11 Recent books by Laura Mamo (2007), Maureen Sullivan (2004), and Amy Agigian (2004) challenge the status of self-insemination as a 'first stop' in a queer woman's attempts to become a parent by pregnancy. Instead they report that lesbians deciding to become parents enter a biotechnological and biomedicalized world of procreation. Agigian writes: 'Today, lesbians almost always practice AI in a way that is both high-tech and profession-ally mediated' (2004, x). There are many factors influencing this, includ-ing the perception that clinical insemination is more effective (especially with the transition to practices of intrauterine insemination) and thus perhaps also cost-efficient. In Pam and Caroline's words, they felt that they really received 'more bang for their buck' by choosing to do med-ically assisted insemination (see chapter 7).

12 See also Lewin (1998b) for a discussion of fertile lesbians.

13 Caroline Gallop (2007) offers candid images of her experiences of under-going hormonal stimulation while attempting to conceive by donor insemination.

14 Although only one of the men would be the donor, both men would fulfill donor roles as 'uncles.' One couple I interviewed had an arrange-ment with a male couple: One partner acted as the donor for their first child, and the other partner became 'donor number two' during their attempts to conceive a second child. Planning a third child, they plan to use sperm from either donor.

15 A number of conception guides advise women to ask for a copy of the test results if they would like to see them (Pepper 1999; Toevs and Brill 2002). One woman I interviewed noted that the requirement of the donor to have an HIV test was included in the donor contract.

16 In the United States the Health Maintenance Organization (HMO) system sometimes restricts queer women's access to queer-friendly health practi-tioners by restricting women to accessing services in defined catchment areas (see Ponticelli 1998).

17 The use of oral contraceptives is associated in the literature with a reduced risk of ovarian cancer. Pregnancy, or rather breastfeeding, is

associated in the literature with a reduced risk of breast cancer. Lesbians, who are thought to have a reduced consumption of oral contraceptives and be less likely to get pregnant, are thus, theoretically, presumed to be at increased risk for both ovarian and breast cancer.

18 The policy statement notes that there is no specific data on lesbian patients and suggests that 'a maintenance-screening interval of three years seems reasonable. Under this circumstance, routine testing for STDs is unwarranted.' (Davis 2000). Emerging research on woman-to-woman transmission of STIs, and broader environmental assessments of 'risk,' challenges such recommendations.

19 *LGBTT* in this instance refers to 'lesbian, gay, bisexual, transgender, and transsexual.'

20 See also Michelle Walks (2007).

21 See the final chapter of Sullivan (2004) and Schmidt and Moore (1998).

22 A case was recently heard in Ontario in which a lesbian declared that she was discriminated against because she could not access fertility services with the donor of her choice. The donor in question was gay and not her sexual partner.

Chapter Eleven

1 There was also a shift from the terminology *AID* (artificial insemination by donor) to *DI* (donor insemination). This may have related to the cultural discourse of AIDS and the too close proximity between *AID* and *AIDS*. It may also reflect a marked transition from the use of *artificial insemination* to *alternative insemination* (still *AI*, but no longer *AID*) or *donor insemination (DI)* by women and men who objected to the designation of assisted insemination as artificial.

2 See Paula Treichler (1999) for a cultural analysis of the politics of knowledge and information dissemination with respect to AIDS, HIV transmission, and scientific uncertainty. Within mainstream donor insemination programs, the association between HIV transmission and donor semen was not made very early. In 1991 a decision in the case of *Ter Neuzen v. Korn*, concerning a woman who became HIV positive following donor insemination at a clinic run by Dr Gerald Korn in Vancouver, found that he had acted negligently. Other experts were called to testify, including a physician who testified that in a letter to the *New England Journal of Medicine* submitted in 1983 she had raised the possibility of HIV transmission by donor insemination. An article in *The Lancet* in 1985 reported on HIV transmission via AI. The decision was appealed, and a new trial was

heard in 1995 (see Hall 1991). In the reports of the case, the sperm donor, who was part of the anonymous sperm donation program run by Dr Korn, is named. Korn has, however, repeatedly been reported to have stated that he would not reveal the identity of sperm donors.

3 The syndrome was informally called *Gay-Related Immunodeficiency* in writing circa 1981 (Treichler 1999).

4 Similarly, other women in my study represented themselves as women without husbands in order to qualify for donor insemination programs that provided services to single heterosexual women but not lesbians.

5 The tension and uncertainty that surrounded conversations of HIV testing at this time contrasts starkly with the matter-of-factness with which HIV testing during the course of clinic-based fertility treatment is currently approached by clinic staff and sometimes, but not always, 'patients' (Gallop 2007).

6 None of the women I interviewed identified as HIV positive, nor was the HIV status of women mentioned in relation to parenting plans.

7 The test is an HIV antibody test, and it tests for the presence of antibodies, an indication of exposure to different strains of the HIV virus.

8 Debates ensued about the minimal attention paid to lesbians and HIV. On the one hand, women countered the lobby for inclusion of woman-to-woman transmission categories, stating that this reproduced a 'sex paranoia.' On the other hand, activists argued that there was no research on which to ground 'no risk/low risk' status. Regardless, women were not being diagnosed with AIDS-related illnesses, and many women died sooner than men following a diagnosis as HIV positive.

9 Although safer-sex campaigns acknowledged that queer women do have sex with men (and have had sex with men), queer women's histories of using contraceptive technologies, contracting sexually transmitted infections, and experiencing unintended pregnancies and abortions are absent from discourses of lesbian health and the broader politics of reproduction.

10 See note 2 above. This case was not mentioned by women I interviewed. See Luce 2009 for a description of the Semen Regulations and designated-donor program guidelines in Canada.

11 The *I* here refers to 'Intersex.'

12 Maria Hudspith, a health researcher and activist based in British Columbia, produced an accessible brochure for health professionals entitled *Caring for Lesbian Health*, published in 1999 in British Columbia and in revised form by Health Canada in 2001 (http://www.healthservices.gov .bc.ca/library/publications/year/1999/caring.pdf, accessed 22 Septem-

ber 2007). The link to the brochure on the *Health Canada* website is, unfortunately, no longer active. Following the '2001: A Health Odyssey – Building Healthy Communities' conference in Saskatoon (Canada), the Canadian Rainbow Health Coalition (CRHC/CSAC), a French and English bilingual network, was formed. See Hudspith M. (1999).

13 This availability was influenced by the relatively non-private location of our meeting, which was also governed by my awareness not to disclose my purpose for being present.

14 The term *sperm donor* is now appearing in reference to heterosexual women's practice of sleeping with men to have children. Recent court cases in the United States have focused on whether it is possible for a woman to 'steal' a man's sperm during consensual sex.

15 Meg claimed, 'It's actually easy to get pregnant,' then qualified her statement by telling me that it took six months to conceive, during which she closely monitored her temperature and ovulation. Six months prior to her trying, her partner had been monitoring *her* cycle, planning to be the one to get pregnant. It was only after they realized that her partner's cycle was irregular that Meg decided to try to conceive. As she explained, she was the one to get pregnant by a simple process of elimination.

16 One woman inseminated and then later that night slept with the man (that is, the 'donor'). A few women experienced pregnancy and miscarriage during periods of 'bi-' or straight sexual activity with men. One woman, who told me she knew she was a lesbian when she got married, stayed with her husband on a 'five-year plan.' She became pregnant, miscarried, and divorced within the five years. One woman unintentionally conceived following consensual sex with a man.

17 Although she and her partner did not share their intention to have a child with the donor during Meg's attempts to get pregnant, once Meg was pregnant they provided him with the option of having a role in the child's life. He did not acknowledge the pregnancy nor has he been a part of the child's life.

18 The use of *donors* here is purposeful in order to point to the significance of the person rather than the substance in this practice.

19 Practitioners at clinics in Canada will not inseminate women with fresh semen from 'unrelated' donors. Women who wish to use known donors and frozen semen can do so through, for example, a directed-donor program at ReproMed Ltd., located in Toronto, Ontario.

20 The connection between the transmission of HIV and donor insemination began to be reported in 1984, according to some sources. The donor

program in Vancouver discontinued inseminations in order to test donors, when reports were more widely circulated in 1985 (Hall 1991). In California, especially in the San Francisco Bay area, where a significant amount of literature on lesbian motherhood emerges (Sullivan 2004; Mamo 2007; Lewin 1993), sperm banks began testing donors for HIV and quarantining frozen semen during the 1980s.

21 Becker points out that the United States is one country that does not require physicians to use frozen semen by law (2000).

22 The assumption that lesbians are not at risk from HIV plays out in strange ways. On the one hand, having sex with a man in order to get pregnant is deemed as low risk because it is not going to be an ongoing activity. On the other hand, inseminating (without sexual contact) seems to make people forget the risk.

Chapter Twelve

1 The women I interviewed in my earlier research on women's embodied experiences of pregnancy (Luce 1997) spoke about losing or gaining weight in order to maximize the chances of pregnancy and to reduce the toll or impact of pregnancy on their bodies. A number of those women who suspected they *could* be pregnant took pregnancy tests at home on the days of weddings or parties in order to know whether or not they could consume alcohol.

2 In some ways, rendering the woman's experience of pregnancy visible makes Pepper's guide seem less 'fetocentric' (Mitchell 2001) than others. Yet, as I have argued elsewhere (Luce 1997), an expectation that women will avoid risks to the fetus facilitates a refocusing on women's bodies and designates pregnant women as responsible for representing repro-ductive normalcy.

3 It is important to note in this section that I am addressing here 'pre-con-ception' screening, that is, women's understandings of genetic knowl-edge that were mediated prior to becoming pregnant or experiencing a pregnancy with a partner. Women in this study also mediated medical information and the meanings of screening technologies that were intended to relate more directly to a specific fetus.

4 The women I interviewed who were adopted did not have access to this information. One woman, after assessing her own genetic health history, decided that she would not conceive a child.

5 Although the concept of genetic determinism is significantly challenged by new developments in genomics (and the complexity of interaction

between genes, proteins, and environment), medical practices and therapies that are available, as well as their use, continue to support the discursive and practical emphasis on particular gene mutations.

6 The fertility clinic which she attended did not have its own sperm bank
or sperm-donor program, but rather semen was obtained from external
commercial sperm banks.

7 See the website at http://www.donorsiblingregistry.com/ (last accessed
on 16 June 2008). Although the registry was established for the purpose
of connecting siblings, in the notices there are also postings by individuals seeking additional vials of semen that others who conceived by the
same donor may still have in storage.

    I find it surprising that such authority is given to the coding system
implemented by sperm banks, with the result that relationships are established on the basis of children being conceived with semen from vials
containing the same number, or from paperwork indicating a choice of
this particular number. This current procedure invests in the accuracy of
coding and everyday practice, which will have their faults, as has been
clearly shown in other assisted-reproduction practices such as IVF, and
events such as the transfer of the wrong embryos. There is a consistent
assumption made that the code number given to a sperm donor remains
consistent over time and is simply a substitute for the name. I have not
yet seen anything written to the contrary; however, it seems strange that
in an industry which has been dominated by discourses of anonymity,
such a direct translation between code and individual has been consistently maintained.

8 On the Donor Sibling Registry website, the postings do not indicate a
donor identification number for those donors who were affiliated with
Dr Gerald Korn's practice.

Chapter Thirteen

1 This is a footnote taken from 'The Queers at the Centre of High-Tech
Reproduction: A Lesbian Body Sells Her Eggs' (Pollock 1998), in which
Pollock explores the normative governance of paid egg donation and her
(queer) participation in the practice. The *they* she refers to are the women
seeking reproductive treatment whom she sees in the waiting room of the
clinic.

2 GIFT involves the extraction of a woman's egg and then insertion of both
the egg and sperm into the fallopian tube. Conception thus does not take
place outside of the woman's body but places the egg and sperm cells in

closer proximity to each other and bypasses the need for the egg to be 'taken up' into the fallopian tube. Interestingly, until recently, if GIFT involved the intended parents' own gametes, it was not regulated by the HFEA.

3 See discussions regarding the 'virgin birth' debates in the United Kingdom (Shore 1992; Franklin 1997).

4 The Warnock Report was published in 1985, followed by the Human Fertilisation and Embryology Act in 1990 and the implementation of the regulatory body, the Human Fertilisation and Embryology Authority in 1991. See Franklin (1997), Steinberg (1997a), and Spallone (1989) for analyses of the development of regulatory processes.

5 When I began research in the UK in 2002, ManNotIncluded, a website-based donor-semen service (not a sperm bank) had just been launched. It was cited as providing lesbians with a necessary service which was otherwise unavailable to them. While single women (lesbian or not) and women partners were gaining access to assisted-reproduction services at clinics across England, access was not a given, and assessment of the context into which the child would be born still took place. It was surprising, though, when discussion about the clause began within the context of the open consultation entitled 'Tomorrow's Children,' to realize how many people had thought that this 'and also the need for the father' advice clause was no longer in force.

6 The Centre for Reproductive Care was closed in March 2009.

7 The 1995 voluntary moratorium on the buying and selling of human gametes (eggs or sperm) was adhered to, in general, by the practice common to fertility clinics in Canada of making arrangements with sperm banks based in the United States (Luce 2009). The commercial transactions of donor payment took place outside of Canada, and women or couples paid fees for the insemination service. The fees, though, were dependent on the currency exchange, as well as on the 'prices' for particular donors set by the sperm bank.

8 See Luce 2009 for an analysis of the unintended and stratified effect of assisted-reproduction governance.

9 See Health Canada's website for a detailed chronology of the proposed bills.

10 The information about the consultation was available at http://www.hc-sc.gc.ca/ahc-asc/public-consult/consultations/col/pgd-dgp/cons1_e.html (accessed 2 September 2007).

11 See http://www.hc-sc.gc.ca/hl-vs/reprod/hc-sc/index_e.html (accessed 2 September 2007).

12 Angela Mulholland, author of an article posted to www.CTV.ca entitled
    'Infertile Couples Disappointed with Cloning Bill' (2004), stated that the
    legislation would ban human cloning and regulate stem cell research,
    and she went on to focus on the implications of banning the commercial-
    ization of gametes (http://www.CTV.ca [accessed 2 September 2007]).
    The Multiple Sclerosis Society also referred to the AHR Act as a cloning
    law.
13 The 1993 final report of the Royal Commission on New Reproductive
    Technologies had also recommended a ban on cloning, but it was
    perhaps not viewed at that time as a pressing issue in need of formal
    governance. It was not necessarily known by which form (that is, by
    which technique) cloning might be possible.

Bibliography

Achilles, Rona. 1993. Self-Insemination in Canada. In *Treatment of Infertility: Assisted Reproductive Technologies Research Studies of the Royal Commission on New Reproductive Technologies*. Ottawa: Royal Commission on New Reproductive Technologies.

Agigian, Amy. 2004. *Baby Steps: How Alternative Insemination Is Changing the World*. Middletown, CT: Wesleyan University Press.

Aird, Elisabeth. 1998. Gay and Lesbian Parents: We Are Family. *Vancouver Sun*, 1 May, final edition, C10.

Almeling, Rene. 2007. Selling Genes, Selling Gender: Egg Agencies, Sperm Banks, and the Medical Market in Genetic Material. *American Sociological Review* 72 (3):319.

Anderson, Lynda, Theresa Healy, Barbara Herringer, Barbara Isaac, and Ty Perry 2001. *Out in the Cold: The Context of Lesbian Health in Northern British Columbia*. Vancouver: British Columbia Centre of Excellence for Women's Health.

Andrews, Lori. 1999. The Sperminator. *New York Times Magazine*, 28 March, 60-65.

Arditti, Rita, Renate Duelli Klein, and Shelley Minden, eds. 1984. *Test-Tube Women: What Future for Motherhood*. London: Pandora.

Arnup, Katherine. 1991. 'We are family': Lesbian Mothers in Canada. *Resources for Feminist Research* 20 (3-4):101-107.

– 1994. *Education for Motherhood: Advice for Mothers in Twentieth-Century Canada*. Toronto: University of Toronto Press.

– ed. 1995. *Lesbian Parenting: Living with Pride and Prejudice*. Charlottetown, PEI: Gynergy Books.

– 1998. Does the Word Lesbian Mean Anything to You? Lesbian Mothers Raising Daughters. In *Redefining Motherhood: Changing Identities and Patterns*. Ed. S. Abbey and A. O'Reilly. Toronto: Second Story Press.

Arnup, Katherine, and Susan Boyd. 1995. Familial Disputes? Sperm Donors, Lesbian Mothers, and Legal Parenthood. In *Legal Inversions: Lesbians, Gay Men, and the Politics of Law.* Ed. D. Herman and C.F. Stychin. Philadelphia: Temple University Press.

Atkins, Jeannine. 1999. *A Name on the Quilt: A Story of Remembrance.* Illus. Tad Hills. New York: Atheneum Books for Young Readers.

Balsamo, Anne. 1996. *Technologies of the Gendered Body: Reading Cyborg Women.* Durham: Duke University Press.

BBC News. 2001. Eggs Fertilized Without Sperm. 10 July.

– 2005. Concern Over Three-Parent Embryo. 9 September. http://news.bbc .co.uk/1/hi/health/4228712.stm.

Becker, Gay. 2000. *The Elusive Embryo: How Women and Men Approach New Reproductive Technologies.* Berkeley: University of California Press.

Beckman, Linda J., and S. Marie Harvey. 2005. Current Reproductive Technologies: Increased Access and Choice? *Journal of Social Issues* 61 (1):1–20.

Bell, David, and Gill Valentine, eds. 1995. *Mapping Desire: Geographies of Sexualities.* New York: Routledge.

Bissessar, Haimant. 2005. Altruism by Law. *The Canadian Journal of Infertility Awareness,* Summer:11–14.

Blackburn-Starza, Anthony. 2008. Equal Rights for Lesbian Parents in New South Wales. *Progress Educational Trust,* 29 April, http://www.ivf.net /ivf/equal_rights_for_lesbian_parents_in_new_south_wales-o3371.html (accessed 29 March 2009).

Blackwood, Evelyn, and Saskia Wieringa. 1999. *Female Desires: Same-Sex Relations and Transgender Practices Across Cultures.* New York: Columbia University Press.

Boston Women's Health Book Collective. 1994. *Our Bodies, Ourselves: A Book by and for Women.* New York: Simon and Schuster. (Orig. pub. 1970.)

Bourassa, Kevin, and Joe Varnell. 2007. Maritime Mothers Plan Childbirth in Exile: Nova Scotian Fights for Wife's Recognition as Parent. Available at http://www.samesexmarriage.ca/advocacy/nsf200407.htm (accessed 20 August 2007).

Bourgeault, Ivy, Jacquelyne Luce, and Margaret MacDonald. 2006. The Caring Dilemma in Midwifery: Balancing the Needs of Midwives and Clients in a Continuity of Care Model of Practice. *Community, Work and Family* 9 (4):389–406.

Bourgeault, Ivy, Jacquelyne Luce, Margaret MacDonald, and Jude Winkup.

2006. In preparation. *Doors Opened, Doors Closed: Integrating Midwives into Hospitals in B.C. and Ontario*.

Boyd, Susan B. 2007. Gendering Legal Parenthood: Bio-Genetic Ties, Intentionality, and Responsibility. *Windsor Yearbook of Access to Justice (2007)*. Available at http://ssrn.com/abstract=962236.

Brill, Stephanie. 2006. *The New Essential Guide to Lesbian Conception, Pregnancy, and Birth*. Los Angeles and New York: Alyson Books.

Burstin, Fay. 2000. Gay Police Clear on IVF. *Herald Sun*, 24 February, 15.

Butler, Judith. 1990. *Gender Trouble: Feminism and the Subversion of Identity*. New York: Routledge.

Byers, F., and J. Malvern. 2007. Lesbian Hits Back in Sperm Donor Support Case. *Times Online*, 4 December, http://www.timesonline.co.uk/tol/news/uk/article2998076.ece (accessed 17 June 2008).

Canada. 1993. Royal Commission on New Reproductive Technologies. *Proceed with Care: Final Report of the Royal Commission on New Reproductive Technologies*. Ottawa: Minister of Government Services.

Canada. 2004. Bill C-6, *Assisted Human Reproduction Act*, SC 2004, c. 2. Available at http://www.canlii.org/ca/sta/a-13.4 (accessed 12 June 2008).

Cannell, Fenella. 1990. Concepts of Parenthood: The Warnock Report, the Gillick Debate, and Modern Myths. *American Ethnologist* 17 (4):667–686.

Capen, Karen. 1997. Can Doctors Place Limits on Their Medical Practice? *Canadian Medical Association Journal* 156:839–40.

Carsten, Janet, ed. 2000. *Cultures of Relatedness: New Approaches to the Study of Kinship*. Cambridge: Cambridge University Press.

– 2004. *After Kinship*. Cambridge: Cambridge University Press.

CBC News. 2007. Ontario Court Says Boy Can Have Dad, Mom – and Mom. 3 January. http://www.cbc.ca/canada/toronto/story/2007/01/03/twomom-court.html (accessed 16 June 2008).

Clarke, Adele. 1998. *Disciplining Reproduction: Modernity, American Life Sciences, and the 'Problems of Sex.'* Berkeley: University of California Press.

Clarke, Adele, and Virginia L. Olesen. 1999. *Revisioning Women, Health, and Healing: Feminist, Cultural, and Technoscience Perspectives*. New York: Routledge.

Coffey, Mary Anne. 1989. Seizing the Means of Reproduction: Proposal for an Exploratory Study of Alternative Fertilization and Parenting Strategies Among Lesbian Women. *Resources for Feminist Research* 18 (3):76–79.

Corea, G. 1985. *The Mother Machine: Reproductive Technologies from Artificial Insemination to Artificial Wombs*. New York: Harper & Row.

Crews, Heather. 2005. Women Be Warned, Egg Donation Isn't All It's

Cracked Up to Be: The Copulation of Science and the Courts Makes
Multiple Mommies. *North Carolina Journal of Law and Technology* 7
(1):141–156.

Cussins, Charis M. 1998a. Producing Reproduction: Techniques of Normalization and Naturalization in Infertility Clinics. In *Reproducing Reproduction: Kinship, Power, and Technological Innovation.* Ed. S. Franklin and H.
Ragoné. Philadelphia: University of Pennsylvania Press.

– 1998b. 'Quit Sniveling, Cryo-Baby. We'll Work Out Which One's Your
Mama!' In *Cyborg Babies: From Techno-Sex to Techno-Tots.* Ed. R. Davis-Floyd
and J. Dumit. New York: Routledge.

– 1998c. Ontological Choreography: Agency for Women Patients in an Infertility Clinic. In *Differences in Medicine: Unraveling Practices, Techniques, and
Bodies,* ed. M. Berg and A. Mol. Durham, NC: Duke University Press.

– *See also* Thompson, Charis.

Dalton, Susan. 2000. Nonbiological Mothers and the Legal Boundaries of
Motherhood: An Analysis of California Law. In *Ideologies and Technologies of
Motherhood.* Ed. H. Ragoné and F. Winddance Twine. New York: Routledge.

– 2001. Protecting Our Parent-Child Relationships: Understanding the
Strengths and Weaknesses of Second-Parent Adoption. In *Queer Families,
Queer Politics: Challenging Culture and the State.* Ed. M. Bernstein and R.
Reimann. New York: Columbia University Press.

Daniels, Cynthia R. 1997. Between Fathers and Fetuses: The Social Construction of Male Reproduction and the Politics of Fetal Harm. *Signs: Journal of
Women in Culture & Society* 22 (3):579–616.

Daniels, K.R., and I. Burn. 1997. Access to Assisted Human Reproduction
Services by Minority Groups. *Australia and New Zealand Journal of Obstetrics
and Gynaecology* 37 (1):79–85.

Davis, Victoria. 2000. Lesbian Health Guidelines. *Society of Obstetricians and
Gynaecologists of Canada* 22 (3):202–205.

Davis-Floyd, Robbie, and Joseph Dumit, eds. 1998. *Cyborg Babies: From
Techno-Sex to Techno-Tots.* New York: Routledge.

De Bruin, Philip. 2003. Lesbians: Biological Parents. *News 24.*
http://www.news24.com/News24v2/Components/Generic/News24v2
_Print_PopUp_A (accessed 17 June 2008).

Demczuk, Irène, Michèle Caron, Ruth Rose, and Lyne Bouchard. 2002. Recognition of Lesbian Couples: An Inalienable Right. Ottawa: Status of Women
Canada. Available at http://publications.gc.ca/pub?id=293729&sl=0
(accessed 3 June 2009).

Duelli Klein, Renate. 1984. Doing It Ourselves: Self-Insemination. In *Test-Tube*

Women: What Future For Motherhood? ed. R. Arditti, R. Duelli Klein, and S. Minden. London: Pandora Press.

– 1987. What's 'New' About the 'New' Reproductive Technologies? In *Man-Made Women: How New Reproductive Technologies Affect Women*, ed. G. Corea. Bloomington: Indiana University Press.

Edwards, Jeanette. 2000. *Born and Bred: Idioms of Kinship and New Reproductive Technologies in England*. Oxford: Oxford University Press.

Edwards, Jeanette, Sarah Franklin, Eric Hirsch, Frances Price, and Marilyn Strathern, eds. 1999. *Technologies of Procreation: Kinship in the Age of Assisted Conception*. New York: Routledge. (Orig. pub. 1993.)

Edwards, Jeanette, and Marilyn Strathern. 2000. Including Our Own. In *Cultures of Relatedness: New Approaches to the Study of Kinship*, ed. J. Carsten. Cambridge: Cambridge University Press.

Egale Canada. 2002. 'Tolerance Is Always Age-Appropriate,' Supreme Court Rules. Press release, 20 December. http://www.egale.ca/index.asp?lang=E&menu=70&item=101.

Englert, Y. 1994. Artificial Insemination of Single Women and Lesbian Women with Donor Semen. *Human Reproduction* 9 (11):1969–1977.

Farquhar, Dion. 1996. *The Other Machine: Discourse and Reproductive Technologies*. New York: Routledge.

– 1999. Gamete Traffic/Pedestrian Crossings. In *Playing Dolly: Technocultural Formations, Fantasies, and Fictions of Assisted Reproduction*, eds. A.E. Kaplan and S.M. Squier. New Brunswick, NJ: Rutgers University Press.

findlay, barbara. 1998. BC Includes Queers in Family Law Act: Children Protected in Amendment. *Siren Magazine*, April–May:5.

Finkler, Kaja. 2000. *Experiencing the New Genetics: Family and Kinship on the Medical Frontier*. Philadelphia: University of Pennsylvania Press.

Fisher, John. 2000. 'Too Little, Too Late': Canadian Alliance Candidate Apologizes for Anti-Gay Slur; EGALE Challenges Alliance MPs to Apologize for Other Offensive Comments. Press release, 6 November. Available at http://www.egale.ca/index.asp?lang=E&menu=102&item=910 (accessed 22 June 2008).

Fisher, Sara. 1995. Lesbian Health Care Issues: A Guide for Gynaecologists. *Society of Obstetrics and Gynaecology in Canada* 17:1077–88.

Franklin, Sarah. 1990. Deconstructing 'Desperateness': The Social Construction of Infertility in Popular Representations of New Reproductive Technologies. In *The New Reproductive Technologies*, ed. M. McNeil, I. Varcoe, and S. Yearley. London: MacMillan.

– 1995a. Postmodern Procreation: A Cultural Account of Assisted Reproduction. In *Conceiving the New World Order: The Global Politics of Reproduction*, ed. F. Ginsburg and R. Rapp. Berkeley, CA: University of California Press.

– 1995b. Science as Culture, Cultures of Science. *Annual Review of Anthropology* 24:163–84.

– 1997. *Embodied Progress: A Cultural Account of Assisted Conception*. London and New York: Routledge.

– 1998. Making Miracles: Scientific Progress and the Facts of Life. In *Reproducing Reproduction: Kinship, Power, and Technological Innovation*, ed. S. Franklin and H. Ragoné. Philadelphia: University of Pennsylvania Press.

– 2006. Embryonic Economies: The Double Reproductive Value of Stem Cells. *BioSocieties* 1:71–90.

Franklin, Sarah, and Susan McKinnon, eds. 2001. *Relative Values: Reconfiguring Kinship Studies*. Durham, NC: Duke University Press.

Franklin, Sarah, and Maureen McNeil. 1988. Reproductive Futures: Recent Literature and Current Feminist Debates on Reproductive Technologies. *Feminist Studies* 14 (3):545–60.

Franklin, Sarah, and Helena Ragoné, eds. 1998. *Reproducing Reproduction: Kinship, Power, and Technological Innovation*. Philadelphia: University of Pennsylvania Press.

Franklin, Sarah, and Celia Roberts. 2006. *Born and Made: An Ethnography of Preimplantation Genetic Diagnosis*. Princeton: Princeton University Press.

Gallop, Caroline. 2007. *Making Babies the Hard Way: Living with Infertility and Treatment*. London: Jessica Kingsley Publishers.

Garden, Nancy. 2000. *Holly's Secret*. New York: Farrar, Straus, & Giroux.

Gartrell, Nanette, Amy Banks, Nancy Reed, Jean Hamilton, Carla Rodas, and Amalia Deck. 2000. The National Lesbian Family Study. Pt. 3, Interviews with Mothers of Five-Year-Olds. *American Journal of Orthopsychiatry* 70 (4):542–8.

Gartrell, Nanette, Jean Hamilton, Amy Banks, Dee Mosbacher, Nancy Reed, Caroline H. Sparks, and Holly Bishop. 1996. The National Lesbian Family Study. Pt. 1, Interviews with Prospective Mothers. *American Journal of Orthopsychiatry* 66 (2):272–281.

Gavigan, Shelley. 2000. Mothers, Other Mothers, and Others: The Legal Challenges and Contradictions of Lesbian Parents. In *Law as a Gendering Practice*, ed. D.E. Chunn and D. Lacombe. Don Mills, ON: Oxford University Press.

Ginsburg, Faye, and Rayna Rapp, eds. 1995. *Conceiving the New World Order: The Global Politics of Reproduction*. Berkeley, CA: University of California Press.

Gravenor, Kristian. 2004. Infertile Ground. *Montreal Mirror*, http://www
.montrealmirror.com/ARCHIVES/2004/081904/cover_news.html
(accessed 13 April 2007).

Grayson, Deborah. 2000. Mediating Intimacy: Black Surrogate Mothers and
the Law. In *Biotechnology and Culture: Bodies, Anxieties, Ethics*, ed. P.E.
Brodwin. Bloomington, IN: Indiana University Press.

Haimes, Erica. 1990. Recreating the Family? Policy Considerations Relating
to the 'New' Reproductive Technologies. In *The New Reproductive Technologies*, ed. M. McNeil, I. Varcoe, and S. Yearley. London: MacMillan.

Haimes, Erica, and Jacquelyne Luce. 2006. Studying Potential Donors' Views
on Embryonic Stem Cell Therapies and Preimplantation Genetic Diagnosis.
Human Fertility 9 (2):67–71.

Haimes, Erica, and Kate Weiner. 2000. `Everybody's Got a Dad.' Issues for
Lesbian Families in the Management of Donor Insemination. *Sociology of
Health & Illness* 22 (4):477–99.

Hall, N. 1991. Infected Sperm Donor Left a Legacy of Death for Victoria
Nurse. *The Vancouver Sun*, 21 November, A1.

Haraway, Donna. 1991. *Simian, Cyborgs, and Women: The Reinvention of Nature*.
New York: Routledge.

Harmon, Amy. 2007. Sperm Donor Father Ends His Anonymity. *New York
Times*, 14 February. http://www.nytimes.com/2007/02/14/us/
14donor.html?ex=1329109200&en=36011329be c29b1e&ei=5088&partner=
rssnyt&emc=rss (accessed 17 April 2007).

Hartouni, Valerie. 1997. *Cultural Conceptions: On Reproductive Technologies
and the Remaking of Life*. Minneapolis, MN: University of Minnesota Press.

Hayden, Corinne. 1995. Gender, Genetics, and Generation: Reformulating
Biology in Lesbian Kinship. *Cultural Anthropology* 10 (1):41–63.

Hennessy, Patrick, and Beezy Marsh. 2006. Fatherless Babies in Fertility Revolution. *Sunday Telegraph*, 11 December.

Hilborn, Robin. 2007. Ontario Law Behind the Times. Boy Has Three Parents,
Ontario Court Rules. *Family Helper News*, 9 January. http://www.family-
helper.net/news/070109threeparents.html (accessed 16 June 2008).

Hoffman, Eric. 1999. *Best Best Colors / Los Mejores Colores*. Illus. Celeste Hen-
riquez. Trans. E. de la Vega. St Paul, MN: Redleaf Press.

Hornstein, Francie. 1984. Children by Donor Insemination: A New Choice for
Lesbians. In *Test-Tube Women: What Future For Motherhood?* ed. R. Arditti, R.
Duelli Klein, and S. Minden. London: Pandora Press.

Hudspith, Maria. 1999. Caring for Lesbian Health: A Resource for Health
Care Providers, Policy Makers, and Planners. Victoria, BC: Ministry Advisory Council for Women's Health.

Hudspith, Maria, with Jannit Rabinovitch. 2002. 'Made in BC': An Overview of Lesbian-Specific Research in British Columbia. Vancouver, BC: Status of Women Canada and Women's Creative Network of BC. Available at http://educ.ubc.ca/faculty/bryson/inqueery/images/bibliography.pdf (accessed 3 June 2009).

Johnston, Josephine. 2002. Mum's the Word: Donor Anonymity in Assisted Reproduction. *Health Law Review* 11 (1):51–55.

Kaeser, Gigi, and Peggy Gillespie. 1999. *Love Makes a Family: Portraits of Lesbian, Gay, Bisexual, and Transgender Parents and their Families.* Amherst, MA: University of Massachusetts Press.

Kahn, Susan M. 2000. *Reproducing Jews: A Cultural Account of Assisted Conception in Israel.* Durham, NC: Duke University Press.

Kaplan, Ann E., and Susan Merrill Squier. 1999. *Playing Dolly: Technocultural Formations, Fantasies, and Fictions of Assisted Reproduction.* New Brunswick, NJ: Rutgers University Press.

Katz Rothman, Barbara. 1986. *The Tentative Pregnancy.* New York: Viking Press.

Kennedy, Elizabeth Lapovsky, and Madeline D. Davis. 1993. *Boots of Leather, Slippers of Gold: The History of a Lesbian Community.* New York: Routledge.

Kinross, Louise. 1992. Breaking the Silence on Donor Insemination. *Toronto Star*, 25 July, G1.

Kissane, Karen. 2000. IVF Doctor to Challenge Laws. *The Age*, 25 February, MEBA1.

Kulick, Don, and Margaret Wilson, eds. 1995. *Taboo: Sex, Identity, and Erotic Subjectivity in Anthropological Fieldwork.* London and New York: Routledge.

Lahey, Kathleen. 1999. *Are We 'Persons' Yet? Law and Sexuality in Canada.* Toronto and Buffalo: University of Toronto Press.

– 2001. The Impact of Relationship Recognition on Lesbian Women in Canada: Still Separate and Only Somewhat 'Equivalent.' Status of Women Canada. Ottawa: Status of Women Canada. Available at http://publications.gc.ca/pub?id=293460&sl=0 (accessed 3 June 2009).

Landecker, Hannah. 2003. Discussant, Genealogical Hybridities Panel at the ASA Decennial Conference, Anthropology and Science, Manchester, UK.

Layne, Linda, ed. 1999. *Transformative Motherhood: On Giving and Getting in a Consumer Culture.* New York: New York University Press.

Lewin, Ellen. 1981. Lesbianism and Motherhood. *Human Organization* 40 (1):6–14.

– 1993. *Lesbian Mothers: Accounts of Gender in American Culture.* Ithaca and London: Cornell University Press.

– 1998a. *Recognizing Ourselves: Ceremonies of Lesbian and Gay Commitment.* New York: Columbia University Press.

– 1998b. Wives, Mothers, and Lesbians: Rethinking Resistance in the US. In *Pragmatic Women and Body Politics*, ed. M. Lock and P. Kaufert. Cambridge: Cambridge University Press.

Lewin, Ellen, and William Leap, eds. 1996. *Out in the Field: Reflections of Lesbian and Gay Anthropologists*. Urbana: University of Illinois Press.

Lock, Margaret, and Patricia Kaufert. 1998a. Introduction. In *Pragmatic Women and Body Politics*. Cambridge: Cambridge University Press.

– eds. 1998b. *Pragmatic Women and Body Politics*. Cambridge: Cambridge University Press.

Luce, Jacquelyne. 1997. Visible Bodies: Revealing the Paradox of Pregnancy. Master's thesis, Department of Anthropology, York University, Toronto.

– 1998. Negotiated Relations: Dykes, Reproductive Technologies and the Politics of Conception. American Anthropological Association Meeting, Philadelphia, United States.

– 2000. Genes and Nations: Cultural Dimensions of Transborder Gamete Transactions. American Anthropological Association, San Francisco, United States.

– 2002. Making Choices / Taking Chances: Lesbian/Bi/Queer Women, Assisted Conception, and Reproductive Health. Vancouver: BC Centre of Excellence for Women's Health. Available at http://www.bccewh.bc.ca /publications-resources/documents/makingchoices.pdf (accessed 20 June 2009).

– 2003. Recording Relatedness: 'Nonbiological Birth Mothers' and Other New Possibilities. Association of Social Anthropologists Conference, Manchester, UK.

– 2004. Imaging Bodies, Imagining Relations: Narratives of Queer Women and 'Assisted Conception.' *Journal of Medical Humanities* 25 (1):47–56.

– 2005a. Egg and Embryo Donation for Stem Cell Research. Paper presented at the Heinrich Böll Foundation, co-sponsored by the Institut Mensch, Ethik und Wissenschaft, 4 March, in Berlin, Germany.

– 2005b. Shelley's Story: A Narrative of Pregnancy Loss. In *Gendered Intersections: An Introduction to Women's and Gender Studies*, ed. C.L. Biggs and P.J. Downe. Halifax, NS: Fernwood Press.

– 2008. Ethics as Capital: Eggs, Research Governance, and the Politics of Representation. In *Mehrwertiger Kapitalismus: Multidisziplinäre Beiträge zu Formen des Kapitals und seiner Kapitalien*, ed. Stephan A. Jansen, Eckhard Schröter, and Nico Stehr. Wiesbaden: VS Verlag für Sozialwissenschaften.

– 2009. Regulatory Borders: Knowledge Politics and Reproductive Science. In *The Social Integration of Science: Institutional and Epistemological Aspects of the Transformation of Knowledge in Modern Society*, ed. G. Bechmann, V. Gorokhov, and N. Stehr. Berlin: Edition Sigma.

Luce, Jacquelyne, with Janet Neely, Teresa Lee, and Ann Pederson. 2000. *Documenting Visibility: Selected Bibliography on Lesbian and Bisexual Women's Health*. Vancouver: British Columbia Centre of Excellence for Women's Health. Available at http://www.bccewh.bc.ca/publications-resources/download_publications.htm.

Mamo, Laura. 2005. Biomedicalizing Kinship: Sperm Banks and the Creation of Affinity-ties. *Science as Culture* 14 (3):237–264.

– 2007. *Queering Reproduction: Achieving Pregnancy in the Age of Technoscience*. Durham and London: Duke University Press.

Martin, Emily. 1987. *The Woman in the Body: A Cultural Analysis of Reproduction*. Boston: Beacon Press.

– 1991. The Egg and the Sperm: How Science has Constructed a Romance Based on Stereotypical Male-Female Roles. *Signs* 16:485–501.

Matas, Robert. 1998. BC Gay Parents Gain Equality. *Globe and Mail*, 5 February.

Mathieson, Cynthia. 1998. Lesbian and Bisexual Health Care. *Canadian Family Physician* 44:1634–1640.

McClelland, Susan. 2002. Who's My Birth Father? *Maclean's*, 20 May, 20–26.

McElroy, Wendy. 2005. Case Could Freeze Sperm Donation. *FoxNews.com*, 31 May 31. http://www.foxnews.com/printer_friendly_story/0,3566, 157553,00.html (accessed 17 June 2008).

McKeague, Paul. 2000. Offspring Plead for Sperm-Donor ID. *Calgary Herald*, 13 August, A7.

McNeil, Maureen. 1990. Reproductive Technologies: A New Terrain for the Sociology of Technology. In *The New Reproductive Technologies*, ed. Maureen McNeil, Ian Varcoe, and Steven Yearley. London: MacMillan.

McNeil, Maureen, Ian Varcoe, and Steven Yearley, eds. 1990. *The New Reproductive Technologies*. London: Macmillan.

Mick, Hayley. 2007. Who's Your Donor? *Globe and Mail*, 24 July. Available at http://www.theglobeandmail.com/servlet/story/RTGAM.20070724.wldo nors24/BNStory/ lifeMain/home#.

Millbank, Jenni. 2003. From Here to Maternity: A Review of the Research on Lesbian and Gay Families. *Australian Journal of Social Issues* (38):541–600.

Mitchell, Lisa M. 1993. Making Babies: Routine Ultrasound Imaging and the Cultural Construction of the Fetus. Dissertation, Case Western Reserve University.

– 2001. *Baby's First Picture: Ultrasound and the Politics of Fetal Subjects*. Toronto: University of Toronto Press.

Modell, Judith. 1999. Freely Given: Open Adoption and the Rhetoric of the Gift. In *Transformative Motherhood: On Giving and Getting in a Consumer Culture*, ed. L. Layne. New York: New York University Press.

Moore, Pamela. 1999. Selling Reproduction. In *Playing Dolly: Technocultural Formations, Fantasies, and Fictions of Assisted Reproduction*, ed. E. Ann Kaplan and Susan Squier. New Brunswick, NJ: Rutgers University Press.

Moran, Nancy. 1996. Lesbian Health Care Needs. *Canadian Family Physician* 42:879–884.

Morris, Rosalind. 1995. All Made Up: Performance Theory and the New Anthropology of Sex and Gender. *Annual Review of Anthropology* 24:567–92.

Mulholland, Angela. 2004. Infertile Couples Disappointed with Cloning Bill. *CTV News*, 4 March (accessed 2 September 2007).

Murphy, Julien. 2001. Should Lesbians Count as Infertile Couples? Anti-lesbian Discrimination in Assisted Reproduction. In *Queer Families, Queer Politics: Challenging Culture and the State*, ed. M. Bernstein and R. Reimann. New York: Columbia University Press.

Nelson, Fiona. 1996. *Lesbian Motherhood: An Exploration of Canadian Lesbian Families*. Toronto: University of Toronto Press.

Newton, Esther. 2001. *Margaret Mead Made Me Gay: Personal Essays, Public Ideas*. Durham and London: Duke University Press.

Nisker, Jeff, and Angela White. 2005. The CMA Code of Ethics and the Donation of Fresh Embryos for Stem Cell Research. *Canadian Medical Association Journal* 173 (6). Available at http://www.cmaj.ca/cgi/content/full/173/6/621.

Peletz, Michael. 1995. Kinship Studies in Late Twentieth-Century Anthropology. *Annual Review of Anthropology* 24:343–72.

Pepper, Rachel. 1999. *The Ultimate Guide to Pregnancy for Lesbians: How to Stay Sane and Care for Yourself from Pre-conception Through Birth*. 2nd ed. San Francisco: Cleis Press, 2005.

Peters, Rich. 2002. Mayor Snubs Straight Pride Day. *365Gay.com*. Available at http://www.Groovyannies.com/news/2002/press28.html.

Pies, Cheri. 1988. *Considering Parenthood: A Workbook for Lesbians*. San Francisco: Spinsters / Aunt Lute.

Pollock, Anne. 1998. The Queers at the Centre of High-Tech Reproduction: A Lesbian Body Sells Her Eggs. *Critical inQueeries* 2 (1):59–66.

Ponticelli, Christy M., ed. 1998. *Gateways to Improving Lesbian Health and Health Care: Opening Doors*. New York: Haworth Press.

Porter, Andrew. 2008. Two Mother IVF Families Enshrined in Law. *Telegraph*, 20 May. http://www.telegraph.co.uk/news/uknews/1996358/Two-mother-IVF-families-enshrined-in-law.html (accessed 12 June 2008).

Ragoné, Helena. 1994. *Surrogate Motherhood: Conception in the Heart*. Boulder, CO: Westview Press.

– 1999. The Gift of Life: Surrogate Motherhood, Gamete Donation, and Constructions of Altruism. In *Transformative Motherhood: On Giving and Getting
in a Consumer Culture*, ed. L. Layne. New York: New York University Press.

Ragoné, Helena, and France Winddance Twine, eds. 2000. *Ideologies and Technologies of Motherhood: Race, Class, Sexuality, Nationalism*. New York: Routledge.

Rapp, Rayna. 1999. *Testing Women, Testing the Fetus: The Social Impact of
Amniocentesis in America*. New York: Routledge.

– 2000. Extra Chromosomes and Blue Tulips: Medico-Familial Conversations. In *Living and Working with the New Medical Technologies*, ed. Margaret
Lock, Allan Young, and Alberto Cambrosio. Cambridge: Cambridge University Press.

Rapp, Rayna, Deborah Heath, and Karen-Sue Taussig. 2001. Genealogical
Dis-Ease: Where Hereditary Abnormality, Biomedical Explanation, and
Family Responsibility Meet. In *Relative Values: Reconfiguring Kinship Studies*,
ed. S. Franklin and S. McKinnon. Durham, NC: Duke University Press.

Roberts, Celia, and Karen Throsby. 2008. Paid to Share: IVF Patients, Eggs,
and Stem Cell Research. *Social Science and Medicine* 66:159–169.

Robson, Ruthann. 1995. Mother: The Legal Domestication of Lesbian Existence. In *Mothers in Law: Feminist Theory and the Legal Regulation of Motherhood*, ed. M.A. Fineman and I. Karpin. New York: Columbia University
Press.

Rockhill, Kathleen. 1996. And Still I Fight. In *Pushing the Limits: Disabled
Dykes Produce Culture*, ed. Shelley Tremain. Toronto: Women's Press.

Rogers, Lois. 2001. Eggs of Two Moms Make One Baby. *Calgary Herald*, front
cover.

Rose, Nikolas, and Carlos Novas. 2005. Biological Citizenship. In *Global
Assemblages: Technology, Politics, and Ethics as Anthropological Problems*, ed.
A. Ong and S. Collier. Malden, MA: Blackwell.

Ross, Lori E., Leah S. Steele, and Rachel Epstein. 2006. Service Use and Gaps
in Services for Lesbian and Bisexual Women During Donor Insemination,
Pregnancy, and the Postpartum Period. *Journal of Obstetrics and Gynaecology
Canada* 28 (6):505–11.

Saffron, Lisa. 1994. *Challenging Conceptions: Pregnancy and Parenting Beyond
the Traditional Family*. London: Cassell.

Schaffer, Rebecca, Kristine Kuczynski, and Debra Skinner. 2008. Producing
Genetic Knowledge and Citizenship Through the Internet: Mothers, Pedi-
atric Genetics, and Cybermedicine. *Sociology of Health and Illness* 30
(1):145–59.

Scheib, J.E., M. Riordan, and S. Rubin. 2003. Choosing Identity-Release

Sperm Donors: The Parents' Perspective 13–18 Years Later. *Human Repro-duction* 18 (5):1115–1127.

Schmidt, Matthew, and Lisa Jean Moore. 1998. Constructing a 'Good Catch,' Picking a Winner: The Development of Technosemen and the Deconstruc-tion of the Monolithic Male. In *Cyborg Babies: From Techno-Sex to Techno-Tots*, ed. R. Davis-Floyd and J. Dumit. New York: Routledge.

Schneider, David. 1980. *American Kinship: A Cultural Account*. Englewood Cliffs, NJ: Prentice-Hall. (Orig. pub. 1968.)

– 1984. *A Critique of the Study of Kinship*. Ann Arbor: University of Michigan Press.

– 1997. The Power of Culture: Notes on Some Aspects of Gay and Lesbian Kinship in America Today. *Cultural Anthropology* 12 (2):270–274.

Shapiro, Julie. 2008. News in Brief – PA Sperm Donor Contract Enforced. Available at http://julieshapiro.wordpress.com/2008/01/03/news-in-brief-pa-sperm-donor-contract-enforced/ (accessed 17 June 2008).

Shore, Cris. 1992. Virgin Births and Sterile Debates: Anthropology and the New Reproductive Technologies. *Current Anthropology* 33 (3):295–314.

Skelton, Chad. 2006. Searching for Their Genes. *Vancouver Sun*, 22 April. http://www.canada.com/vancouversun/news/observer/story.html?id=f0 257a1a-b7d4-4872-a1b2-06747a933fd6&p=1 (accessed 22 June 2008).

Smith, Miriam. 2007. Framing Same-Sex Marriage in Canada and the United States: Goodridge, Halpern, and the National Boundaries of Political Dis-course. *Social Legal Studies* 16 (1):5–26.

Solarz, Andrea, ed. 1999. *Lesbian Health: Current Assessment and Directions for the Future*. Institute of Medicine (United States) Committee on Lesbian Health Research Priorities. Washington, DC: National Academy Press.

Spallone, Patricia. 1989. *Beyond Conception: The New Politics of Reproduction*. Basingstoke, UK: Macmillan Education.

Spallone, Patricia, and Deborah Lynn Steinberg, eds. 1987. *Made to Order: The Myth of Reproductive and Genetic Progress*. Oxford: Permagon.

Spousal Rights Pass in BC. 1997. *Xtra! West*.

Squier, Susan Merrill. 1994. *Babies in Bottles: Twentieth-Century Visions of Reproductive Technology*. New Brunswick, NJ: Rutgers University Press.

Stanworth, Michelle, 1987a. Reproductive Technologies and the Deconstruc-tion of Motherhood. In *Reproductive Technologies: Gender, Motherhood and Medicine*. Cambridge: Polity Press.

– ed. 1987b. *Reproductive Technologies: Gender, Motherhood, and Medicine*. Cam-bridge: Polity Press.

Steele, L.S., and H. Stratmann. 2006. Counseling Lesbian Patients About Getting Pregnant. *Canadian Family Physician* 52 (May):605–611.

Steinberg, Deborah Lynn. 1997a. *Bodies in Glass: Genetics, Eugenics, and Embryo Ethics*. Manchester: Manchester University Press.

– 1997b. A Most Selective Practice: The Eugenic Logics of IVF. *Women's Studies International Forum* 20 (1):33–48.

Strathern, Marilyn. 1992. *Reproducing the Future: Anthropology, Kinship, and the New Reproductive Technologies*. Manchester, UK: Manchester University Press.

Sullivan, Maureen. 2001. Alma Mater: Family 'Outings' and the Making of the Modern Other Mother (MOM). In *Queer Families, Queer Politics: Challenging Culture and the State*, ed. M. Bernstein and R. Reimann. New York: Columbia University Press.

– 2004. *The Family of Woman: Lesbian Mothers, Their Children and the Undoing of Gender*. Berkeley: University of California Press.

Terry, Jennifer. 1999. Agendas for Lesbian Health: Countering the Ills of Homophobia. In *Revisioning Women, Health and Healing: Feminist, Cultural, and Technoscience Perspectives*, ed. A. Clarke and V.L. Olesen. New York: Routledge.

Thompson, Charis. 2005. *Making Parents: The Ontological Choreography of Reproductive Technologies*. Cambridge, MA, and London: MIT Press.

– *See also* Cussins, Charis M.

Tiemann, Kathleen, Sally Kennedy, and Myrna Haga. 1998. Rural Lesbians' Strategies for Coming Out to Health Care Professionals. In *Gateways to Improving Lesbian Health and Health Care*, ed. C.M. Ponticelli. Binghamton, NY: Harrington Park.

Tober, Diane M. 2001. Semen as Gift, Semen as Goods: Reproductive Workers and the Market in Altruism. *Body and Society* 7 (2–3):137–169.

Toevs, Kim, and Stephanie Brill. 2002. *The Essential Guide to Lesbian Conception, Pregnancy, and Birth*. Los Angeles and New York: Alyson Books.

Treichler, Paula A. 1999. *How to Have Theory in an Epidemic: Cultural Chronicles of AIDS*. Durham, NC: Duke University Press.

Tulchinsky, Karen. 1999. Two Moms, Better Than One? Staking Claim to Mother's Day. *Vancouver Sun*, final edition, 8 May, E5.

United Kingdom. 1990. Human Fertilisation and Embryology Act, c. 37. Available at http://www.opsi.gov.uk/Acts/acts1990/Ukpga _19900037_en_1.htm (accessed 22 June 2008).

– 2008. Human Fertilisation and Embryology Act, c. 22

United Kingdom Human Fertilisation and Embryology Authority. 2005. *Tomorrow's Children: A consultation on guidance to licensed fertility clinics on taking in account the welfare of children to be born as a result of assisted concep-*

tion treatment. London: HFEA. Available at http://www.hfea.gov.uk/docs
/TomorrowsChildren_consultation_doc.pdf (accessed 4 June 2009).

Valverde, Mariana, and Lorna Weir. 1997. Regulating New Reproductive and
Genetic Technologies: A Feminist View of Recent Canadian Government
Initiatives. *Feminist Studies* 23 (2):419–23.

van Dijck, José. 1995. *Manufacturing Babies and Public Consent: Debating the
New Reproductive Technologies.* New York: New York University Press.

Villarosa, Linda. 2002. Once-Invisible Sperm Donors Get to Meet the Family.
New York Times, 21 May.

Von Radowitz, John. 2005. Boy Traced His Sperm-Donor Father Using DNA
from Saliva. *Independent* (London), 3 November.
http://findarticles.com/p/articles/mi_qn4158/is_20051103/ai_n15824894
(accessed 17 April 2007).

Walks, Michelle. 2007. Queer Couples' Narratives of Birthing: A BC Focus on
the Intersections of Identity, Choice, Resources, Family, Policy, Medicalization, and Health in the Experiences of Queers Birthing. Master's thesis,
Department of Sociology and Anthropology, Simon Fraser University,
Burnaby, BC.

Watt, Nicholas. 2008. MPs reject 'need for father' in IVF bill. *The Guardian,* 20
May. Available at
http://www.guardian.co.uk/politics/2008/may/20/health.health
(accessed 17 June 2009).

Weschler, Toni. 1995. *Taking Charge of Your Fertility: The Definitive Guide to
Natural Birth Control, Pregnancy Achievement, and Reproductive Health.* New
York: Harper Collins.

Weston, Kath. 1991. *Families We Choose: Lesbians, Gays, Kinship.* New York:
Columbia University Press.

– 1996. *Render Me, Gender Me.* New York: Columbia University Press.

– 1997. The Virtual Anthropologist. In *Anthropological Locations: Boundaries
and Grounds of a Field Science,* ed. A. Gupta and J. Ferguson. Berkeley, CA:
University of California Press.

White, Jocelyn, and Valerie Dull. 1997. Health Risk Factors and Health-
Seeking Behaviour in Lesbians. *Journal of Women's Health* 6 (1):103–112.

Wilkes, Susan. 1985. Lesbians Trying to Get Pregnant. *Rites,* 13.

Williams, Clare, Steven P. Wainwright, Kathryn Ehrich, and Mike Michael.
2008. Human Embryos as Boundary Objects? Some Reflections on the Biomedical Worlds of Embryonic Stem Cells and Pre-Implantation Genetic
Diagnosis. *New Genetics & Society* 27:7–18.

Williams, Rachel. 2007. Sperm Donor to Lesbian Couple Forced to Pay Child

Support. *Guardian*, 4 December. Available at http://www.guardian.co.uk /politics/2007/dec/04/gayrights.immigrationpolicy/print (accessed 17 June 2008).

Winnow, Jackie. 1992. Lesbians Evolving Health Care: Cancer and AIDS. *Feminist Review* 41:68–76.

Wolf, Deborah C. 1982. Lesbian Childbirth and Artificial Insemination: A Wave of the Future. In *Anthropology of Human Birth*, ed. M.A. Kay. Philadelphia: F.A. Davis.

Wozniak, Danielle. 2001. *They're All My Children: Foster Mothering in America.* New York and London: New York University Press.

Wright, Janet M. 1998. *Lesbian Step Families: An Ethnography of Love.* Binghamton, NY: Haworth Press.

– 2001. 'Aside from One Little, Tiny Detail, We Are So Incredibly Normal': Perspectives of Children in Lesbian Step Families. In *Queer Families, Queer Politics: Challenging Culture and The State*, ed. M. Bernstein and R. Reimann. New York: Columbia University Press.

Yanagisako, Sylvia, and Jane Fishburne Collier. 1987. Toward a Unified Analysis of Kinship and Gender. In *Gender and Kinship: Essays Toward a Unified Analysis*, ed. J.F. Collier and S.J. Yanagisako. Stanford: Stanford University Press.

Yanagisako, Sylvia Junko, and Carol Lowery Delaney, eds. 1995. *Naturalizing Power: Essays in Feminist Cultural Analysis.* New York: Routledge.

Index

abortion: experience of, 27, 241n13; as a new reproductive technology, 221n1; women's health movement and, 161

access to fertility services: discourses of, 163–5, 169, 180; ethics of 155, 162; gay men, 38, 184, 186, 228n21, 240n5; HIV and, 117, 187; information about, 42, 97; known donors, 38, 155, 184, 186, 228n21, 240n5; legislation, Canadian and, 14–17, 169, 209, 211; legislation, UK and, 11–14, 159, 205, 245n7, 253n5; recommendations about, 17, 117, 169, 172; single women and/or lesbians, 5, 6, 35, 99, 106, 108, 110, 145, 159, 184, 186, 209, 211, 223n12, 227n15, 228n21, 247n16, 253n5; US-based, 106, 108, 110, 161, 223n15, 228n16; women's health movement and, 161, 177, 235n19

Achilles, Rona, 95, 161

adoption: anonymity and, 115, 125; associated costs of, 18, 242n17, 243n23; birth certificates and, 84, 147–51, 232n1; decision about, 39, 103, 108; discrimination and, 242n16; domestic, 143, 145, 242n14; donor insemination compared with, 114; of embryos, 117, 124, 126; genetic identity and, 108, 114, 125; genetics and, 121; international, 84, 144, 146, 242n17, 242n18, 242n20; and known donor, choice of, 110, 133–140; legal parental status and, 83, 84, 131, 133, 146, 147, 206; legislation, 17, 78, 79, 90, 105, 129, 131, 133, 226n5; as a parenting option, 77, 235n12; second-parent, 18, 19, 78, 105, 110, 117, 133–40, 144, 147, 240n7; sperm donors and, 79, 90, 110, 133–40

Adoption Act (British Columbia), 17, 33, 78, 79, 90, 105, 129, 133, 134, 137, 143, 146, 224n16, 226n5, 235n13, 240n5, 242n14

Agigian, Amy, 19, 96, 170, 228n16, 228n21, 234n2, 239n10, 244n4, 247n11

AIDS. *See* HIV

Aird, Elisabeth, 72, 77, 85

Almeling, Rene, 228n19